Also by Mike Matson

Spifflicated

COURTESY BOY

A TRUE STORY OF ADDICTION

MIKE MATSON

www.mikematson.com

Cover design by Clare McClaren
www.claremcclaren.com

Back cover author photo by Keshia Ezerendu
Instagram: @keshia_ezerendu

ISBN Paperback Version: 978-1-953583-14-7
ISBN Electronic Version: 978-1-953583-16-1

Library of Congress Control Number: 2021916294

Printed in the U.S.A.

ʬFlint Hills Publishing
Topeka, Kansas
www.flinthillspublishing.com

For information on addiction prevention and recovery, contact:
Mirror, Inc., Drug and Alcohol Addiction Treatment, Newton,
Kansas   855-396-1199
www.mirrorinc.org

For Rex and Lane

FOREWORD

This is a story of ruin and redemption, of falling down hard and fumbling one's way to the life one desperately wants. It's the story of my brother's journey to sobriety.

In these reflections, Mike offers a clear-eyed view of the insecurities, frailties, and deep empty places that led him to drink when he was barely old enough to drive, and which kept him in the throes of addiction for the better part of two decades.

We've got the dreaded addiction gene in our family. In a previous book, *Spifflicated*, Mike offers something of a biography of that particular gene, capturing in compelling narrative how it took root in our ancestors and wreaked havoc with several lives through the generations. With that book, and with this one, he helps us understand how he (we) got from there to here.

One of the traits of families of alcoholics is that we don't see what we don't want to see. During the years Mike was drinking, I was creating my own life, coming to terms with my own insecurities and frailties, oblivious to what he was going through. I knew the headlines: Mike is in Minneapolis at broadcasting school, Mike got married, Scott was born, Mike and Sharon are divorced, Mike is working for the governor. But I had no idea of the stories behind the headlines.

This book fills in the details. For those of us who had lost him for a period of time, this can be a painful read. *If only, if only, if only.* Yet ultimately, this is a story of hope and healing. Mike shows us the paradoxical truth that owning up to our worst moments can make us more whole.

One Christmas when Mike was newly-sober and still finding his legs, we were gathered at our Mom's house. I was doing something in the kitchen when I began to hear someone fingering the piano. I peeked around the corner to see that it was Mike. He was trying to find the notes by ear to *Amazing Grace*. He had never had piano lessons, but there he was, stumbling a bit but staying with it until we could make out what it was.

I once was lost, but now I'm found
Was blind, but now I see.

To say that I am proud of him doesn't do justice to how I feel. It's more like pride, relief, respect, love and affection, all rolled into one. I got my brother back. Amazing grace, indeed.

Viki Matson
Nashville, Tennessee
Autumn 2021

PREFACE

For most of my life, I've known I would write a book. Or a major motion picture screenplay. That knowing was always accompanied by a powerful fantasy of seeing my name on the *New York Times* best-seller list for weeks in a row, or watching the credits scroll on the big screen, "Written by Mike Matson."

The fantasy was always more powerful than the realities of making it happen.

I imagined myself at the Dorothy Chandler Pavilion, resplendent in my tux, graciously accepting the Oscar for Best Original Screenplay. Or Best Adapted Screenplay—adapted, of course, from my best-seller. My acceptance remarks would seem off the cuff, but every syllable, inflection, and breath would have been carefully and purposefully planned.

The narrative would be shaped during red-carpet interviews, where I would offer humble platitudes about the simple sufficiency of the nomination. Modesty and humility can be scripted, and mine would be so finely honed, everyone would think it was genuine.

From early childhood, the behaviors and traits that would lead to addiction were there.

Obsessions, impulsivity, and a nagging sense that everyone is looking at you, judging, following your every move. Dishonesty. Insecurity. The fear that you can't be happy alone and the feeling that life lacks meaning without a partner and a relationship.

There was manipulation, control, and the tendency to arrange circumstances (and, eventually, people) to serve my purposes. But there was also the persistent fear of rejection and a constant need for reassurance. Even as a little kid, I was always asking my mom, "What's the matter?" For me to be okay, I needed her to be okay.

The Oscar acceptance speech fantasy isn't really a stretch, when you consider my career path: radio deejay, radio news, television news, press secretary to a governor. It's almost as though there's a line on my business card, right below my name, that says, "Look at me."

No one aspires to addiction as a life goal, and it's difficult to explain using words—you have to experience it (and you really don't want to experience it). But since this is a book, books are full of words, and I'm writing it, let's give it a shot.

Addiction is a compulsive condition, resulting in the repetitive pursuit of a destructive substance or behavior despite negative consequences. Essentially, you are driven toward your own ruin.

The traits and behaviors associated with addiction aren't unique to me. I have come to believe that not only was I born with a biological genetic predisposition to addiction, the life I designed as a young adult, based on childhood experiences, set me up for it. Had I known then what I know now, would I have made different choices? Maybe, but I also believe I am in recovery from addiction for a reason.

We'll get to that at the end of the book.

Everything described in these pages happened, and everyone here is a real person. Some names were changed, while others gave permission to use their real names. One, in fact, insisted on it.

In describing his memoir, Steve Martin nailed it when he called it a biography, because he was writing about someone he used to know.

Same here.

My early adult life unfolds chronologically in these pages, but addiction itself is not linear. It's an insidious mosaic of multi-layered behaviors, circumstances, traits, and events that eventually leads to a perspective that can only be gleaned, accurately and wholly, in hindsight.

This is the reconstruction of that mosaic.

"Midnight creeps so slowly into hearts of men who need more than they get."

Boogie Wonderland, Earth Wind & Fire ft. The Emotions

WOODGATE

1.
May 27, 1975

Panic seized him immediately upon hearing the first rule.

"Rule number one: Boys are to pair up with girls—you have five minutes to find a partner!"

The Wichita Heights High School assistant wrestling coach didn't relish babysitting seniors at commencement practice, and with three months of freedom looming, he was eager to get this little chore behind him.

"No grab-ass, just pair up! Then line up, double file!"

It was left unsaid, that absent some action in the form of a purposeful choice, the leftovers would be relegated to the back of the line. Having failed this one final assignment of their dozen years plus kindergarten of organized state-mandated public education, they would be default-coupled with one of the same sex.

Jocks paired up effortlessly with cheerleaders; debaters and thespians wasted no time connecting; the German Klub *verbinden mit* the French Club; the National Honor Society hooked up with Quill and Scroll; and, of course, band and orchestra geeks found one another—female cello, male trumpet; strings and brass.

Mike Matson glanced at his watch, lamenting, at least for the moment, his clique-less nature. The five minutes was hauling ass.

When the deadline came, those who made choices (and those who didn't) were to descend in pairs from the upper level to the floor of Henry Levitt Arena, past beaming parents, grandparents, and various well-wishers on hand to witness this significant life milestone. Each couple was to make their way across the arena floor to the center aisle of nearly 400 chairs, divided evenly into a dozen sections—six on either side—each designated by two or three letters.

After that, the alphabet took over, and the boy-girl pressure was off. Tonight they'd do it all over again for real, boys in black gowns and mortar boards, girls in white.

Built only a generation ago, when a round basketball arena was perceived as state-of-the-art—if not ahead of its time—this building was known as "The Roundhouse." He often thought the whole city would have been better off, and their collective municipal vernacular elevated a tad, had the meeting where they came up with that name lasted another half hour.

Mike had traveled to commencement practice with Andy Wagner, a kid he'd known since fourth grade. Andy was big-boned and unathletic, with a reputation of coming on too strong with girls. He was, however, sufficiently self-aware to be hip to this shortcoming, and after hearing the first rule, abandoned any thought of walking with a girl. Andy just assumed he'd walk with the friend who brung him.

"No offense, Pando, but walking with you totally screws up my self-image," he said, departing before Pando could offer a useless counterargument.

Andy, who had been dubbed Pando Bear in junior high owing to his size, shrugged and blended in seamlessly with a group of kindred high school spirits—members in good standing of the Chess, Key, and Bible Clubs. Sadly, a high school diploma would not be enough to burnish some images.

Tick-tock.

Mike saw three girls standing by themselves, did his best to muster a crooked smile, and made his way over. He knew all their names but had never spoken to two of them. The third, Sherry Johnson, was in his first semester American Government class.

In October, right before the 1974 midterm elections, the teacher had asked the class to organize and name their own political parties. Despite being fellow travelers in the same political party seven months ago (dubbed the Honesty Party, post-Nixon resignation), their only communication had been an occasional Heights hallway "Hi." Not much of a platform on which to build a post-Watergate manifesto, much less a commencement procession invitation. But desperate times called for desperate measures.

"Hi, Sherry. Wanna walk together?"

This greeting had already exceeded their previous longest conversation by four words. He could tell she was doing the math (three girls, a double-file procession). Sherry made momentary, fleeting eye contact with her two friends as she calculated, then announced, what he accepted was an unemotional numbers-driven decision.

"Sure."

Breathing a little easier, Mike offered her his arm. She smiled, hooked hers through his, and they pomp-and-circumstanced their way down the steps toward their alphabetically-assigned seating sections, hers to the left, his to the right. He glanced to see Pando behind him, fidgeting and uncomfortable, walking at arm's length with another boy, a few degrees geekier.

Thank God. Everyone will see me walking with a girl, and they won't think I'm a loser like Pando.

Sherry was a dishwater blonde, straight on top, parted down the middle, spilling into curls three or four inches below her shoulder. Blue eyes that didn't sparkle and a smile that didn't dazzle, not the kind of girl who drew enduring attention from the boys.

She interrupted the awkward silence as they descended the stairs.

"What are you doing this summer?"

"I work at Mr. D's IGA in Sweetbriar. Moving into an apartment next week. Woodgate. With Endler and Inglewood."

Mr. D's was a family-owned supermarket chain where the three of them worked.

She nodded like she knew them, or maybe it was just an acknowledgment nod (with 400 kids in the graduating class, no one knew everybody), but she did seem to sense his genuine excitement about the new place.

"What about you?"

"Working at Peter Pan on North Arkansas Avenue, then WSU in the fall," she said. "I'm majoring in accounting."

WSU came out "dub-yes-you." Like all south-central Kansans, Sherry pronounced the avenue and the river which flowed through Wichita "are-KAN-zuhz."

Sherry was in the clear majority in transitioning to Wichita State University, where there were more parking lots and fewer dorms. Most dub-yes-you students lived at home and commuted, and the university had earned and owned the nickname, "Hillside High."

"Woodgate?" She tilted her head and looked at him. "Where's that?"

"Just east of Oliver on 21st. It's a brand-new complex. Our pad overlooks the pool."

He didn't share his notion of becoming a Major League Baseball play-by-play announcer. It wasn't a goal, and you couldn't really call it a dream, just a vague, faraway hope and an answer for his father and other authority figures interested in his life plan.

Mike knew two things: He loved the sport and, with zero experience, was already better than Curt Gowdy, who consistently screwed up names and facts while calling balls and strikes on NBC's *Game of the Week*. He had no clue how one goes about becoming a Major League Baseball play-by-play announcer and wasn't really worried about it.

It was an idea, and that's all it was. He could discern good ideas from crappy ones, and the good ones nearly always resulted in a self-driven outcome. It was a good idea because it helped him reach a desired end. Bad ideas don't, and they just fade away.

There was no plan to achieve the idea. The plan would come, and he had nothing but time. He intended to work full-time for a year, then sometime in his nation's Bicentennial year, assess his options.

A few couples up, he saw his buddy, Robbie Lang, walking with Lisa Criss (trombone-violin). Robbie had lusted after Lisa since junior year and enrolled in orchestra class with the express intent of getting closer to her. For two years, Lisa's cold shoulder was consistent, including a now infamous between-classes incident in the Heights commons area the previous winter when Lisa very publicly encouraged him to "pound sand."

Mike glanced at Robbie, offering a telepathic, Fonzie-inspired thumbs-up, which was returned with an approving raised eyebrow and nod toward Sherry.

Robbie (and everyone else, really) would logically assume he'd already taken Sherry to Cinemas East to see *Tommy,* wowed her with his knowledge of Daltrey, Townshend, Clapton, et al, and that halfway through the movie, she'd leaned in close and whispered sacred permission to bring his own interpretation to see me, feel me, touch me.

After the movie, in the back seat.

But Sherry wasn't a see-me, feel-me, touch-me kind of girl. She was an unassuming girl, likeable when you got to know her, who would scoop Peter Pan ice cream this summer; matriculate to Hillside High; spend four years learning the nuances of present value and owner's equity; earn an undergraduate degree in accounting; and become an unassuming counter of beans.

And make unemotional, numbers-driven decisions.

Assumptions generally contained at least a thread of truth, and the reputations built around these assumptions stuck. Sherry Johnson's reputation lined up with her actual persona, so his post-*Tommy* fantasy died a quick death.

Mike flashed back briefly to his stage management connected to senior prom, just a month earlier. He wanted desperately to go and had most of the ingredients in place for a grand evening, having already picked out a natty, powder blue, double-knit tux with royal blue piping and matching royal blue velvet bow tie.

All he lacked was a date—truth was, he was oh-for-2 securing a prom date. And as much as he wanted to go, he was even more desperate not to be oh-for-3, or oh-for-4.

He told people he had to work that night. He didn't, but to lend plausibility to the story, he'd traded his Saturday morning shift at Mr. D's with a kid who was down to work Saturday night.

At least they'll admire my work ethic.

In anticipation of commencement photos, when the night came, he wore white pants and black platform shoes, polished to a fare-thee-well. The white pants would contrast nicely with the black cap, gown, and shoes.

Growing up, he was always either the shortest or second-shortest kid in his class. The growth spurt came in junior high, but short kid stigma isn't easily forgotten, and the platforms brought a measure of emotional equilibrium.

After the ceremony, he rounded up Endler and Inglewood to finalize their Woodgate move-in logistics. This work was conducted in Inglewood's '65 Barracuda. He was first to call shotgun, so Endler sat in the back and took charge of beer distribution—Miller Lite—because it was still a relatively shiny new product, and because at 17, Mike was unduly influenced by new and shiny. Bottles, because it was a special occasion.

"Everything you've always wanted in a beer," Endler said, leaning forward and hoisting his high.

Three relatively-shiny new adults, freshly minted and diploma'd high school graduates, now roommates. He and Inglewood recognized their cue and clinked their bottles with his.

"And less." In unison.

2.
June 2, 1975

Tap, tap, tap.

Three thin metallic clicks, in rapid succession. A nearly-empty aluminum beer can tapped against the leg of a nearby end table—it was a brash young drinker's habit and a signal. A hard-surfaced floor would have provided more sound resonance, but it was a newly-built apartment and the shag carpeting still held its showroom smell.

John Francis Endler leaned back in the beanbag chair, threw his head back, held the same nearly-empty Olympia beer can within an inch of his mouth, and captured the last few precious drops.

TAP. TAP. TAP.

Mike had known John Endler for a half-dozen years. In the seventh grade at Pleasant Valley Junior High, every male student rebelled against The Man by growing their hair long. Except John. Endler was short hair, National Honor Society, straight As and horn rims. John was Junior Achievement, long before it was forced upon him in high school.

The long hair of the Class of 1975 was a hard-earned badge of honor. The Summer of Love was a lifetime ago and involved their older siblings, not them. They were not protesting the war. It's over. America lost. Three weeks before descending the stairs at Levitt Arena, America had pushed South Vietnamese helicopters off her aircraft carriers. We abandoned our allies. We bugged out.

His classmates suspected Endler's strict Catholic

upbringing and his parents' Kansas conservatism explained John's short hair. Nearly all their parents listed to starboard politically. Boys negotiating at arms-length distance to keep their long hair and Dingo boots. For the girls, this diplomacy resulted in really short skirts and halter tops.

If his dogmatic iconoclasm bothered him, John didn't let it show. It didn't stand in the way of making friends, and he made up for it with his intellect, which commanded respect. Out from under Mom and Dad's roof, like his two shiny new roommates, John was now free to do what came naturally.

"She's supposed to pick up on the cue, regardless of the surface upon which the empty can is tapped," Endler said, as he leaned over and once again knocked the vanquished soldier against the end table leg, this time with extreme prejudice.

TAP.   TAP.   TAP.

They were all smartasses, but Endler's was tinged with a layer of above-the-fray intellectualism Matson genuinely admired but didn't yet possess. Endler floated through high school like it was simply a box to be checked.

John had walked into the Woodgate leasing office—where the rules said you could have just two people, each at least 18, to a two-bedroom apartment—and walked out with a signed lease allowing three people, one underage at just 17.

"We're not breaking the rules, we're just bending them a bit," Endler had explained. "There's still plenty of slack. It's the way of the world, my young friend."

Mike had offered to use his fake ID to sign the lease. His most prized possession was Wes Gordon's draft card, a kid two years older, who had given it to him in exchange for an introduction to his sister. Matson got the fake ID, the kid chasing his sister got the cold shoulder.

"No, let me and Inglewood sign the lease," Endler had

said with the confidence of a man who'd been spearheading real estate transactions for decades. "Legally, you can't sign dick until you're 18. We'll still split everything three ways, but this way, you're covered and protected."

It made so much sense, and there was no argument. Not only had Endler taken charge, he had taken responsibility.

They all knew Endler was destined for success because he had already succeeded as a teenager. While Matson and Inglewood lived Mr. D's paycheck to paycheck, Endler was loaded, thanks to his mastery of American capitalism since age eight, when he started his own business painting street address numbers on curbs throughout Wichita.

Decades before emergency response systems mandated it, young John Endler had envisioned it.

His sales pitch was honed by experience: "Good morning/afternoon/evening, ma'am/sir. My name is John Endler, and I'm earning money by painting street address numbers on curbs. I paint a white rectangular background, roughly twice the size of a license plate, then apply your street address number on top. You have your choice of colors for the numbers—black, burnt umber, deep burgundy, or navy blue.

"Only three dollars!"

John would purposefully wear ratty clothes and wrap black electrical tape on the bridge of his hornrims to give the impression he really needed the dough. And if a chatty homeowner asked the bright young entrepreneur how he intended to spend his earnings, John would reply he was "trying to help my family."

Endler, *aka* "Moneybags," never talked about how much he had saved, but his roommates suspected it was plenty. Shortly after the Woodgate move-in, Endler quit his job at Mr. D's, which seemed counterintuitive to Matson.

Now that we're paying rent, don't we need the jobs more than ever?

The nicknames started at Heights, mostly sprouted organically through groupthink, but Mike proved proficient at cultivating and developing options derived from personal characteristics.

As first-chair trombone, Robbie Lang became "Bones." High school radio station disc jockey John Messman was known as "J.B. Mezz." Another kid who pumped gasoline and washed windshields after school was tagged "Gas Jockey." Owing to his business acumen and financial prowess (and the fact they all knew he was going to become a millionaire), John Francis Endler became "Moneybags." He did not object.

While Matson viewed Woodgate as a seminal life moment—both an end to itself and escape from the oppressive paternal thumb of seventeen-and-a-half years—it was merely a convenient waystation for Moneybags. Endler was planning an undergraduate degree in three years: a year at dub-yes-you, the final two at the University of Kansas in Lawrence. He was already knocking out what he called some "pud prerequisites" during the summer at Hillside High.

"Three taps with the empty is her signal to bring me a fresh brewski."

John met the girl of his Pavlovian empty-beer routine at Mr. D's. Cindy was a checker and he was a "courtesy boy," Mr. D's homespun euphemism for polite young men hired to sack and carry out groceries.

The Sweetbriar Shopping Center sat four blocks south of West 25th Street North, the school board's boundary separating Heights Falcons from North Redskins. As a result, Mr. D's teenage human resources repped both high schools. Cindy was North, they were Heights and damn proud of it. Members in good standing (actually, now alumna) of the

Mighty Falcon Marching Band.

Endler was first chair trumpet; Inglewood was third chair French Horn; and Matson was treble clef baritone after bailing on the trumpet between junior high and high school. The story he told his mother was he wanted to branch out, expand his musical horizons. The truth was, Mike sucked at trumpet because while all the other trumpet players practiced and improved, he watched *Star Trek* reruns.

I cannae change the laws of physics!

It's hard to get demoted from last chair. It's easier to quit and do something else.

From the kitchen, they could hear Cindy's steps toward the fridge, a crack/whoosh of the pull-tab, and the metallic scraping of its top popping off. She wiped overflow suds on her high-waisted blue jeans with her right hand, passing the fresh Oly to Endler with her left.

Then, looking at Mike expectantly: "Can I get you one?"

Matson was matching Endler brewski for brewski, but it felt wrong somehow to ask another man's girlfriend to get it for him.

"No thanks, Cindy Sue."

She smiled at this, an acknowledgement that, however badly John treated her, there was at least one other person in the room who thought enough of her to give her a nickname.

Maybe some courtesy boys were more courteous than others.

At 19, Cindy was Class of '74, a year ahead of them, but still lived at home with her parents. Her name was Cynthia Lynn Revell, and when she introduced herself, she'd say "ruh-VELL, emphasis on the last syllable." When they first met, Mike suggested "em-FOSS-us on the last suh-LOB-ul," and the Matson-inspired lingo stuck.

If it bothered John, he hid it well.

The John and Cindy relationship was complicated. On the one hand, she seemed to embrace the opportunities the women's movement had made possible in the mid-1970s, but she was also Endler's "step and fetch it" girl. They knew she was on the pill, but they were unsure if it was liberation, convenience, or because John insisted. She was caught in the tricky transitions of culture clinging to its old ways and the status quo.

Cindy once told Mike, "Nobody likes a smart woman."

They both knew who she meant.

He was never sure if Endler really felt this way, or if it was just an act.

Mike knew Endler's Catholicism brought patriarchal deference. He was also a proudly vocal conservative Republican, who was always recruiting his friends to the Ronald Reagan bandwagon. At 18, Endler was well on his way to the split-level rancher in the suburbs, two cars, a boat, Stepford wife, cabin at the lake, and a once-a-week cleaning lady with an apron and sensible shoes.

"Individual judgment and personal responsibility, boys," Endler would soapbox. "These are the things that will ensure our freedom and liberty."

The more Matson experienced John Francis Endler as a roommate, the more he leaned toward believing the disrespectful treatment of Cindy was '70s false bravado, a schtick for the guys.

People don't really feel that way, do they? And even if they do, they sure don't want to let on that they do. My God, what would people think?

3.
June 5, 1975

"Why Olympia?"

Mark Inglewood was carefully arranging the boxed components of his stereo, still cocooned in the original Styrofoam molds. After several carloads of clothes and furniture, Inglewood's stereo was the last of the man's worldly possessions to make the move from the bedroom in his mother's Sherwood Glen basement.

"It's the water."

They were best friends, but disassembling, moving, and reassembling Inglewood's stereo was a delicate "trust-no-one-else" operation that fell beyond even the bounds of friendship.

"It's like, naturally pure from Artesian wells in Olympia, Washington. Besides, they couldn't exactly use, 'It's the 3.2 percent alcohol.'"

"Jesus, Matson, you sound like a friggin' radio commercial."

Inglewood suspected some brewery flunky connected a rubber hose, cranked the spigot, fired up a smoke, and came back 15 minutes later when the vat was filled with city tap water.

"Artesian water, my ass." Then, because they were best friends, "But it's better than Schlitz, I'll give ya that."

He met Inglewood in Drafting 1, sophomore year at Heights. His first impression was this guy seems sullen, almost sad.

Drafting 1 gave way to Drafting 2 and Drafting 3, which

was basically Architecture 101. Senior year, they each designed houses. His, a Brady Bunch-esque split-level rancher with two fireplaces, a wet bar, and laundry chute. Inglewood's was a postmodern monstrosity with curved walls and a Batcave-inspired hidden garage.

Mark got Mike his first real job, bussing tables at Angelo's Italian restaurant at 26th and Amidon. When together they grew weary of scrubbing baked-on mozzarella remnants from lasagna tins at 2 a.m. and traversing Wichita coated with a patina of olive oil, they hatched a plan to walk away from Angelo's for jobs as courtesy boys at Mr. D's.

Less greasy, more... courteous.

Three years before Drafting 1, on a Saturday morning when Mark and his three pajama-clad younger siblings were glued to the Bugs Bunny/Roadrunner Hour, their father walked out the front door of their south Wichita home and never returned.

Joe Inglewood owned a coin shop in downtown Wichita, where he trafficked in rare coins, mystery, and intrigue. He owned the largest nationwide wholesale coin business in the country and, on the day he vanished, was seen at the Wichita airport and main downtown post office, signing for shipments of rare coins.

The cops found signs of foul play at his shop downtown, which led the family to assume the worst. Inglewood eventually came to suspect his father was involved in shady business with shady characters and dealt with accordingly.

Sullen and sad. No damn wonder.

Matson was allowed to put together the glass and veneer-covered particle board display case that housed the stereo, while Inglewood gingerly and meticulously connected all the wires and cords on the back sides of the receiver, cassette deck, turntable with a bronze Plexiglas cover hinged at the back, and the *pièce de résistance*: the Marantz 1090 integrated amplifier.

Separate, stand-alone electronic components with transistors, diodes, and integrated circuits—no vacuum tubes or solid-state components that don't move. Alone, they were worthless. But ensembled, they created audible art. Something beautiful.

"What's that actually do?"

Inglewood was the only friend of whom he could ask such basic questions and not be held up to ridicule.

"The amplifier receives the input signal from one of these other sources and makes the signal bigger."

More than sheer volume, a fullness of sound.

In the arc of apartment complex lifespans, their new abode still held its original luster.

Built in 1973, Woodgate featured 239 units in 13 separate buildings. Two bedrooms, one bath, 830 square feet, fully loaded with garbage disposal, dishwasher, refrigerator/freezer, stove/oven, central air, glass shower doors, metal miniblinds in the bedrooms, curtains in the living room, and covered parking.

Real estate developers in the early '70s didn't need complicated market analyses to recognize there was money to be made in apartment complexes. The Heights Class of '75 numbered nearly 400, and it was the smallest of eight Wichita high schools. The final wave of baby boomers leaving the nest would need a place to live, and apartment complexes had sprung up all over town, each designed specifically for a young, unmarried adult audience.

There was something else unique about that demographic.

Their Midwest-raised, rule-following older siblings would have considered swanky apartment life an extravagance, but the trailing baby boomers expected it and wanted that swimming pool, clubhouse with a bar, tennis courts, and in-building laundry.

He and Inglewood had carefully examined a half-dozen apartment complexes in Wichita and liked them all, but Woodgate was close to dub-yes-you, which was important to Endler. That point sealed the deal, and with rent at $245 a month, it broke down to 82 bucks per roommate.

Endler got the solo bedroom because he said he got it. Inglewood put up a mild argument but caved when Endler reminded them that when it came to the depth of the triumvirate friendship, he was the outlier. Again, Endler's logic had proven flawless.

Inglewood was a true friend. Moneybags was an ambition.

Like Endler, Woodgate was temporary for Inglewood. In six months, he intended to become fluent in avionics by enrolling in the Spartan School of Aeronautics in Tulsa. That left the summer and fall to party.

Inglewood's nickname wasn't really a nickname, but his surname, sung aloud, matching the tones of the NBC chimes, used originally by the radio network as a cue to affiliates for station identification, still ubiquitous on TV.

Three notes. G, up a major 6th to E, down a major third to C. Every time he approached, one of them would sing, "ing-GULL-wooooood," often holding that last suh-LOB-ul for em-FOSS-us.

Before he met Mark Inglewood, Mike's fear-driven reaction to circumstances around him was dictated by his father's "Shape up, mister" hard line. In his best friend—just beneath the sadness—was a newly developing layer of confidence that Mike sought to emulate. Mark had all the answers and offered a connection unlike any he'd ever experienced.

He quit complaining about his own old man's harshness the time Inglewood cut him off, sadness elbowing aside confidence.

"At least you have a father."

He also admired Inglewood's way with electronics, cars, and girls. Inglewood appreciated Mike's imagination. Their friendship endured through minor infractions—like a spilled McDonald's chocolate milkshake on the new blue-and-white shag carpeting they'd spent all day installing in Inglewood's 1965 Barracuda and his own 1970 Ford Falcon—and through major ones involving accusations of girlfriend stealing.

"Man, she came on to me," Matson recalled, pleading his case and having no idea what it took to negotiate a successful outcome of such a sticky situation, genuinely fearful it could cost him his best friend.

"I know," Inglewood eventually allowed. "I could see it coming."

Mike's was an all-in-one, off-the-shelf stereo purchased at David's, a discount department store in Sweetbriar. Inglewood once told him it was a rip-off, and the first time he heard Inglewood's state-of-the-art system in the Sherwood Glen basement, he couldn't argue. Twist the knob on Inglewood's receiver, and it spun up and down the AM/FM frequency range and didn't stop until the kinetic energy dissipated. But twist the corresponding knob on Matson's stereo and it went only as far as the applied fingertip torque.

"We'll use yours in the bedroom, mine out here."

Neither of them intended to spend much time in the bedroom, other than for its intended purpose.

"Which reminds me, we gotta figure out some sorta signal if one of us is in there with a girl."

Inglewood was giving him the benefit of the doubt.

"If you see a sock on the doorknob, sleep on the couch."

Clearly, Inglewood had given this some thought.

Inglewood slipped an album out of a thin brown paper bag: "Check it out. I heard these guys on KEYN."

He ran his thumbnail through the cellophane, retrieved the record, flipped it with the deftness and alacrity one would expect from the owner of a stereo featuring a Marantz 1090 integrated amplifier, and placed it on the turntable, tossing Mike the album cover.

"They're sort of a cross between Chicago and the Ohio Players."

Twin guitars kicked off the Average White Band lead track with an upbeat funk/soul line. Eight seconds in, a drum riff with tenor sax melody hot on its heels. At 23 seconds, they were enveloped by the vocal emanating from Inglewood's twin JBL speakers, each with a foam rubber checkerboard grill affixed with Velcro strategically positioned to fill the entire apartment with full sound—woofers for AWB's funky bass line and other low notes; midrange drivers bringing the middle frequencies; and tweeters ensuring the high frequencies weren't lost.

"We could connect your speakers to this system," Inglewood mused out loud before realizing that would leave them speaker-less in the bedroom.

"Quadrophonic?"

Matson knew it was cutting edge and that it involved four speakers, but his knowledge stopped there.

"Nah, just stereo twice. Quad's a flash in the pan. Too impractical."

In the nearly three years of their friendship, he had seen Inglewood's sadness give way to a bit of an edge that Matson had grown to admire. Instead of a sad story about a father disappearing and, "Oh, please feel sorry for me," Inglewood's 1975 persona was more, "Yeah, the old man was shady and now he's gone, and fuck you, I know what I'm doing."

Joe Inglewood's less-than-above-board business dealings may have cost him his life. Or maybe he was sitting on a beach in the South Pacific, sleeping late and sipping Mai Tais. Mark seemed at ease with either possibility.

Inglewood cranked the stereo, now fully constructed and operational, to full sound and retired to the bedroom to unpack his clothes.

Socks, within easy grasp.

Mike snagged a fresh Oly and stepped out onto the balcony, closing the screen and sliding glass door. The central air conditioning was on, and he had no desire to cool the whole complex on their dime. Then it hit him.

That's a James E. move.

He shuddered a little, took a deep pull on the beer, reached back, slid the door wide open, and communicated telepathically with his father.

Fuck you. I know what I'm doing.

Surveying his domain, he remembered telling Sherry Johnson at commencement practice about their pad overlooking the pool. When they were apartment shopping it was a requisite for him, and Inglewood went along. A swimming pool may have been an extravagance to some, but this was the life he was purposefully seeking.

He wanted to be the poster child for the easy living, single young adult.

Take a picture of me right now, for the glossy tri-fold Woodgate promotional brochure.

Sandals, cutoff blue-jean shorts, Oxford shirt with the sleeves rolled up, long hair wafting in the south Kansas wind, leaning on the balcony railing and enjoying a cold one. So what if he was only 17? He would be legal in six months.

Matson had been designing this life for years, and one of his first steps would be making new bikini-clad friends at the pool.

Hi there. Perhaps you've seen me around? Me and my 1970 Ford Falcon with the blue-and-white shag carpeting throughout. My place is right up there (leaning in and pointing nonchalantly, beer in hand). Maybe you'd like to come up and listen to some music on my all-in-one, off-the-shelf, rip-off stereo from David's discount store in Sweetbriar?

You strike me as a Doobie Brothers aficionado. Olivia Newton-John? Elton John? I have all the Johns. I'm also becoming well-versed on the Average White Band. They're sort of a cross between Chicago and the Ohio Players.

Please remind me to hang a sock on the doorknob. I'll explain later.

The upper reaches of a massive, fifty-year-old cottonwood tree rustled in the south wind. As a man who had already designed a house, he was impressed that the developers had enough wisdom and foresight to design and construct this complex around a healthy grove of the official Kansas state tree.

Beyond the pool were two tennis courts, where he envisioned mixed singles with the local Chrissie Evert. He would holler, "AD-IN!" and thwack an ace for victory. Hurdling the net with perfect grace and aplomb, he would invite freshly vanquished local Chrissie to the clubhouse for a postgame libation.

The trees had begun shedding massive amounts of cottony seeds, making it look like a dusting of June snow on the Woodgate sidewalks and grass. He inhaled the musty-sweet aroma of cottonwood in bloom. His mother, who had grown up in Rooks County, had taught him it didn't get much better than Kansas in the late spring.

He made a mental note to call his mom this weekend on their new candy apple red, trimline push button telephone. Mom would answer at home on her avocado green, rotary dial wall phone, take a seat at the kitchen table, and sip weak Butter-Nut coffee from a brown melamine cup perched on a form-fitting white melamine saucer.

Voices, male and female, carried to his balcony from the Woodgate picnic area. New friends would be made over there with a couple of T-bones, grilled to medium-rare perfection on the complex's built-in barbecue.

Say, chums! I'm a close, personal friend of the butcher's apprentice in the Mr. D's meat department. Stick with me, I can get you a real deal on Porterhouses and sirloins!

There could be a weekly gathering with fellow late-wave baby boomers in the clubhouse for a weekday night poker game. He would spear a pair of olives on a plastic toothpick designed to look like a little sword while constructing a Dagwood sandwich from a heaping platter of cold cuts.

Boys, if we play our cards right...

He plunged his olive-laden sword deep into the Dagwood as the sound of Inglewood's voice interrupted his reverie.

"I gotta split. Thanks for your help with my stereo."

His help. Mark's stereo. Best friends, but boundaries.

"That Olympia's like bear piss. I'll bring home some Budweiser tonight."

You can keep your rhinoceros-piss Budweiser.

Side 1 of the AWB album was playing out. At least his best friend trusts him to turn off his precious stereo. The exact moment that thought entered his mind, the stereo turned itself off.

Solid state. No moving parts.

Individual components make a stereo, allowing the sounds of the Average White Band to fill one apartment. This one, and 238 others filled with like-minded, single young adults. Each with a stereo: AWB here, the Carpenters upstairs, Led Zeppelin across the courtyard, and John Denver on the north side.

A community of friends, waiting to be made.

Three friends—two who were close, plus an outlier—become roommates and personify a new definition of home.

The things that make a friendship don't move. Friendship is supposed to be permanent, and best friends are supposed to be roommates as young adults. Society expects it. Hell, demands it. Or was that a vestige of his parents' generation?

Three young men living together are supposed to meet girls, hang socks on the doorknob, host parties, and play music at high volume and full sound. It's what they do.

They are supposed to drink beer. Lots and lots of beer. So much beer that you can construct a pyramid of empty Olympia cans against the dining room wall. Every can perfectly aligned facing forward.

Meticulous.

Perfect.

Don't sit in the dining room chairs on that side. It obstructs the view of the pyramid.

You might accidentally bump into it.

You can add your empties but be careful. Make sure they're aligned. This only works one way.

He said some of these things out loud.

These are the things you can't do when you live at home with your solid, respectable middle-class white-bread parents, whether your old man is a hard-ass, a possible fugitive on a South Pacific beach, or Howard Cunningham from *Happy Days*.

It's a work of art. It will not move until we move out. To a place even swankier. It's reflective of this time of transition in our lives.

Bigger transitions were in play. We lost the war. The President resigned. Women are more than bikini-clad fantasies.

It was not solid state. The parts were constantly in motion. Both his roommates clearly considered Woodgate as temporary. He liked thinking of it as home. A bright line. Out from under the asshole's thumb.

Finally.

4.

August 9, 1975

Nancy Ellis' popcorn went airborne the moment Ben Gardner's one-eyed head floated into the shark-made hole in the boat's hull, and she grabbed Mike's arm with both of hers. *I'll have to remember this Spielberg guy. He knows how to make movies.*

Nancy was two years behind him at Heights and she seemed excited when he called to ask her out. He tossed her empty popcorn box in the trash as they filed out of Cinemas East. As a courtesy, Mike had invited her to their party at Woodgate after the movie. She wanted to come, but when her parents found out their daughter's date was living the young, unattached singles life in an apartment complex, the edict came down.

So, he walked her to the front door and kissed her goodnight. He promised to call again soon and hustled back to Woodgate in the shagged Falcon. Nancy was a sweet girl, but she was still in high school and didn't fit his new image and lifestyle.

"Get in her pants?" Endler smirked as he looked up from his task of removing 12-ounce cans of Coors from their cardboard six-pack containers, transferring them to the bottom two shelves of the fridge.

"Yeah, 'dja get any on ya?"

Inglewood grinned from the dining room, where he was moving the table even further from the empty Olympia beer can pyramid.

And these are the guys I want to emulate?

They told people to show up around nine, but young, unattached singles-lifestyle etiquette meant folks would show up at least 30 minutes late, maybe an hour. There were no formal invitations or RSVPs, just word of mouth and a few phone calls. The three of them had no idea how many to expect.

Their intent had been to host this affair in the clubhouse, with targeted side visits of three or four at a time to show off the apartment (or if the need arose to hang a sock on the doorknob). But they waited too long—it had already been reserved—so they told themselves it was a chance to showcase the place. It was a convenient justification.

"You know, that prolly won't survive the night," Inglewood motioned with his head to the pyramid.

"Sure it will, if we keep people away from it," Mike said, thinking he didn't relish the notion of playing pyramid cop all night. "Thanks for moving the table out further, though."

Inglewood reached into a box and arranged bottles of Smirnoff, Jose Cuervo, Wild Turkey, and Cutty Sark. With his roommates in charge of alcohol, Matson's responsibility was ice procurement, and he had evenly distributed two 10-pound bags from QuikTrip into three cheap Styrofoam coolers.

He had a fleeting thought to ask James E. if he could borrow his prized Coleman camping cooler, but the thought left almost as soon as it arrived. And then it hit him that he had achieved what he set out to accomplish with the Woodgate move—he hadn't thought about his father in weeks.

"You guys keep the receipts?"

Endler, household financier, sought to ensure three-way party expense equity. Inglewood reached into his now empty box of liquor, held the receipt high, then pocketed it for safe keeping. Matson patted his front left pocket, signaling peace of mind to Moneybags.

When he saw the cocaine, he wasn't concerned about cops or getting arrested. They would only come around if there were noise complaints, and Inglewood kept the stereo volume modulated for that reason. The receiver was tuned to The Rock of Wichita, KEYN, which was easier than changing records and tapes (or trying to manage partygoers tempted to play DJ).

He wouldn't have been able to describe it as such, but image-and-reputation management considerations moved to the forefront. If he didn't toot, people might think he was chicken.

He also had trouble shaking the sixth grade propaganda— a stern lecture delivered by uniformed community-outreach officers from Wichita's finest back at South Pleasant Valley Elementary. If he found himself doing lines of stardust only two months into the young, unattached singles lifestyle, how long would it be before he was mainlining heroin in the hand-me-down orange, frieze-upholstered swivel rocking chair inherited when he left home?

The chair had once belonged to his mother's parents, wealthy from western Kansas oil, who traded furniture like other people changed their underwear. What would Grandma think?

Afraid to get caught? Afraid he would like it too much? Afraid it wouldn't work? Afraid of what his party peers might think if he didn't?

His best friend already knew this and let him off the hook when time came to pass around the little spoon. It wasn't a huge concern.

"Suit yourself," Inglewood said, tilting his head back and shaking long hair out of his eyes.

Surely I can live the unattached singles lifestyle without a monkey on my back.

Since so many of the partygoers worked at Mr. D's, they inevitably talked shop. A former Mr. D's colleague had recently defected catawampus to Safeway in Twin Lakes and lit into them about their "dogshit tan" aprons. Aprons worn by Safewayers were sea green, and as the chemical-fueled repartee escalated, minor concessions were allowed regarding dogshit tan, while firing back at the turncoat with "puke green."

He was outnumbered, so the traitor launched into a condescending drunkalogue about wages. Safeway was a union shop, where workers earned more but had to sell their soul. Endler had schooled them on that and waited for his opening.

"You wanna offer up your first-born male child to Jimmy Hoffa?" Endler sought to quash the debate. "Who, by the way, has been missing now for more than a week."

"Write this down," holding court and turning to Cindy Sue, who pantomimed a secretary taking dictation. "Hoffa's dead, they'll never find him, and it's the beginning of the end of corrupt labor unions."

With a brilliant smile, big glasses, and ever-present headscarves, Sheryl Gray's whole demeanor screamed friendly and approachable. She was a colleague from Mr. D's, and Cindy Sue had brought her to the party. Sheryl's personality leaned cynical and loud, and it was on that plane she and Mike connected.

A 1975 graduate of nearby Goddard High School, just west of Wichita on U.S. 54, economies of scale had brought Sheryl to the big city. Small town, finite number of jobs. Big city, more opportunity.

No one else in their peer group commanded respect like Sheryl. She worked in the Mr. D's courtesy booth, where all manner of business was transacted: checks cashed, pop bottle deposits returned, money orders issued, film from a myriad of cameras dropped off for developing, vendors signed in and out, cash counted and locked into zipper bags to be handed off to armored-car drivers. On the post office-side of the booth, stamps were sold, and proper postage was determined through careful management of outgoing packages.

This full-service model was the cutting edge of the 1970s supermarket business, and Mr. D. liked to be cutting edge. Any moron who could sack, carry, and stock groceries could be a courtesy boy. A warm body and the hint of a personality were all that was required. It took an extra layer of skills to work in the courtesy booth: pleasant, fast on your feet, and the ability to multi-task.

Sheryl Gray was all that.

The courtesy booth was platformed a foot higher than the rest of the supermarket, which allowed a clear view of the front end and the power to manage the human resources needed for smooth operations. Sheryl was often the only female in the booth, was smarter than her male counterparts, and was typically the one called upon for vital impromptu decisions. Had she been born 20 years later, she would have been obvious management material.

Sheryl didn't hire courtesy boys or sign their paychecks, and she couldn't discipline or fire them. Her authority came from friendship, respect, and goodwill. No one had ever seen her get pissed, and it was as though she had learned how to manage her emotions in a professional work setting in a way most of her fellow 17 to 20-year-old peers had not.

"Why do they call you Duck?"

He pulled Endler's beanbag up next to her. Sheryl was seated in his grandmother's swivel rocker, next to the stereo, and just like when she was in the courtesy booth, she was a good foot above him.

"When I worked at Pizza Hut, they said I waddled like a duck, so it stuck."

The scarf wrapped around her head was tied off with a bow on one side. The two trailing ends moved with the wind every time someone came in and out of the balcony sliding glass door.

"You don't mind?" He hadn't yet called her Duck, only Sheryl.

"Nope. I love it," she said, giving him tacit permission to call her by her nickname. "What's your nickname?"

"Don't have one."

He said nothing else. It must have registered on his face.

"What's your middle name?"

"James. It's my old man's first name."

Her scarf fluttered. Someone had opened the sliding glass door and a wave of pot fumes washed over them.

"Ah, the gateway drug," she smiled as a doobie on a hemostat made the rounds on the balcony. "Wow, a hemostat! I usually only see alligator clips. You guys are high-class here at Woodgate."

He was unsure how to approach the relationship. Until now, with every girl there had always been some sort of a romantic or sexual endgame, at least in his own mind. When

Nancy Ellis lost her popcorn and grabbed his arm, she hung on for the rest of the movie. He knew how to manage that—kiss her good night and promise to call her again, even if he had no intention to.

He probably could have brought Nancy to the party and hung a sock on his doorknob but chose not to. The very existence of this party was evidence to him he had moved beyond high school thinking. He had no romantic interest in Duck, but of the two girls with whom he had meaningful communication that day, Duck was the one he most admired.

Duck swiveled the rocker and leaned toward him: "You like *Star Trek*?"

"Beam me up, Scotty," he replied.

"Getting drunk, getting high, it's like the chemical has been applied directly to the center of our molecules while being scrambled in an Enterprise transporter," she said, her eyes big and animated. "When we materialize on the surface of the M class planet, we're completely high."

That is exactly what it feels like.

"To all those nameless red-shirted transporter technicians who valiantly boosted the gain," he smiled and hoisted his Coors can toward her.

Sheryl dropped her lowball tumbler down to meet his hoisted can, "Live long and prosper!"

She was drinking tequila and orange juice on the rocks in a lowball tumbler. Rocks that had been distributed evenly in those three cheap Styrofoam coolers and placed purposefully where party invitees could construct their own libations.

Four months from his 18th birthday, he pondered a new dilemma: How can you be just friends with a girl?

He had heard the word "platonic" before and always assumed it meant the guy struck out but was still in there swinging. What do you do when you want to play the game but actually have no interest in even swinging at pitches? When he looked it up the next day he found, "...rising to levels of closeness to wisdom and true beauty and, eventually, union with the truth."

He wasn't sure what that meant, not even sure it was something he wanted, but it sounded like a helluvan aspiration.

Roughly three hours deep into the party, the Olympia beer can pyramid came crashing down. A 60-day monument to his hard-won freedom, the visual tribute to young, unattached singles lifestyle was scattered all over the dining room floor and spilled into the kitchen.

"Smooth move, Ex-Lax!" Inglewood hollered at the perpetrator, then glanced over at Matson and offered a non-verbal, eyebrows raised, "told you so."

He was too lit to be upset and was coming around to Inglewood's bear piss-interpretation anyway. Now there was a legit excuse to switch over to Coors. Maybe it was time to move beyond such childish frivolities.

He looked up just in time to see Craig Donovan, his best friend from fourth grade at South Pleasant Valley Elementary, walk face first into the sliding glass door. Fourth grade had been traumatized by the mid-year death of their teacher. They came back from Christmas vacation, and no Mrs. Balzer. Ever again.

The glass door didn't give, and Donovan ended up on his back, on the floor.

"You all right, man?" Matson leaned over, inspecting the damage. No blood, but Craig was bound to have a lump and maybe a shiner in the morning.

"Hey, is Mrs. Balzer really dead?" Craig's eyes swam for a minute before locking on to his fourth grade best friend's dusty greens.

After receiving assurances that she was, in fact, Donovan switched into performance mode, the purposeful, attention-getting manner one employs when one has committed an embarrassing *faux pas* in front of a multitude.

"Ouch!"

Why not milk it?

"If I can have everyone's attention, please?! Friends, please take note, there's a glass door right there," Craig pointed vaguely, while flat on his back. "It's not open, even though it looks like it is."

After the last guests departed, the three roommates gathered in the living room for a quick debrief. Inglewood declared the bash a success and peeled off for bed.

Matson's new rectangular fabric wall hanging, four diagonal lines of varying widths (orange, black, beige, and white) was hanging 45 degrees askew on the wall above the couch.

"Lowball tumblers, silver coke spoons, and hemostat roach clips," he said, straightening the wall hanging. "At our first party. Not sure how we can improve on it."

Endler, always a decade ahead of the curve, wasn't convinced.

"We have a ways to go," he complained. "Too many of those people still think of 'party' as a verb."

5.
September 19, 1975

"The Kansas City Royals edged the Minnesota Twins last night, 4 to 3. Amos Otis was the star of the game, homering in the first, then knocking in Freddie Patek at the top of the seventh with what turned out to be the game winner. Harmon Killebrew also homered for the Royals. More sports at 2:50, right here on 1240 KAKE Radio."

The radio in the Falcon was still tuned to KAKE, because he'd been listening to the game the night before. Royals baseball was the only reason to listen to KAKE radio. Their adult contemporary format was designed specifically for the same target audience as Mr. D's. KAKE served up Streisand and Manilow the way Mr. D's offered weekly specials on Log Cabin maple syrup and True Value brand honey in a squeezable container shaped like a bear.

Mike thought about the Fat Kid as he punched the car radio over to KLEO (1480-AM). It was the nickname big league pitcher Jim Bouton hung on Killebrew in *Ball Four*, his baseball culture, envelope-expanding diary of the 1969 season. The Fat Kid led the majors in home runs and RBIs that year and powered the Twins to their first-ever American League West Division title and playoffs, where they lost the pennant to Baltimore.

He loved that book for two reasons: baseball, and the fact that it showed big leaguers for who they really were, not the sanitized version Curt Gowdy spouted in NBC's *Game of the Week*. Mike was 12 years old when he stumbled across Bouton in the Sweetbriar branch of the Wichita Public Library five years earlier, and it was the first time he'd been exposed to dark humor and cynicism. He also began to realize the difference between reality and the story someone wants you to know.

Killebrew was 39 years old and didn't have much left. He knew the Royals signing him after the Twins cut him loose was just a stopgap. The Royals were on the ascent with new skipper Whitey Herzog poised to lead them to the postseason promised land. After beating the Twins last night, they were now 18 games over .500 and on track to finish in second place in the West.

Pretty damn good for an expansion team only seven years old.

Mike had no way of knowing the Fat Kid's solo shot to deep left for the Royals against the Twins in Minnesota would be the last of his career, and he was pondering who would replace the Fat Kid next year at DH for the Royals as he entered Mr. D's and tied on his apron.

Duck saw him, and they exchanged smiles as she motioned with her head to the cash registers, where it was clearly busy. He kept walking, nodding toward the back of the store, and snapping his leather Garvey price-marker holster to his belt, just below his right kidney.

It was hot, and he would rather stock dairy than carry out. The Kansas wind always did a number on his long hair, and he was constantly running to the bathroom to comb and primp. After all, you gotta look good for the KAKE Radio/Mr. D's target demographic. He was half-a-cartload of Steffen's whole and 2 percent milk into his excuse when he heard Duck's voice.

"We need all courtesy help up front, please."

It wasn't the volume, but the tone of voice that dictated how fast the courtesy boys would make their way up front.

"All courtesy help, up front!"

Supermarket intercom protocol demanded that the message be repeated. This occurred naturally, since you couldn't hear everything the first time in a big and noisy store. He looked up from his milk gallons and saw a couple colleagues making their way up front.

That'll take care of it.

He rotated what little remained of the Steffen's whole milk stock. Oldest in the front, newest to the back.

Since most everything in the store cost less than a dollar, most courtesy boys left the cents symbol static on their Garveys, and just adjusted the numbers. So, the few Steffen's gallons that remained in the case were stamped 159¢.

It's not 159 cents, you clueless bastards, it's a dollar-59, adjusting his Garvey to read $1.59 before stamping. *What the hell is the target demographic gonna think when they see 159¢ stamped atop these plastic milk jugs? They're gonna think Mr. D. employs a bunch of fools who are too goddamn lazy to adjust our Garveys, that's what they're gonna think.*

kuh-CHUNK, kuh-CHUNK, kuh-CHUNK.

"Mike, courtesy help up front, please. Mike, courtesy help."

There are three Mikes who work here. She must mean one of the other two.

Garveys were assigned after 90 days. Some guys washed out long before Garvey issuance. If you passed the 90-day muster, a Garvey became a visible sign of courtesy boy self-worth. His was brand-new, its shining stainless stem topped by a green metal knob. They were spring-loaded, returning on the upswing to an ink pad to imprint the selected price on the foodstuff.

When business was slow and courtesy boys were called to

stock, the mechanical sounds of price-stamping would emanate throughout Mr. D's.

Libby's Creamed Corn on Aisle 3, 49 cents.

kuh-CHUNK, kuh-CHUNK, kuh-CHUNK.

One-pound cans of Folgers coffee on aisle 8, $1.69 (not 169¢).

kuh-CHUNK, kuh-CHUNK, kuh-CHUNK.

Twenty minutes in the dairy cooler, and he was ready for some warmth. He made his way up front, where the rush had subsided, and Duck motioned him over to a corner of the courtesy booth.

"Why didn't you come when I called?" She had found a balance between indignation and genuine concern.

"Stocking dairy. It was nearly empty."

They both knew that checking, sacking, and carrying out trumped all other work at Mr. D's. The customer always comes first.

"Yeah, but I called you twice, once by name."

He thought she sounded more disappointed than pissed.

"I thought you meant Mike Lancaster." She gave him a "horseshit, you know better" look, and he made his way to the checkouts for sacking and carryout duty.

The rest of the evening, he was able to zero in on the housewives he found particularly attractive, chat them up while carrying out their groceries, then fantasize after slamming the tailgates of their new Mercury Marquis Colony Park station wagons.

Manilow, huh? Well, you know, here at Mr. D's we can't smile without you, but I'm really more of an Aerosmith guy.

Still seeking warmth.

About a half hour before the end of the shift, he was sweeping the floor in the backroom after arranging stock carts for the overnight shift when Duck came on the intercom.

"Mike Lancaster, Mike Seeley, Mike Matson, please come to the courtesy booth." Duck's voice was polite, almost singsongy. "Lancaster, Seeley, Matson, to the courtesy booth, please."

Now what? Doesn't seem very courteous to call us by our last names. At least she said please.

They stood before her like subjects in a royal court.

"There's too many of you guys with the same name."

Problem-solving was not a requisite for working in the courtesy booth, but it sure helped.

Pointing to Lancaster, "You will be called Mike."

Seeley was next in line, "You will be Michael."

Seeley shrugged and nodded.

"And you, my friend," she paused for dramatic effect as though tapping him on the shoulders with a sword and bestowing him with Courtesy Boy Knighthood, "henceforth, heretofore, and from now on, you will be known as Michael J."

Mike and Michael departed. He and Duck smiled broadly at each other.

"Like it?" She was pulling the cash drawer from the Post Office.

"I love it!" In fact, he thought it captured his persona perfectly. "Thanks, Duck."

He rushed to the back, found the strips of paper designed specifically for the Mr. D's nametags, and wrote MICHAEL J. in the same block lettering he'd used to design the house in Drafting 3, and proudly reaffixed the nametag to his dogshit tan apron.

Like the Fat Kid, he had a nickname.

Finally.

He snagged the pair of Coors six-packs he had set inside the freezer a half-hour ago. They would be ice-cold for the trip home to Woodgate. He would also want some tomorrow afternoon at the pool.

The other two Mikes, each six to 12 months behind him in the young, unattached singles lifestyle, had expressed interest in popping over after work. The ambience would speak for itself, so he wouldn't have to work very hard to show off. It was Friday night, and there was bound to be a party at the pool or clubhouse. Plus, it was still officially summer, so the hot Kansas wind would be blowing, and the girls would be bikini-clad.

Hi girls, please forgive the intrusion and allow me to introduce my friends, Mike Lancaster, (you can call him Mike) and Mike Seeley (you can call him Michael). They're kicking the tires on our lifestyle, and I think they like what they see!

Of course, you already know me. But henceforth, heretofore, and from now on, you can call me Michael J. I think it apropos, capturing my casual, laid-back essence, wouldn't you agree?

He would run his hand through his hair on that last question.

6.
October 21, 1975

The sacks were all paper. Brown paper.

Small, flat sacks, into which greeting cards could be slipped, protecting them from condensation from a milk carton. Double-lined thermal sacks designed specifically to hold a half-gallon carton of Steffen's Butter Brickle Ice Cream. Drippy, cut-up chicken and whole fryers were to be double-bagged. He learned early on the housewives appreciated it when he would reach for the thermals to wrangle the messy poultry.

But the large utility sacks, designed to hold 12 pounds of groceries, were the money bags. The Mr. D's logo, red and black italicized block lettering with the finishing stem of the capital "M" doubling as the starting stem of the capital "R," was imprinted on both sides, about three-fourths of the way up from the bottom. This sack had succeeded an earlier version that listed the address of every Mr. D's in Wichita. The junior marketing account exec in charge of transitioning to a cleaner, simpler sack must have thought he had stumbled into an epiphany.

"Boys, it's silly to list the street addresses for all the stores on these sacks! It's not like the lady of the house will scrounge for a sack currently serving as a wastebasket liner beneath the sink. Is she really going to study the grease-splotched list of addresses and decide to drive across town to shop at a different Mr. D's, eschewing the convenience of Mr. D's Sweetbriar in her own neighborhood?"

Then, a grizzled veteran at the marketing firm would be forced to verbalize the dirty little secret: "Ever consider that Mr. D. himself likes seeing a long list of every store in his kingdom plastered all over every sack of groceries that leaves every one of his stores?

We have an audience of one. And don't use 'eschewing.' No one knows what it means."

Sacking groceries became an art form, and Michael J. took it seriously. Heavy stuff, like cans and five pound bags of flour, went on the bottom. Glass jars and bottles were separated with bags of pasta, baking goods, or anything that would cushion the blow. Meat and ice cream wrapped up in the thermals. Bags within bags. Eggs and bread on top.

Cereal boxes were the easiest to sack. Four boxes of family-sized Cheerios, laid sideways, would completely fill a Mr. D's carryout sack. Every inch of space taken. Maximum efficiency.

The two-wheeled standup carryout dolly cart was a vital tool of the courtesy boy trade. Four feet tall with an upper retractable top shelf that could hold three full-sized paper sacks—two lengthwise and one widthwise in front with the Mr. D's logo face-up—all held in place with a swing bar. The bottom held more sacks of groceries, gallons of milk, and eight-pack returnable bottles of pop. When ice was on the list, those five and 10-pound bags would anchor loose items in place on the bottom.

Otherwise efficient courtesy boys had to master their center of gravity and expend just the right amount of body English on the cart to keep everything secure through the often perilous parking lot journey. Chunks of ice in the winter.

Pothole caused by the chunk of ice in the summer.

He became proficient quickly and could maneuver two dolly carts at a time—lead with one, trail with the other. It wasn't rocket science, but customers seemed to appreciate his sacking skills and friendly demeanor.

"October in Wichita is awfully nice, huh?" He had become a pro at chatting up the housewives. "Pretty windy sometimes. Some days even a wind surge."

Checkers grooved on his speed and adeptness and would ask for him by name.

"Michael J., courtesy help on 3, please."

A courtesy boy hitting on all cylinders made for better all-around supermarket life.

Michael J. was also responsible for the development and dissemination of a closely-held Mr. D's lingo. For ordering and inventory purposes, every product on every shelf was identified by a number on a postage stamp-sized sticker, designed specifically to slide into the front facing of the shelf. Space for individual product data was limited, so the sticker space allotted for a standard size can of Del Monte Cut Green Beans would read:

DM CGB
4.5 oz
76561

Long before the advent of barcodes, managers would walk the aisles with a hard copy list of products corresponding to shelf stickers. If they were short on product #76561, he'd write down how many cases were needed to fill the shelf and stock the storeroom, then phone in the order using only the numbers.

Matson wasn't breaking any new linguistic ground. He was simply taking existing abbreviations and saying them out loud. As a result, cut green beans became CGBs; early June peas, EJPs; whole kernel corn, WKC; strawberry preserves, SP; crunchy peanut butter, CPB; paper towels, PTs, etc.

A layer of complexity was added when brand names came into the picture. A checker couldn't just get on the intercom and say, "Michael J., need some CGB's up here on register 4!"

One needed to be more specific.

"Uh... we got yer DM CGB's (Del Monte), yer FP CGBs (First Pick), and yer GG CGBs (Green Giant), that are actually cut diagonally, which sorta makes them GG DCGBs. What's your pleasure?"

He knew he was onto something when he overheard a couple of the managers speaking the language.

The lingo became an essential component of effective courtesy boy know-how and another rallying point for the clique of like-minded young supermarket professionals. Since he was the one who came up with it, deciding who was (and wasn't) included in the clique fell to him. When someone outside the clique attempted the lingo, snickers would often ensue.

Register 1 was the domain of Veda Barnett, the checker with the most seniority. Hers was the checkstand closest to the courtesy booth, and all the regulars stood in Veda's line, even if it meant a longer wait. They had been checking out with Veda for years, and their friendly relationship with her was a vital aspect of their shopping experience.

She was in her 50s, and if she had a bad day, it never showed. Veda wore a peaceful smile that reflected the confidence of a generation that had tamed the Great Depression and won a World War.

"Mike, will you please run and fetch a pair of two-pound bags of C&H brown sugar for Mrs. Turner here?"

Nicknames carried no truck with Veda.

"Delighted. C&H BS. Check."

"Such foolishness," Mrs. Turner said under her breath.

Veda's peaceful smile descended into a peaceful frown, and she gave Mrs. Turner a look that said, "I agree with you wholeheartedly, but I have to work with them."

This would contrast with Diana Adams on register 2, who was in her mid-30s and eager to fit in.

"Michael J., three-pound MHDG on 2, please."

On the intercom, he would often throw in fake static noises between sentences, to lend some authenticity to the storewide communication: "Maxwell House Drip Grind. (STATIC NOISE). Three-pounder. (STATIC NOISE). 10-4. Be there PDQ ASAP."

"Attention, Mr. D's shoppers! For the next three minutes, and three minutes only, we are thrilled to offer you huge savings and what will doubtless prove to be a cherished memory of your time with us here on this October afternoon at Mr. D's Sweetbriar. THREE 46-ounce cans of Hi-C fruit-flavored drinks for only ONE DOLLAR!"

It didn't take long for Duck and the other courtesy booth managers to seek him out when it came time to announce these limited-time specials over the intercom. The voice, sure, but also a knack to wing it, which infused some excitement into otherwise mundane supermarket bargains.

"Make your way to the north end of aisle four, where

you'll find courtesy boys ready, willing, and able to mark the three-minute sale price on orange, grape, cherry, orange-pineapple, pineapple-grapefruit, apple, and something called 'Florida fruit punch,' which remains somewhat of a mystery here in Kansas, but the folks in Miami Beach have REALLY nice things to say about it!"

He enjoyed doing it but, even more, he liked being sought out to do it.

"Hi-C is enriched with Vitamin C and contains 10 percent fruit juice... little unsure about the remaining 90 percent, but man, is it tasty! Aisle four. North end. Hi-C. Three for a dollar!"

And so on. For three minutes straight. Mr. D. moved some slow-moving inventory, shoppers got a price break, and Michael J. freebased his ego.

7.
December 25, 1975

"I Love Music" blared from KEYN on the clock radio.

I do love music, but I also love sports. Sorry, O'Jays.

He tuned the radio to KFH (1330-AM), to catch the sportscast for some followups to the news two days earlier that had rocked Major League Baseball. A court-appointed arbitrator had relegated baseball's reserve clause to the ash heap of history, declaring Andy Messersmith of the Dodgers and Dave McNally of the Expos free agents. The game would never be the same.

He lay in bed wondering if Ewing Kauffman would now shake loose some of his millions to bring some proven lumber to Royals Stadium, especially with Harmon Killebrew now retired. The Fat Kid lasted one year in KC.

Mr. D's had gone silent at midnight. Christmas was the only day of the year the supermarket closed, and Mike was among a group of courtesy boys tasked to turn the place upside down looking for the keys to Mr. D's automatic doors. When you only lock up once a year, keys are only needed once a year and easy to misplace.

No Christmas Eve parties, as Inglewood and Endler had already gone home to their nuclear families.

He squinted in the dark before reaching for his glasses: 7:15 a.m. The time was displayed in actual white-on-black numbers that flipped, sort of like a time-keeping Rolodex, no big hand or little hand. He used his fingers to count forward and backward. It had been six hours since he went to bed, and he still had six hours before he was expected home.

Home. It was a mental slip—he was already home. It hadn't taken long to really, truly, deeply believe that Woodgate, not Pleasant Valley, was home.

Christmas dinner was set for 1 p.m. He was eager to see his mom; his older sister, now in her third year at a small, liberal arts, church-affiliated college in Oklahoma; and his younger brother, a sophomore at Heights. He could get there early, but why?

A 12:50 p.m. arrival felt about right.

He would dress for dinner, though, so he could show off his new brushed-denim leisure suit with tan piping, a gem picked up at A.J. August. He had polished his tan, leather, high-top zip boots that matched the piping on the leisure suit. When he bought them senior year, his father had called them "fruit boots."

His father came out to greet him as he pulled into the driveway.

"You and I are going to have a little talk after dinner, mister."

He hadn't talked to James E. Matson since leaving home, a week after graduation last spring. Once every couple of weeks, he would phone his mom to check in. She never handed the phone to his father, and Mike wasn't about to ask.

Father and son with matching false pride.

As a kid, there was really only one way to do business with James E. Matson, and that was his way. You bent to his will or you suffered the consequences, which were sometimes physical, always emotional, and always painful. He never talked back, and even when he got old enough to think about talking back, it was as though James E. read his mind and the emotional gamesmanship was elevated to a new level.

His father was strict, rigid, often loud, and profane. There were no beatings, just swats on the ass with a plywood paddle (a weekend woodcraft project in the garage), and corralling his son firmly by the neck. Mike learned early on that survival meant acquiescence.

As Mike reached into the backseat to retrieve his gifts for the family, James E. made a mental note of all the empty beer cans. At least a dozen, maybe 20.

Merry Christmas to you, too.

"Okay."

He was his own man, but 18 years of fear-driven behavior dies hard.

"You've already frittered away the fall semester."

It was James E.'s after-dinner opener as he plopped into his vinyl, harvest-gold La-Z-Boy, directing his son to a corner of the living room couch.

"If you enroll at dub-yes-you for the spring semester, I'll pay for it."

James E. saw it as a compromise. He didn't object to his son working and had encouraged it since age 12. He knew his son wasn't crazy about the notion of college and thought by removing the barrier of financing, the leap to yes would be shorter.

I wouldn't call it 'frittering.' I now have a nickname and built an Olympia beer can pyramid that just so happened to be the envy of Woodgate.

His father did have sort of a point.

As a youngster, because he had never had to work hard to

succeed, he didn't. When the elementary school straight As slipped to junior high Bs, Cs, and the occasional D, it had nothing to do with brainpower. It was because he lacked the discipline to study and was not inclined to develop it.

James E. was still disappointed about Mike's senior year at Heights.

He had entered with a goal of carrying as few textbooks as possible, ending up with two in the fall, one in the spring: First semester American Government with Sherry Johnson and the Honesty Party, which he aced, and Algebra 2, which he flunked. Mostly because it was second hour, and it was easier to pile into Inglewood's 1965 Barracuda or Robbie Lang's 1970 pale yellow Malibu after first-hour band class and head to an arcade in Park City to play foosball, drink rhino piss, then ease back for third-hour orchestra.

After spending junior year as a jack-of-all-trades on the yearbook staff, Mike started senior year as yearbook editor. He stepped down from that job when it became clear he would have to work harder than he wanted to.

Throughout his childhood, college had been the expectation. In the driveway during junior high, he would imitate Lon Kruger's jump shot and dream about Kansas State. His Drafting 3 teacher encouraged him to study architecture.

Some kids from the yearbook staff spent a week at yearbook camp at Bethany College in Lindsborg the summer between junior and senior year. The highlights of that week were twofold: driving Mark's Barracuda home after Inglewood fell asleep at the wheel and ended up in the median, and sneaking out one night to drive to Salina for beer. High jinks aside, Matson was struck by the campus and briefly entertained the notion of an intimate, small-school undergrad experience.

James E. had some skin in his son's first forays into the

Wichita labor force, arranging a paper route at age 12 and a gig as a janitor's assistant at 15.

The *Wichita Eagle* was to be on Pleasant Valley front porches by 6 a.m., and the *Wichita Beacon* was to be delivered by 5 p.m. The job also demanded his evenings, when he went door to door securing weekly subscription fees—"collecting" in paper boy parlance. It involved a zippered cash bag and pocket-sized hard copy register, which detailed names, addresses, and individual subscriber specs. "M" meant customers consumed their daily news in the morning; "E" denoted evening subscribers; and "S" was for Sunday.

Most subscribers were MES; some were MS or ES; and there was even an occasional ME, who apparently preferred to keep Sundays free from accounts of the outside world. Some math was required since each newspaper bore a different price. Paper boy'ing also helped him burnish his people skills.

One little old lady with fading faculties on Carlock Street proved to be a chronic pain.

"Manson?" Every week, the same thing, when he rang the doorbell and introduced himself. "Manson?"

He had scant patience for little old ladies who struggled to distinguish a clean-cut, 12-year-old Pleasant Valley white boy from a crazed California cult leader bent on starting an apocalyptic race war.

Helter Skelter, lady. You owe me two-fifty.

He'd return from his paper route shortly after 6 a.m., and James E. would be the only one awake. In the winter of his 13th birthday, after a frigid morning of slogging through snow and ice, his father offered him a cup of Butter-Nut Regular Grind, percolated from the bottom up on the stove, served in a brown melamine cup form-fitted to a matching white melamine saucer.

It was as close as James E. got to expressing pride in his son.

When Mike's brother reached the age of 12, their father decided it was time to hand down the paper route and introduced Mike's next gig—a summer job as a janitor's assistant at Amelia Earhart Elementary on North are-KAN-zuhz Avenue in USD 259, the district where James E. was a veteran teacher.

On his mental list of Things to While Away the Summer Hours, serving as a janitor's assistant ranked low, but the James E. decree was loud and clear.

A month and a half into the new job, he couldn't shake the nagging feeling that being a janitor's assistant fell well below his expectations. At 15, he wasn't sure he could verbalize what he wanted out of gainful employment, apart from the paycheck, but a job that essentially boiled down to cleaning up after others did not make the grade. He drew the conclusion after thoughtlessly sizing up and categorizing the janitor.

On the day he walked off the job, he had been assigned the task of scrubbing dozens of plastic chairs in a half-dozen classrooms.

This soap isn't strong enough to get the job done, and now this cheap-ass scouring pad is falling apart. What does this guy know, anyway? If he's so smart, why is he still a janitor?

"Every one of these chairs is still dirty."

One classroom full of chairs done, Mike was standing for inspection before proceeding. The janitor was leaning over to closely eyeball what he expected would be smudge-free, pristine chairs.

"Start over. And turn that damn thing off!"

Matson's transistor radio was tuned to KLEO, which was currently broadcasting the Raspberries' tale of a paramour encouraging consummation.

All of a half-dozen chairs into his re-do, Mike reached a conclusion. He was done. He stood up and tossed the scouring pad into the bucket of weak suds. He briefly considered just walking out the door, but something made him go in search of the janitor.

"I'm done."

He expected an argument, maybe a confrontation, but had no intention of engaging and began walking away.

"Whaddaya mean, done? You've only been at it for an hour."

The janitor scowled, wishing he didn't have to babysit this ingrate while still humping all day to get his own work done.

"I mean, I quit." He didn't want to explain himself, he just wanted out. "I'm not gonna do the same work twice."

He was on foot, a few blocks south on are-KAN-zuhz Avenue, no thought given to whether he had even done the work once, when he heard the janitor hollering after him.

"The keys!" The old man was huffing and puffing as he got to within about a dozen yards. "You can't leave with the keys!"

Matson reached into his pocket and felt the ring of keys that would grant entry to Amelia Earhart Elementary and open any door within. He had been entrusted access, at age 15, with a job in a huge bureaucratic system, secured on the good name of his father, a vital cog in the same system.

So much for a clean getaway.

He didn't want to explain his motivation, and he was already embarrassed by such an impulsive action. Pride wouldn't allow him to save face, and he wanted no more interactions, so he reached back and tossed the ring of keys to the man, who until five minutes ago, was his boss. A nice, soft, underhand lob designed for little leaguers and old man janitors.

There would be hell to pay once he got home, but he had been weathering James E.'s verbal blasts for 15 years. Maybe he was developing immunity. Or apathy.

Maybe it was a defense to justify an impulsive decision that, deep down, he knew was wrong.

"WHY did you do that?"

The tone was unmistakable and familiar in a way that led him to question all his assumptions about father-son relationships. It was a voice that for 15 years, had immediately rocketed him into a position of fear. There was no gently sloping trend line. Zero to 60 in three seconds. Impulse power to warp speed.

"Answer me, goddamn it!"

Short of total and complete capitulation, nothing he could say would diffuse his father's anger.

James E. wanted a heartfelt *mea culpa* and a verbal commitment that his son throw himself on the mercy of the old janitor at Amelia Earhart, and that was never going to happen. The son's heart didn't feel that way and, deep down, the father was afraid for his son. That fear morphed seamlessly into another layer of anger, which only served to fortify the wall between them.

Even had the words been verbalized, neither side would feel good about it. With the sum total of 15 years of emotional wherewithal and imagination, the son's reaction to these assaults remained consistent, and nothing changed. When the attacks commenced, he had one goal: to extricate himself and find relief.

James E. was glaring and poked an index finger into his

son's chest: "You're gonna go back there, mister, explain that you made a goddamn mistake, and GET THAT JOB BACK!"

With the second poke, the son pulled away from the father, made direct eye contact, and returned the glare.

A first.

The fear remained, but something else was crowding in. It wasn't courage, and it wasn't pushback. He couldn't even chalk it up to anger or resentment. It was resistance. The commitment was shaky, and the outcome remained uncertain.

He was too big for swats on the ass with the plywood paddle, and James E. had never crossed the unspoken, ill-defined line between socially acceptable corporal punishment and assault and battery.

Mike half-hoped for a backhand. No idea about the consequences and no idea how James E. would react if he actually found himself backhanding one of his children, but Mike had a suspicion it could go one of two ways: carpet-bombing Hanoi or a moratorium. Morality-driven self-analysis was out of the question.

The unspoken but crystal clear implication, expectation, and result of every confrontation with James E. had been that Mike would bend to his father's will. But he did not want to go back to Earhart, hat in hand, and ask if he could please start scrubbing plastic classroom chairs again with weak soap and a cheap-ass scouring pad.

A clash of personalities.

He didn't go back to Earhart, but it didn't feel like a victory.

James E. saw his son's shortcomings as a failure of responsibility—immaturity; lack of stick-to-itiveness—and an inability to understand the importance of doing things the right way. The father's analysis of the problem and resulting conclusions were spot-on, but his potential solutions fell drastically short of effectiveness.

Instead of helping his son understand and learn from his mistakes, he just got pissed and yelled. At 15, Matson was stuck living with a man who held a polar-opposite view of responsibility as it applied to the relationship between a father and son.

After Earhart, Mike decided he would find his own jobs. Within six months he was a busboy at Angelo's, courtesy of Inglewood, who had preceded him there as a dishwasher earning $1.60 an hour. No one asked specifics surrounding the departure from his most recent job, and he didn't volunteer any.

He had just turned 16 when he started at Angelo's, where his busboy duties included bringing cases of bottled beer from a walk-in cooler in the kitchen to the front of the restaurant— Coors, Miller High Life in clear glass, gold foil-topped Michelob, and rhino piss in stubby little brown bottles.

A new professional colleague introduced him to the concept of hiding out in the walk-in cooler and cracking open a cold one.

His first regular access. The gateway cooler.

A year later, when employment prospects took him six blocks south to Mr. D's, he discovered a similar walk-in cooler with an even wider selection. With his newfound mantle of courtesy boy leadership and responsibility, Michael J. recruited new colleagues and introduced them to this unwritten fringe benefit.

Paying it forward.

Mike promised his father to give dub-yes-you some thought but kept coming back to why? Where's it written? What chapter and verse in the Epic Tome of Societal Expectations does it dictate that the only way for young people to succeed is by going to college?

He had once overheard his father say he could relate to older children much easier than younger ones. As he grew older, he kept waiting for that to manifest itself in their own relationship. Now that he could, a big part of him liked imagining a middle-finger response to any of his father's ideas.

Growing up, the descriptive noun that always seemed to accompany Mike was "potential." James E. saw it, but his overall demeanor and attitude toward his middle child resulted in a brick wall.

Fuck potential. Mike had 18 years of resentments to catch up on.

His children and even his wife didn't know it at the time, but James E. had endured a colorful, but less-than-idyllic, childhood.

His father, J. Ellsworth Matson II, known as Ell, was a ne'er-do-well motorcycle daredevil who skirted the edge of norms and societal expectations. His mother, Victoria Maday, was a devout Roman Catholic raised on the southern Minnesota plains.

When he was conceived out of wedlock in the Twin Cities, his parents quickly married, then left on a houseboat honeymoon voyage down the Mississippi River. Upon reaching New Orleans, they sold the houseboat; bought a motorcycle with a sidecar; and made for Spokane, Washington.

The idea was to get to Spokane in time for James E.'s paternal grandfather, a medical doctor, to deliver the baby, gratis. They fell 153 miles short, and the kid was born—a month premature—in Walla Walla. His parents dubbed him Champ, "A name he can grow into."

A hard-charging drinker, Ell's work for FDR's New Deal Bureau of Reclamation took them all over the West. Western American expansion and government money put men to work, helping them regain a sense of self-worth in the heart of a Great Depression.

As a land surveyor, Ell helped lay out, map, and establish boundaries for reclamation projects throughout the West—Grand Coulee Dam, northwest of Spokane; Shasta Dam in northern California; irrigation dams in Arizona. When World War II began, the family of three was in Anchorage, Alaska, where Ell was surveying ground for military bases.

His mother used the fear of a Japanese invasion of Alaska in the weeks after Pearl Harbor as camouflage to pack up her son and leave Ell for keeps. As a single mother, Victoria then embarked on her own tragic, alcohol-fueled narrative that featured a revolving door of husbands who ran the gamut from standup decency to criminal violence.

Once, when a drunken suitor had beaten his mother to a bloody pulp, 14-year-old Champ ran the man out of the house with a shotgun.

During Mike's 17-and-a-half years living with his father, this childhood was whitewashed. James E. held his mother at arm's length until her death in 1972, and his father was never mentioned.

Champ looked to the Navy for structure and escape from his mother. The day after his graduation from Plainville High School in 1951, he was on a train to San Diego for basic training. His emancipation included a new name. He chucked Champ and became James E. Matson, Jim to his friends.

One of his mother's revolving-door husbands was from Plainville, and he came home, wife and stepson in tow, the summer before Champ's sophomore year in high school. In study hall, he met Geraldine Ordway, daughter of Victor Ordway, an outgoing, community-minded entrepreneur whose father-in-law, Fred Bemis, had struck oil twenty years earlier.

The Bemis Pool, deep below the Saline River Valley in southern Rooks and northern Ellis counties, would become the largest producing oilfield on the continent.

Jim and Geri were married halfway through his four-year Navy hitch. He was honorably discharged, and the couple spent another four years in Manhattan, Kansas, where Mike and his older sister were born. Armed with an undergraduate degree in agronomy from the land-grant university, James E. moved his young family back to Plainville, and Victor set them up on the farm where his daughter had grown up.

Calves in the early spring; wheat harvest in the summer; grain sorghum in the fall; fixing fence and equipment in the winter. Debt, year-round.

Because of his father-in-law's fossil fuel collateral, James E. could get operating loans on a handshake at the bank in Plainville. But he was irritable and restless on the farm and sought job security with a steady paycheck. So, they sold the farm, paid off the debts, and used a portion of the proceeds to finance a graduate degree in education from nearby Fort Hays Kansas State College.

In the summer of 1966, the family moved to Wichita,

where James E. had accepted a job teaching 8th grade biology at Brooks Junior High.

The neighborhood was a textbook byproduct of postwar suburban creep. Pleasant Valley was white, middle class, homogenous. The men went to work in the morning while women stayed home, raised the baby boomers, and drove station wagons to Mr. D's to stock up on CGBs, Hi-C, and minute steaks.

The Steffen's Dairy milkman, with a six-inch ring on his belt holding keys to every house in Pleasant Valley, delivered a weekly 10-gallon box of milk that took up an entire shelf in the avocado green General Electric refrigerator.

Their house on St. Clair Avenue was three doors down from Pleasant Valley Junior High School, which stood adjacent to South Pleasant Valley Elementary. A dozen houses the other way, the neighborhood bumped up against the Big Ditch, a postwar flood control project that funneled water out of basements and into the are-KAN-zuhz. On the far side of the Big Ditch, North PV was just a few doors down from Inglewood's mother's house in Sherwood Glen.

After a few months of trial and error, Jim and Geri found a church home in Pleasant Valley United Methodist, where all the congregants looked, acted, and thought just like they did.

It's almost as if founding father John Wesley had the 20th century Kansas agrarian culture in mind when he urged Methodists to "do all the good you can, by all the means you can, in all the ways you can, in all the places you can, at all the times you can, to all the people you can, as long as ever you can."

It appealed to Geri's nature. James E.'s too, on the rare

occasions when he took his wife's nature seriously.

Geri sang in the choir, and James E. served on the church governing board. He was full of creativity and innovation, but his consensus-building skills were limited to expecting everyone else to come along, based solely on the merits of his arguments, and then privately disparaging them when they didn't.

At home, and in front of the classroom, James E. Matson was large and in charge.

Methodists believed in something they called prevenient grace. God's love is omnipresent and comes before humans do what comes naturally (which is to screw up). Wesley believed this grace was Point A, with repentance and faith found at Point Z.

The Methodist Youth Fellowship was designed to set junior high and high school Methodists on this straight-and-narrow path, but Mike's curiosity in discerning Points B through Y tended to take a back seat to chasing girls.

James E. and Geri's Methodist friendships led to a quintessential 1970s cultural phenomenon called "sharing group," where a half-dozen couples would take turns hosting a weeknight evening of conversation, generally culled from some larger pressing societal concern.

Between bites of chocolate sheet cake and sips of Butter-Nut brewed in a poppy-red, 32-cup electric percolator, the sharing group would dive into cutting edge, psyche-exploring notions like transactional analysis which posits that humans front themselves in one of three ways: the parent, the adult, or the child.

The parent relies on "tapes" from childhood: external influences a child has observed and from watching adults.

James E. came away from sharing group not thinking how

he could help others, but how he could help himself. He saw nothing innately wrong with this worldview. He saw it as a way to inform his own thinking about himself, but it didn't translate into better relationships with his wife, children, or mother.

Geri was naturally social and genuinely cared for her sharing groupies. James E. was intellectually curious and eager to harvest pearls of wisdom. Their childhoods were Venus and Mars. She got a baby grand piano for her 16th birthday. He ran a drunken wife-beater out of the house with a shotgun at 14.

After the life he had led, Pleasant Valley was the pinnacle for James E. When your childhood is strewn with abandonment, neglect, violence, and other assorted alcohol-fueled drama, structure and consistency become an aspiration.

A generation later, Mike was seeking an anti-Pleasant Valley life and reputation. Not counterculture or hippies—the youngest from that crowd were five years older—their time had come and gone. He had no clue what his life would look like, other than it would be away from James E.

He thought a lot about his parents' friends in the sharing group, especially George Landon, who was kind and supportive and whose children adored him. George served meals to shut-ins and had brought Mike along on a couple of recent rounds, no doubt to expose him to the concept of selflessness.

He wondered what it would be like to have a father who was supportive and encouraging like George.

He wondered what you had to do to be worthy of such things.

Like Messersmith and McNally, he was a free agent—players create the economic value now. Messersmith signed a million-dollar contract with the Atlanta Braves, and McNally retired. Matson took his potential and set up housekeeping at

Woodgate.

Home.

Pleasant Valley was where he learned a sense of fair play, right from wrong, and the tenets of Christianity through MYF. Do all the good you can, by all the means you can. All the ingredients for a life of integrity were there, at his disposal.

All he had to do was live it.

8.
January 7, 1976

"MAAAKUL J., WE GAWD INNY MOW-ER O' THAY-UM THREEFERDOLLER AH-GEE-A BRAY-UHND MANDARIAN ORN-JIZZ?"

Michael J. and the new guy stopped stocking 18-ounce boxes of Duncan Hines Brownie Mix and looked at each other. Unsure of courtesy boy protocol for such announcements, the new guy tried hard not to laugh until he saw Matson break into a big grin and chuckle.

"That's Virginia on register five, platinum hair piled high, held in place with a can of Aqua Net a day," Mike said, getting up to fetch the mandarin oranges. "She's an Ozarks refugee. Sort of a female Mr. Haney from *Green Acres*."

"Cultivated and harvested in Mandaria?" New guy Duane Smith wanted to fit in. "Governed by a strongman who stifles dissent, but he's our strongman?"

Intelligent, above the fray, with an innate talent for using humor to diffuse uncomfortable situations. Intended or not, Duane's intellect and ability to accurately size up people and situations, then crack wise about them, was his entrée to relationships. As a result, there wasn't much of a murky middle. You either liked the guy or you didn't.

Yet to pass 90-day muster, Duane was Garvey-less, so to give him something to do, Michael J. handed over his box cutter, a single edge razor blade slipped into a thin, retractable aluminum sheath, but not before demonstrating how to open cases of brownie mix without slicing into the product. Then, he led the new guy on a Mr. D's tour d'horizon, where Matson shared vital courtesy boy knowledge, such as rotating the stock.

"I encountered some cans of Hormel Chili the other day that looked like they'd been there since Nixon resigned."

"We prefer Ford administration chili," Duane said. "Less greasy. Got it."

New guy opened the cases, while Michael J. Garvey-ed .49 on each package (or 49¢, either price presentation acceptable in this case, he explained). They took turns arranging brownie mix on the shelves, then breaking down and flattening the empty boxes. Within 30 minutes, the two of them had constructed an end-of-aisle display the envy of any supermarket in the Great Plains.

Even if the store wasn't busy, courtesy boys were expected to be doing something: grab a broom, straighten up the sacks, face the shelves (where all the products were pulled to the front of the shelf, which gave it a neat and organized look).

"I get it. Serves two purposes," Duane replied. "Spiffs up the appearance and provides an outlet for the OCD."

"Exactly."

Michael J. had no idea what that meant and wasn't about to ask. He was the one imparting knowledge in this relationship, not seeking it. But he couldn't quit thinking about it and worried what the new guy thought of him.

This new guy seems decent enough. He seems to catch on quickly to rotating the stock and facing. Just like my Olympia beer can pyramid— every can facing forward. Consistency is a good thing. Appearances matter.

"That new guy's a goofy fucker! He acts like he's smarter than the rest of us."

Steve Walters was a short kid who compensated by being

loud, boisterous, and filterless. He lived on a farm near Andale and lacked the pretension and skills to fully appreciate Duane's "humor as deflection" strategy.

"Nah, the guy just needs a nickname," Matson replied, ignoring the obvious.

The nickname was of vital importance and should be approached with great care. Done well, it built *esprit de corps*, bestowed legitimacy, and signaled a worthiness to join the courtesy boy brotherhood. Done really well, it elevated one's stature and brought the bestowee a deeper level of self-worth.

People don't really change after they get a nickname, they just feel better about themselves. Michael J. thought that was important.

Duane had been sent up front to sack and carry out, but next on the new-guy learning curve was to get schooled on the intricacies and nuances of "doing bottles."

The consumption of carbonated soft drinks in the 1970s was a labor-intensive enterprise. The cycle started when a Mr. D's shopper would pick up an eight-pack carton of 16-ounce glass bottles of Coca-Cola. Maybe someone in the family turned up their nose at Coke, so Mom would swap out a couple of bottles of Coke for Sprite.

When all eight bottles were consumed, Mom brought the carton of empties back to the Mr. D's courtesy booth. Or, if pressed for time, she left them in her shopping cart until reaching the checkstand. Refunds were returned as cash or a credit on Mom's grocery tab.

In the booth, the empty bottles were stowed in 6 x 2 x 4-foot carts. When full, a courtesy boy wheeled them to the back and slammed through the swinging metal doors between the eggs and beer. There was an unspoken competition among courtesy boys to produce the loudest slam.

Roughly one-fourth of the backroom storage space was allotted to the organized sorting and stacking of empty pop bottles—four cardboard cartons of empties per one wooden case, stacked six feet high, against the wall, then building out into the open space.

Sprite goes with Coke. Teem goes with Pepsi. Dr. Pepper and Fanta go with 7UP.

Four times a week, the delivery drivers from Coke, Pepsi, and 7UP arrived, dutifully checked in and out by anyone on the flow chart higher than a courtesy boy. They arrived bearing cases of full cartons of glass pop bottles and departed with empty ones.

He and Walters heard the metal doors open, and a cart of bottles gingerly rattled and clinked toward them. They exchanged "gotta be the new guy" glances.

Hesitant and uncertain with what to do with the bottles, Duane stopped the cart just a few feet into the hallway after clearing the doors.

"Jesus Henry, new guy! Slam that cart through there like you got a pair!"

Walters' nickname was "Sticky," mostly because he tended to end up wearing bottom-of-the-bottle residue when he sorted empties, though among the ranks of courtesy boys, Steve's nickname had evolved into dual interpretations—based on Walters' self-professed exploits on the farm.

Duck's voice on the intercom interrupted them: "Michael J., please check on register 6... Michael J., check on register 6!"

"This is Steve Walters, he'll check you out on bottles," Michael J. said before departing the backroom for register 6. "I may have mentioned—everyone here has nicknames. Henceforth, heretofore, and from now on, you'll be known as 'Duane the Man.'"

"Seems fitting," he replied. "Does it come with a decoder ring or engraved certificate on parchment, suitable for framing?"

"You're so full of shit! Duane the Man, my rosy-red ass!" Walters countered, frowning as he hoisted two eight-packs of 16-ounce Pepsi empties from the cart. "You're gonna be Duane the BOY—Duane the boooeey."

"DOO-WAYNE GEH-*BOOOOOEY*," throwing some wooden cases in the general area that would eventually be filled with empties and duly stacked. "C'mon Gebooey, these pop bottles are callin' your name. Watch and learn, new guy."

Duane the Man was perfectly content to lean on the cart, asking Sticky the occasional cogent pop-bottle sorting procedural question, all the while not lifting a finger.

Watching and learning.

Michael J. squinted against the setting sun shining directly in his eyes.

At about three-fourths of the way up the ladder, he wasn't high enough above sea level for the acrophobia to kick in, and it gave him the breathing room needed to hang a sign in the plate-glass window. It was one of two remaining chores that stood between courtesy boys and cold beer.

"We hang these half-dozen signs, burn those last three carts, and we're history."

Duane thought in terms of divide, conquer, get to the beer faster. "You wanna do these, and I'll burn?"

"Nah, this is a two-man job."

It wasn't really. He would still need to climb up and down the ladder six times, because there were six signs for six different plate-glass windows, but the window on breaking in the new guy was closing rapidly, and Michael J. would cling to one-upmanship as long as he could.

A half-dozen massive window signs arrived each week from the Fleming Foods warehouse, neatly rolled up in a cardboard tube, to promote the top six IGA food bargains of the week. Michael J. had tackled this chore enough times that he could get them all hung, true and square, in less than 20 minutes.

Weekly bargain-sign hanging brought a new use for the courtesy boy's box cutter. Pull the razor blade out of its box-cutting position, slide it into the slot on the bottom, and it became a tape scraper. Rip the old signs down; scrape the four corners of last week's tape; unroll the new sign; apply twice as much tape on top than the bottom; then repeat times five.

"Make any difference which sign goes where?" Duane looked up, holding the tape and the tube.

"That's a responsibility that falls to the courtesy boy who bears the actual signs," Matson replied, signaling for him to hand up a sign, any sign.

"Cudahy Sliced Bacon. A dollar-29 a pound," Duane the Man read aloud as he handed it up. "You won't find these bargains at Safeway—union shop, puke green aprons."

One-upmanship demanded a response. "Unorganized, free market, dogshit tan here at Mr. D's."

"A complete new experience in food shopping," Duane added. "It says so right here on our name tags, em-FOSS-us on 'new.'"

One day on the job, and the new guy was hip to culture and lingo.

If it could be burned, Mr. D's burned it.

Every single flattened cardboard box, fresh produce leavings, fat trimmed from steaks and roasts in the meat department, all manner of solid waste generated in the daily machinations of keeping Mr. D's a complete new experience in food shopping, was destroyed.

The incinerator was a red brick, cylindrical smokestack that rose high above the store and spewed ash and toxicity over the general vicinity. A fixed metal grate over an ash pit was accessed from the outside, to clear out ashes.

Matson often wondered, if you put stuff in the incinerator to get rid of it, where do you get rid of what comes out?

Behind a pair of massive steel doors, the beast was driven by unseen cables and pulleys. When he pulled the giant lever counterclockwise, one steel door went up while the other went down, revealing the blaze inside.

As he opened the incinerator, Matson reflected on his new life: parties every weekend and making new friends at Woodgate. A leader of courtesy boys and checkers. Actual women who asked for him by name. Creator of supermarket lingo. Intercom ad-libbing prowess. He loved this job.

Then there was the beer, and the freedom and blissful feeling that came with it.

Their trash cart was jammed with flattened boxes that had until very recently contained Dole Yellow Cling Peaches in Heavy Syrup, True Value Frozen Sausage Pizza, and pastel-colored Northern 2-ply Bathroom Tissue (pink, yellow, green, and blue). Within the incinerator, a fire burned slow and constant, waiting to be fed. The key to successful incineration was to feed the fire at a speed that increased the burn velocity. Too much, too fast, and it was smothered.

It was like drinking. Slow and steady wins the race to a mellow feeling of euphoria. It was everything he had dreamed about as a kid and better than he had expected.

He had been chasing the feeling for a year and a half since that first bottle of beer in the Angelo's cooler. Lately, he had begun to experience a relaxed, confident peace of mind if he even anticipated the drinking that would ensue after they got off work. He would visualize holding the glass at an angle, pouring beer from a pitcher to keep the foam at a minimum. Some days, he kickstarted the feeling with visits to the walk-in cooler.

The state of euphoria was out there, and he had enough experience now to know it would come if he was patient. The problem was, he was naturally impatient, a trait inherited from James E.

He couldn't remember being happier. It's exactly how he envisioned life when he thought about escape from James E. He was free from oppression and abuse, and the feeling produced by alcohol added unexpected value and made it even better.

The fire was raging now, so hot that he donned gloves to keep his hands from getting singed. The remnants of last week's window signs went up in flames in about the same amount of time it took him to chuck them in the incinerator, wiping out any traces of what had been.

Courtesy boy banter tended to revolve around one of three subjects: cars, girls, or beer. As they made their way to the parking lot at the end of their shift, conversation transitioned to the former, and it was the first time all day he had seen the new guy's eyes light up.

Duane's new-to-him 1972 Datsun 240Z brought to life the notion that the car you drive can, at least partially, make up for personality deficiencies. Behind the wheel of the Z, he no longer needed the humor façade. It was a sleek, aerodynamic, coffee-colored image-elevator.

"The ads for the Z say 'sexy, powerful, agile, and impressive.' This baby is all those things and more—get in, I'll show you."

It was the first time Duane hadn't cracked wise within a conversation all day.

That's the thing about advertising. You're attracted to the product, because the ad takes you by the hand and shows you a perceived gap in your life. Or it offers an impression of yourself that, deep down, you wish to see. Experiencing the product in its best light makes you want it even more.

The only two seats in the car were reclining buckets. After climbing in, he was struck by how low the Z ran to the ground. Leather interior, 4-speed stick. The radial tires allowed lane-to-lane movement, seemingly at will.

"I barely have to steer—the radials do all the work."

This Z put Matson's Falcon to shame. He was embarrassed just thinking about it.

If this dweeby new guy can drive a superfine machine like this, then by all means, I deserve something similar, more befitting of my image.

"What's the story on that short guy?"

Instead of braking, Duane downshifted from fourth to third as they passed the Twin Lakes Theatres. The marquee advertised moviegoers their choice of Diana Ross in *Mahogany* or *Mother, Jugs & Speed*, with Bill Cosby and Raquel Welch. After careful consideration, they reached a consensus that you couldn't go wrong either way, Diana or Raquel.

"Walters is harmless, but loud," Matson offered, glancing west to see if the Pogo's crowd had begun to form. "If you don't want 'Duane the Man' to become 'Duane Gebooey,' you might give some thought to making friends with him."

They were speeding south on McLean Boulevard, which transitioned from Amidon at 21st, to parallel the curves of the are-KAN-zuhz River. Duane shifted into fourth, eased around a '74 Oldsmobile Delta 88, and knifed through the air like a missile.

"I'm not too worried about it."

That's the problem with nicknames. Some people just didn't worry about them enough. Or maybe some people just didn't spend as much time as he did, worrying what other people thought.

South on Seneca, west on Douglas, past NuWay Crumbly Burgers to Meridian, then back north to McLean and the river. The Z hugged the pavement, weaving in and out of Buicks, Lincolns, and Chryslers. Back in the Mr. D's lot, Duane dropped him off behind the shagged Falcon, and Mike was glad Duane made no automotive choice comparisons. He was growing weary of defending it.

Before the ride in the Z, he was leaning toward Sticky's "Duane Gebooey" interpretation of the new guy. As Duane laid rubber on asphalt and sped off in the general direction of David's department store, Matson had changed his mind.

Sure, he's a dweeb, but with that car, this guy is definitely Duane the Man.

He decided on the spot to lose the Falcon—1976 would bring some wheels more befitting his image and new life. The promises were coming true. As good as it all was, it would soon get even better.

127 beats-per-minute better.

9.
February 7, 1976

He grouped the dozens of young Wichitans lined up on the sidewalk into three categories. The tiers existed in the broader world, and he had been stereotyping since his days sizing up janitors at Amelia Earhart Elementary. Among the disco demographic, people were easy to size up and silo.

Pogo's was a disco, but it was still Kansas, light years behind coastal trends. When it opened its doors on November 1, 1975, Pogo's immediately became the city's destination nightspot for the trailing end of the baby boom generation. It was the best possible kind of promotion: attraction and word of mouth.

First-tier girls, a small, boutique subset, were sophisticated and fashionable. They wore rabbit-fur waist jackets, polyester that would cling to all the right spots or post-hippie, gauzy fabric blouses with big, flowy sleeves. Hip-hugging blue jeans or equally-flowing skirts and boots or platform shoes (sometimes strappy, high-heeled platforms) completed their look.

They highlighted their cheekbones and wore eye shadow on a spectrum ranging from gold to smoky brown, with some hints of purple. Lips filled with color from a lipstick, touched up with gloss. Not a hair out of place.

Guys in two to three-inch platform heels, Levi Button Fly 646 Bell Bottoms (or at least flared), and skin-hugging polyester shirts, with the top couple of buttons undone.

The guys' togs came from Henry's or A.J. August, a store

permeated by the smell of Naugahyde. The girls' garb came from Parrot-fa-Nalia, on the city's east side, or Cricket Alley, in upscale Twin Lakes on the west side.

Those in the upper tier didn't need to look down their noses on the two tiers beneath them. In the rarefied air contained within their superior bubble, the lower two tiers were not acknowledged. So, did they really even exist?

The single most important characteristic of the middle tier was their desire to think of themselves (and, consequently, be thought of by others) as capable of moving into the upper tier. Middle-tier apparel looked the same, but came from David's or Sears, and those wearing it often gave off an unmistakable air of self-consciousness.

Mike knew he fell solidly into this category and spent considerable energy trying to mask it. Eight out of 10 encounters with girls in the upper tier ended in failure, but the two that led to a dance, or an invitation to join their friends at the table, proved strong enough evidence that he belonged, that he could fake his way up and in.

It was like golf—one good swing in a round of 18 holes kept you on the course in pursuit of replication.

It happened once, so it could happen again. He also took solace in the disco census, where the middle tier vastly outnumbered the upper tier.

The bottom tier was occupied by a mass of human flotsam, easily distinguished by their inability to coordinate their attire. Oblivious to the unwritten rules of the tiers and worse, woefully lacking even the awareness of the level of sophistication demanded to operate and maneuver in the disco.

In the interpersonal relationship realm where boys meet girls and nature takes its course, the physics was nearly immutable—you could always count on working your way down the ladder, but rarely up.

Light and variable Kansas breezes swirled in and around the sidewalk throng. The two girls standing in front of them struck him as solid second tier, comfortable with their second-tierness, or maybe self-confident enough to know that any attempts to fake it would be transparent.

"Charlie, correct?"

Duane the Man thought the odds were with him since the few girls he'd been close to wore Charlie. Behind their ears, where the scent often filtered through the hair and dual dabs on the inside of each wrist. If forced to testify under oath whether girls applied their perfume in more private zones, Duane would not be able to speak from personal experience, only conjecture and hearsay.

"Nope."

Feathered blonde with an athletic build, the alpha female of the pair, turned around and looked directly at Mike.

"You wanna take a guess?"

He leaned in close enough to get a whiff, but purposefully not so close as to have his motives misconstrued.

"Love's Baby Soft," he declared with certainty.

"That's right!"

"I'm Tracie," dazzling smile, blue eyes brightening, as though discerning and naming popular perfumes infused him with disco legitimacy and bona fides. "This is my friend, Debbie."

Debbie made fleeting eye contact, then looked back down at the sidewalk. Matson lowered his assessment of Debbie. On the borderline between middle and lower tier. Could go either way.

"Michael J.," he said, extending his right hand before Duane could interject. "This is Duane the Man."

Why couldn't he say, "My friend, Duane the Man," or, "My buddy, Duane the Man?" In a camaraderie-building work setting, the nickname worked, but in a social setting it was too easily misunderstood.

They were met with smiles and an almost imperceptible giggle. He picked up on it. Maybe he said "Duane the Man" to elicit the giggle.

"We'll see you guys in there," Duane said. "Save us a dance."

More smiles, but no firm commitments.

On the sidewalk, they could feel the beat from inside—a steady, uniform, accented four-on-the-floor beat. It wasn't a live band playing hard rock, this was new and different, more vibrant and predictable. That feeling of knowing what to expect, even in the next song, filled him with a sense of control.

As the throng inched toward the entrance, bouncers stood like sentries on the left. They'd engage with the girls and ignore the guys.

Matson had been legal for two months. His days of using Wes Gordon's draft card to get into bars and buy beer could now fade into storytelling. It had never failed him, and for two months he'd still been using it out of habit. The notion he was breaking the law never entered his mind. No one ever asked for his driver's license and if they had, his plan was to say he must have left it in the car, leave to get it, and never come back.

The truth was bartenders, waitresses, and convenience store clerks cared more about the money in his wallet than the fake ID. At Pogo's, because there was always a throng, the ticket-takers/ID checkers did a cursory glance—enough to cover their ass if the sky fell—and moved on to the next customer.

Now inside, they trod red shag carpeting that didn't stop at floor's end but also covered the walls and went all the way to the ceiling.

Matson handed over the $2 cover charge, and a ticket was dispensed from a slot that sat flush with the counter. Up a flight of four stairs, he handed the ticket to another employee, who stamped his hand. He looked to his right to see a coat-check clerk, behind whom were rows and rows of waist-length rabbit-fur, corduroy, and fleece-lined jackets.

"Track them," Matson said quietly to Duane, nodding to Tracie and Debbie, who were still in front of them. "Make sure you find out where they're sitting."

Duane nodded and made a couple of noises designed to mimic submarine sonar pings. Matson shot his friend a quick furrowed brow, worried his bona fides would take a hit if Tracie and Debbie (or anyone else, for that matter) heard Duane's would-be underwater girl-tracking antics.

"Run silent, run deep."

"Roger."

It was a dark, cavernous, warehouse-sized space, which sort of swallowed them up, but the bars were brightly illuminated. In keeping with the times, it was split-level: bars, tables, and a game room up top, with more tables and a deejay booth on the lower level overlooking the dance floor. And then there was the music—continuous, uninterrupted music. The songs changed, but the beat was constant, deafening, throbbing.

Matson walked in like he'd been there before, consciously

working to give off an upper-tier vibe. He shook back his hair, which was parted down the middle and feathered down to his shoulders. They found a table upstairs and ordered a pitcher of Coors.

"Check out the setup," Duane the Man said and pointed twice. "The traffic patterns are engineered so people can see other people, and everyone has a direct sight line to the bars. Smart business model."

Michael J. didn't know a business model from a fashion model, but he felt immediately at ease, as though everything about this place was designed to meet his every need.

Beer, girls, uniformly accented loud music.

The problem with mastering the Hustle was there was really no place to practice, except the place where mastery was demanded. The last thing he wanted was to perform a half-assed Hustle, so when bodies poured onto the floor, he always tried to position himself in the middle. He knew better than to get on the back row, because at some point during the song, the back row would become the front row and his shortcomings would be exposed.

On display for all to see.

The dance had three components, each with eight things to do: starting with the back leg, back three steps, feet together, forward three steps, then move the left leg, feet together. Step to the right, spin 360 degrees to the left, step to the right, feet together, clap. Same drill the opposite way.

Standing still, seat belt up and down (the signature disco move) through eight beats, two rolls of the arms, hands on hips thrusting your chest in a chicken move for two beats. Still standing in place, thrust the right foot forward, backward, out to the right, then feet back together. Pivot 90 degrees and start over.

A mob of bodies lined up, side by side, almost like a marching band formation, maneuvering as one with the same moves, pointing four different directions.

Tracie helped him with the steps. They saw each other in separate lines, and she motioned him to hers. She had the steps down cold and gave him a glance that communicated, "Do what I do." Then she smiled and bumped her hip into his.

"North. '76." She leaned in close in order to be heard. Love's Baby Soft again.

"Heights. '75."

They were arch-rivals—on the gridiron, basketball court, and in overall-worthiness pecking order, especially among the Pleasant Valley kids.

Built in 1929 on the Little are-KAN-zuhz River, just north of 13th Street, North High was the city's second high school and reflected community demographics of the time, which meant students were mostly white.

Heights, which didn't open until 1961, was at 53rd and Hillside, far north of even the northernmost Wichitans and miles north of North High. As Wichita's white families migrated north and west, Latino families supplanted them. By the middle 1970s, Heights was fed by two junior highs: the mostly white Pleasant Valley and the predominately Black Brooks. North was still mostly white, but the Latino trend line was heading up.

The Heights kids felt superior to their North counterparts because of their racial diversity. In the late 60s and early 70s, tension ensued, and race riots followed. But by 1975, they had embraced diversity—at least that's the story the school board and liberal-leaning parents liked to tell. The truth was more of an uneasy détente and only isolated pockets of social interaction between kids of different races.

North High kids were all second tier. Except Duane, he was all right. And now, Tracie. Could his stereotypes have been wrong?

The familiar fuzzy taste coated the inside of his mouth, but he wasn't worried about beer breath. If he got close enough for a girl to notice, she'd have it too. That was the thing about Pogo's—it was legally a tavern, which meant you had to be 18 to get in, and they couldn't serve anything stronger than 3.2 beer.

On draft, you had one choice: Coors. You could order a "blushing bull," (beer mixed with grenadine), bottles of Michelob, Löwenbräu, or rhino piss, but Michael J. and Duane the Man drank faster than one bottle at a time, so pitchers of Coors became the staple. Sometimes two, even three, at a time. Everyone drank beer, and when you cut to the chase, young men and young women had the same goals.

The lighted floor, the shag carpet on the walls, the rhythmic thumping of the music's beat, the dancing, it was all just ambience and camouflage for real intentions.

He knew enough about the infrastructure of music to recognize the four-beats-to-the-bar time signature and that the bass drum was being struck on every beat. Up-tempo, guitar-driven energy with syncopated bass lines. Escapist lyrics about love, dancing, and sex.

An entire business model designed around young adult hormones.

At Pogo's, three mirrored disco balls reflected rotating spotlights. The lighted dance floor took up nearly the entire lower level, its bright colors changing with the beat of the music. Strobe lights were timed with reverberated vocals, and thousands of glimmering patches scattered like chaff before the wind.

They were showered with light in all directions from the disco balls, and during those brief, finite interludes, it was like stop-motion action. A visual representation of life, frozen and bright, a millisecond at a time.

He felt immediately at ease in the sense that this was where he was supposed to be. Everything came together—the feathered hair, pretty girls, pitchers of beer, the platforms, and selling himself as a member in good standing of the upper tier. It was a feeling of mastery, maybe superiority, over the lower tier.

The four-on-the-floor beat became a new and natural life rhythm. Hard rock was marijuana, disco was cocaine. Hard rock was loud, disco was loud and shiny.

A common feeling descended over the disco, where inhibitions gave way as Wichita's last wave of baby boomers came of age together, an ocean of bodies, on a lighted dance floor, at 127 beats per minute. It was exhilarating, pseudo-sophistication, and they could actually feel it in their bloodstream.

"Whaddaya think?" Matson twirled Tracie and shimmied up next to Duane the Man, who was dancing with Debbie. She looked different in the strobes. Middle tier, after all.

"I think," Duane yelled, "we're gonna be a goddamn subculture."

10.
June 9, 1976

Mike felt the wind in his hair as he gunned it, top down, Woodgate in the rearview mirror, westbound on 21st Street, toward the setting sun or Mr. D's, whichever came first.

A glance to the southeast corner at Oliver and a line on the marquee in front of the Unity Church of Wichita caught his eye: "The truth that is taught in all religions, simplified."

When he thought about it, which wasn't very often, that's where he landed. He took his cues on religion from his grandfather.

"It's the same God in every church," Victor Ordway would say. He was a self-made man who tended to trace systems upstream. "The rest is just window dressing."

As president of the Pleasant Valley United Methodist Youth Fellowship in high school, Mike would call the meeting to order and decide which songs to sing. Even under "new business," redemption and salvation never made the agenda. Point Z.

Until now, there was always a huge chunk missing from his persona, and it gnawed at him constantly. The facts were simple and obvious for all to see—he could not be a young man on the move driving a 1970 Ford Falcon.

As he passed the Y-Not bar on the north side of the street, he made plans to swing in there and work on his pool shot. That was another missing component—he didn't aspire to hustler status, but he would be happy to break even and not embarrass himself.

He was approaching dub-yes-you and the Corbin Education Center, designed by Frank Lloyd Wright. He saw Wright's linear frame of reference during a Drafting 3 field trip and had admired it ever since. He had no clue what specific sort of education was proffered in the Corbin Education Center, but a building on campus designed by Wright elevated the collective esteem, and dub-yes-you'ers were almost certain to mention it.

He and Inglewood had tricked out the Falcon with shag carpet and re-upholstered the vinyl dashboard, and the Falcon got him from point A to point B. If one looked at it solely from a perspective of reliable transportation (as would James E.), the Falcon more than adequately served its purpose.

But there was just no getting around it, the Falcon was beneath him.

Cessna Stadium with its cement-hard Astroturf field came up fast on the left. Shocker football was never particularly good, and the program had never recovered from a plane crash in the Rockies five-and-a-half years earlier that killed almost everyone on the team. It's hard to rebuild amid such grief and sadness. He remembered post-crash football coach Jim Wright, unveiling new black and gold uniforms, spinning, "We'll look a lot like the Pittsburgh Steelers."

Until the ball is snapped.

Levitt Arena flashed by, and he punched it hard. It had been almost a year since pomp and circumstance.

Much of his the-car-makes-the-man frame of reference was informed by Inglewood, from whom he gleaned the young-man-on-the-move automotive pecking order and Mark wasted no opportunity to pile on the Falcon-inspired insults.

"You can put lipstick on a pig and call her Antoinette, but she's still a pig."

When you base your self-esteem on what other people think, other people will drive your decisions.

"Okay, wise guy, you're right, so help me find something better."

Inglewood knew a guy, who knew a guy, who had a cousin who lived way the hell and gone out west near Goddard. Michael J.'s something better turned out to be a 1971 MGB convertible. Forest green. Tan leather interior. Four-speed stick. Two seats.

On the day of purchase, he mastered the stick traversing Kellogg eastbound from Goddard. He stalled at a half-dozen stoplights but gained vital clutch-accelerator-transmission timing experience with each stall. In high school, James E. had tried to teach him how to master a manual transmission in the family's 1973 yellow VW bug, but his father's short temper left no margin for trial and error.

Crossing Hillside, he had come to recognize the cross-street names as synonymous with what his parents' generation referred to as the "inner city." Volutsia, Estelle, Grove, Minnesota, Minneapolis, Moseley. Three years earlier, his younger brother was plucked from the comforts of Pleasant Valley and bused six blocks from here to L'Ouverture School for sixth grade. Likewise, Black students were bused to schools in white neighborhoods.

His brother thrived at L'Ouverture and could have been a poster child for forced integration. He adored his teacher, and his class was like something right out of *Sesame Street*. At the opposite end of the spectrum, race riots at Heights that same year shocked the sensibilities of the lily-white suburbanites.

By 1972, their parents were worn out. Weary of Cronkite's nightly body counts, assassinations, protests, long hair, and bell bottoms. When violence broke out at Heights, even the most open-minded began having second thoughts about forced integration.

Welcome to the Land of Baloney on White Bread with Miracle Whip. Now, assimilate.

He had reached the halfway point of his east-to-west commute on 21st Street.

As Wichita developed from its cowtown days, Chisolm Creek, which ran through the heart of the city, became a drainage canal, eventually paved with concrete. The concrete freeway above the canal it straddled became the Canal Route. What they lacked in creative labeling, they gained back in motorist efficiency. He eased beneath the Canal Route, formally Interstate 35W, just the way it was drawn up.

No Frank Lloyd Wright luster here.

The first of two sensory affronts hit him hard, and it took a minute to determine why. Then he realized there was no protection from the stink in a convertible.

On the north side of 21st Street, the Derby Refinery was a massive, sprawling, industrial complex with what seemed like miles of intertwined pipes, tanks, stacks, and an ever-present flare of excess hydrocarbon gas burning from its highest stack. The smell was intense, like a wave of rotten eggs mixed with rotten cabbage. It rolled across the hood, over the windscreen, and landed in his nostrils.

He shifted into fourth and drove directly into another invisible cloud of yet another distinctively unpleasant aroma. Wichita's stockyards stood as a living, breathing, malodorous symbol of the city's origins, built upon a marriage of the railroad and the Texas cattle trade.

The first stockyard stink smelled of burning hides, which wasn't unpleasant. It reminded him of the time he had used a woodburner to imprint his initials on a baseball glove. But that smell quickly ceded to the rancid odor of packing and rendering, which was the sort of smell one might expect of a business that was turning thousands of animals inside out on a daily basis.

It was bad in the Falcon with the windows rolled up, but in the B, with the top down, the stench was so overpowering that his eyes watered. He considered putting the top back up, but self-image trumped even stink, so he eventually took to wearing a bandana around his neck to cover his face from the Canal Route to Broadway.

Long-haired train robber in a British sports car.

Petroleum and cattle, both on the same mile, on the north side of 21st Street in Wichita. Two of Kansas' leading industries, emblematic of 20th century cutting-edge commerce and wealth creation. Old-timers called it the smell of money.

The smell of someone's money.

About a dozen sets of railroad tracks bunched together right before Broadway. The tracks bore the trains that carried raw products in and refined products out. There was little, if any, effort to bring the pavement surface even with the tracks, and the result was a bone-jarring gauntlet to cross.

He tried attacking them diagonally and speeding over them, top up, then top down. The only way across without rattling the teeth out of his head was to crawl over them gingerly. He thought that made him look like an old man, so he sped over them and lived with the cumulative wear and tear on his suspension.

It was as though there was a push-pull tension when it came to transportation infrastructure pecking order. The Canal Route was designed to make life easier for the car and truck motorists. Just a mile to the west, at the railroad track crossing on 21st just east of Broadway, the railroads still held the upper hand.

The light turned yellow at Waco, and he downshifted without using the brakes. He was getting more comfortable with the stick. In the adjacent lane, he saw a housewife and pulled next to her, looking straight ahead but running a hand through his hair in a purposeful gesture of nonchalance.

She's looking at me. I'm not looking at her.

Just past are-KAN-zuhz Avenue, he caught the deep-fried scent of the Colonel. On the south side of 21st, Kentucky Fried Chicken was a James E. favorite. He had been known to make the occasional Sunday evening trip from Pleasant Valley for a bucket of original recipe.

As he zoomed past the pool house at Woodland Park, Michael J. was eager to see how the B handled the curves as 21st Street bent north to accommodate the Little are-KAN-zuhz. He looked up. Sunlight kaleidoscoped through the trees, creating an almost disco ball-inspired effect.

Taco Tico on the right, where the Pleasant Valley United Methodist Youth Fellowship dined on Americanized Mexican food after analyzing *Jesus Christ Superstar*, coming to the logical conclusion that since there was no resurrection depicted, all of Christianity must now be called into question.

Downshifted again, changed lanes, and slid past a geezer in a 1975 Cadillac El Dorado as he crossed the river.

Heads Together up on the right. It was not a barber shop, it sure as hell was not a beauty parlor. He couldn't bring himself to call it a salon. Decorated with Peter Max posters in chrome frames and ferns in ceramic pots suspended from the ceiling by elaborate macramé plant hangers, Heads Together was the quintessential unisex hair styling outfit.

He always looked forward to his appointments at Heads Together. Denise Benson was his personal stylist, and her Ciara perfume fulfilled its intended purpose—a pleasing amalgamation of lemon, sandalwood, cedar, and musk. It didn't hurt that Denise tended to lean in close to her work. Just because he had long hair didn't mean fewer haircuts. It was almost worth wearing his hair shorter to have more appointments with Denise.

Almost.

Twin Lakes State Bank was on the left. James E. banked there, which was sufficient reason for him not to.

Approaching Amidon. Almost there.

The intersection of 21st and Amidon had evolved into one of the most successful retail intersections in the city. Twin Lakes on the southeast, Sweetbriar on the northwest, with defined but unspoken lines of socio-economic demarcation.

In Twin Lakes, Orr's sold fine gifts and office supplies with a slot car track winding in and around the merchandise. Over in Sweetbriar, David's sold fine gift/office-supply knockoffs. Henry Levitt sold men's and women's fashions in a palatial split-level store in Twin Lakes. You could get a good set of whitewalls at Otasco in Sweetbriar.

Twin Lakes featured a private dinner club overlooking one of the lakes, while Sweetbriar had a McDonald's carved into the parking lot.

Twin Lakes boasted Wichita's first dual movie theater, where he had been wowed by *2001: A Space Odyssey*, and his mother heard Ali McGraw tell Ryan O'Neal that love meant never having to say you were sorry. Sweetbriar had a branch library, where love ran shallow and the apologies were implied.

Safeway in Twin Lakes. Puke green aprons.

Mr. D's in Sweetbriar. Dogshit tan.

His sense of confidence was now complete. It was easily definable. He had the togs, the hairstyle, Saturday nights at

Pogo's, the apartment. He even had the job. And now, he had the car. He hadn't felt himself smiling, but when he glanced in the rear-view mirror, there it was.

The car was an enormous component of his self-esteem, and it gave him that little edge in his continual quest to fake his way into the first tier.

Three other courtesy boys were working the same shift today. He whipped the B into Sweetbriar a full 10 minutes early and circled the parking lot a few times until he saw a couple of them arrive. He was intentional about pulling in right after they did.

What good was finally having a car that matched his self-image if others weren't aware?

11.
October 23, 1976

"Struck out."

Often there was an entire pride of young lions, who, after prowling the lighted dance floor in what nearly always turned out to be a vain pursuit of a mate, would make their way across the street to satiate another vital animal need. The hunt pivoted from a search for Ms. Right, or even Ms. Right Now, to a different form of sustenance. Pan-fried beefsteak cutlets coated with seasoned flour. Tonight, it was just him and Duane.

"Again."

On a directional 21st and Amidon axis, Pogo's was to the southwest, Mr. D's to the northwest, and Kings-X was midway between the two.

Kings-X served what their parents described as stick-to-your-ribs food, amended to stick-to-your-arteries by their children. Like Mr. D's at its pinnacle, Kings-X had propagated throughout Wichita in recent decades in direct proportion to the demographically driven desire for sit-down, rib-sticking fare in a benign family atmosphere, punctuated by flocked wallpaper and Knights of Normandy faux *objets d'art*.

At just 12-years-old, this location was the newest in the chain, adjacent to Sweetbriar and catawampus from Twin Lakes, just as postwar shopping center developers intended. Shop all day, shove your purchases in the back of the wood-paneled station wagon, swing by Kings-X for a steaming plate of homemade chicken and noodles over mashed potatoes, and a side of Del Monte CGB's dug from an institutional-sized can with a restaurant institutional-sized spoon.

They always preferred a table in the middle versus a booth by the windows, for a very compelling reason. A group of guys sitting next to each other in a booth was bad optics. Four or five young men, all clad in tight polyester, perched that close in the wee hours of the morning?

What would the Wichita night owls think?

"I wish girls would ask guys to dance more often," Michael J. complained. "Of all the couples on the floor, I bet 80 percent, maybe 90, are guy-instigated."

Since it was just the two of them, he could be more open and not have to work so hard at saving face.

They had closed down Pogo's. Again. There was something jarring about the way the white fluorescent lights flickered on at closing time.

Assumptions made in the dark, unraveled when the lights came on. A girl sitting still in the bright white light looked different than the same girl dancing with a strobe-lit disco ball reflecting in her eyes. A big wet splotch on your Levi Button-Flys from a knocked-over glass of beer made it look like you peed your pants.

When the clock struck midnight, shit got real.

The enhanced heartbeat four-on-the-floor pulse that had reverberated through them for hours dissipated like beer foam on the inside of a nearly-drained pitcher. The final jolt came when the deejay set aside Donna Summer and Silver Convention and cued up the last song of the night—Roy Rogers and Dale Evans, a stark reminder that for all their glittery pseudo-sophistication, they were still in Wichita, Kansas, a cow town.

"Happy trails to you... until we meet again."

The croonings of Roy and Dale pained their ears, and Michael J. became convinced that "Happy Trails" was a purposeful strategy to clear them out that much faster.

"There're two categories of chicks who do that," Duane explained. "The desperate, who tend to be bow-wows, and the take-no-prisoners libber, who'll grab you by the nuts and lead you down the primrose path directly to the gates of Hen-Pecked City."

While Duane the Man definitely had answers when it came to girls, he lacked actual experience.

"Be careful what you wish for," he said.

Nights at Pogo's always had the same ultimate goal, which had, so far, proven elusive. Lately, they had brought their sights down a level, and success was now defined as leaving with a girl's phone number.

Since the music was so loud, conversation using mere words generally proved an ineffective means of communicating hopes and dreams. That left the visual—togs and moves. Though you saw a few, two-piece leisure suits were considered too dressed up, even for the hippest disco in the cow town.

The standard uniform, top-to-bottom: long hair; a loud and flashy polyester shirt—always formfitting, with the top two buttons left open. Maybe a gold chain or puka bead necklace (he had one of each, both understated); Levi's, of course; socks of a solid color that matched an understated hue from the flashy shirt; and, finally, black platform shoes that were parade-gloss polished.

Further down on the girl-impressing spectrum, and of significantly more importance, was one's ability to dance. Anything short of dancing proficiency carried the risk of being tagged immediately and scorned forever as a third-tier loser.

If you looked like an idiot on the dance floor, you were an idiot.

These types of warnings circulated quickly through the disco. Girls had their own, higher-level modes and methods of communication that only they could decipher.

Freestyle dancing was the easiest way to embarrass yourself. There were no formal steps, just moves. His technique, adapted by watching guys who knew what they were doing—and more importantly, girls' reaction to them—was to gyrate the hips, spin, grab his partner by the hand, then twirl, specifically on the backbeat.

Slow dancing was the pinnacle. It offered the opportunity to whisper well-rehearsed lines directly in her ear.

"I always get the sense they think we want more than just to dance," Michael J. mused.

He was washing down the chicken fry with a Pepsi in a translucent plastic glass, imprinted with a decade-old Pepsi logo. Come alive, you're in the Pepsi Generation.

But I'm not. The Pepsi Generation died in Vietnam.

"Well, don't we?" Duane liked cutting to the essence of any given circumstance or question.

"Maybe. Probably," Michael J. replied. "But I try hard not to show it."

"Quit trying. We're guys, it's written all over our faces. We can't hide it!"

Duane the Man pulled himself away from his own chicken fry and pointed his steak knife in the air to drive home his point: "Don't kid yourself. Pogo's is not really a disco, it's a goddamn meat market."

They were focused on new tactics to achieve their goal. There was absolutely no reason a pair of young, reasonably intelligent, well-dressed and coiffed, red-blooded American males should walk away from four or five hours in a disco without a girl's phone number. They compared slow-dancing lines.

"Mine's, 'Where have you been all my life?'"

"Here's my go-to: 'You were easy to spot,'" Duane said, then leaned in, "'you give off an aura of fill-in-the-blank,' which is adapted to my first impression of that specific girl."

"Friendliness, sweetness, sexuality?"

Michael J. was now attacking the ice water, also in a plastic Pepsi Generation glass.

"Feathered hair, visible tan lines, poontang."

He knew Duane the Man was embellishing. Even completely hammered, there was no way nice, polite, mama's boy Duane William Smith would walk up to a girl and say, "You give off an aura of poontang."

They were seeking the same thing, but Michael J. wanted something deeper, what he would call true love. He could not yet define it, but like Potter Stewart and obscenity, he knew it when he saw it. He also knew what it was not and needed only to think of his parents for that shining example.

He thought vaguely of respect and loyalty. He knew he wanted something deeper than any boy-girl relationship he had experienced so far in his 19 years. When he considered the idea of true love, a notion of security entered his mind, but he had no idea how to get it.

Michael J. wanted to bring it up now, not because Duane the Man was the font of experience-based wisdom—he clearly was not, and they both knew it—but he had come to respect Duane's opinions. Duane the Man had a way of thinking about a problem, visualizing solutions, and taking action to get there.

It was a helluva skill, and he had grown to admire it. That's one of the reasons he's Duane the Man.

"You want someone like Cindy Sue."

"No. Well, maybe," Michael J. said. "That kind of adoration'd be nice, but I would treat her better."

He wanted to move the conversation from poontang to love, but he didn't know how. Plus, he was already uncomfortably far out on an honesty limb.

"It's a two-way street," Michael J. continued. "In the end, don't they want what we want?"

His guard was coming down about 30 minutes ahead of his buzz.

"Abso-fucking-lutely! And if you're lucky, you'll find one who wants it 'in the end,'" Duane added, still wielding his fork and steak knife, air quotes on the last three words.

"Buh-doom. *Tshhhhh...* " Without missing a beat, Michael J. abandoned any hope for a deeper conversation and pantomimed a rimshot.

Back to comfortable and familiar. Back to what came naturally. Back to what they knew.

They both laughed, and he speared his two last greasy french fries and swooshed them around in what was left of the gravy. The clock on the wall showed the big hand on three, little hand on the one, atop an armored knight's helmet adorned by a feathered plume.

"Let's boogie."

They settled the bill, left a hefty tip, and departed. The size of their tip always rode entirely on the attractiveness of their waitress. A judgment call, but they knew it when they saw it. In the parking lot, the two of them made tentative plans to do the same thing again next Saturday night.

The phone numbers were out there, and they were now girded with another week of experience.

"Mañana, dude!" Duane shot him a wave as he folded

himself into his 240Z and sped off.

Both of them were slated for the Sunday shift at Mr. D's. They loved working Sundays because of Bill Walty, Mr. D's hand-picked Sunday manager, whose *laissez-faire* approach to supermarket managing actually made it fun to be at work.

Michael J. eased into the B and headed east on 21st, Woodgate-bound.

Three things were coming down: his mask, his guard, and his buzz. He wasn't sure how to feel about the first two, but he knew how to manage the buzz. He had four, silver-foil wrapped, green bottles of Löwenbräu waiting for him at home in his Woodgate fridge. Just the thought gave him a sense of ease and comfort.

He was eager to get home and crack one open, then a second, possibly a third, and why not a fourth, before calling it a night.

Poontang. Chicken fried steak. Roy Rogers. Cow town.

Nightcaps.

It's the way you ride the trail that counts.

12.
December 31, 1976

In regaling the story later, Duane would say Mike's taillights were the last thing he saw before careening into the Joe Vosburgh Wallpaper storefront. In an instant, red vertical taillights were right in front of him, mindlessly guiding him around the corner, off Washington, and onto Douglas.

The next instant: no taillights, no street, and a hard jolt over the curb on useless brakes. Wide-eyed New Year's revelers jumped to get out of the way as he slid and stopped with the awful, deafening sound of plate glass shattering.

Duane the Man would try to make a car accident that was his fault sound exciting. Perceptions count, even if people didn't buy them.

"This is a little embarrassing," Duane said, entirely for the benefit of his passenger, Danny Ramirez.

Danny, another Mr. D's colleague, was breathing hard and trying to collect himself, checking to see if anything was broken as they sat amid tinkling glass shards and smashed wallpaper samples.

"No nookie tonight," Duane allowed, knowing that, like his car, his New Year's Eve had just come to an abrupt halt.

Up ahead in the B, Steve Walters was riding with Matson. The four of them were bringing in the New Year barhopping. The chances of the evening ending with any of them securing overnight female companionship were remote. Privately, they all knew it, though they clung fast to the fantasy.

They had just left the Red Garter, which featured cold beer and bikini-clad women dancing in cages. Their departure was expedited when Duane breached the unspoken caged dancer/bar patron neutral zone. The caged dancer reciprocated by maneuvering her toe within the cage and deliberately tipping a pitcher of rhino piss in Duane's lap.

Turnabout is fair play. Even if the rules are unwritten. Maybe especially if they're unwritten.

When they got to the Red Garter it was snowing. By the time they left, it had transitioned to freezing rain.

At the moment of wallpaper storefront impact, they were bound for Pogo's. On rare occasions, tonight's agenda had proven an effective formula: Start with the visual; add beer; move to the meat market; then more beer for courage, at which point, the desired objective often seemed within reach.

The more beer, the more realistic the desired objective seemed. It was a comfortable weekend pattern, regardless of its illusory success.

"Gebooey missed the turn!"

Initially, Matson was convinced it was more of the same ol' Sticky, purposefully loud to get attention. But when he saw Steve's face, he knew it was legit.

"He smacked into the building!"

Better him than me.

With flashing lights entering his rear-view field of vision, he tried hard to remember quantities. They had been drinking since getting off work at 6 p.m. The Red Garter was the second bar on their hop. All four of them were clinically and legally "under the influence."

Christ, with the snow and ice, it's dangerous enough out here before you consider all the drinking.

How many glasses of beer had Duane the Man pounded before wearing that final pitcher? Six? Eight? Regardless of Duane's consumption, he harbored a raw and nagging fear. He had had more.

Michael J. always seemed to have had more.

Deep in the recesses of what passed for a conscience, on nights when his barhopping buddy didn't plow his car into a downtown Wichita storefront, he didn't worry about quantities consumed.

He did understand that if he drank too much and got behind the wheel, he ran the risk of getting pulled over and arrested. Lately, he had begun to mindfully drive the speed limit after imbibing. And since acquiring the B, he had always kept a couple of large fast-food drink cups behind the seat, into which he could pour a beer. It was a convertible, after all.

It never entered his mind that he might get in an accident; that he might injure or kill a bystander; that he might skid on the ice rounding the corner, bump the curb at Douglas and Washington, and plow the car into a plate-glass storefront of a wallpaper merchant.

Or that a friend would.

Big picture, the life he was leading was what society expected of a 19-year-old, red-blooded American male. He was normal. He shared the three interchangeable priorities: cars, girls, and beer. Family wasn't on the list; friendships didn't make the cut.

Michael J. knew that Duane would be shook, and therein was his dilemma.

"Matson, ya daffy fuck, turn around and go back! Those guys are probably sliced to ribbons by all that glass!"

Steve was alternating between sticking his head out the window and straining back to see through the small plastic window in the rear of the B's ragtop.

The Z was a hardtop, so the serious injuries would be emotional, Michael J. rationalized. He was grasping at straws to come up with plausible justification to keep his own New Year's Eve from coming to a screeching halt. They still had more than two hours until 1977.

Back at the Red Garter, before the caged dancer dampened Duane's ardor, the conversation had turned to time.

"I'll be 20 years old in '77. Two entire decades," Matson said it as though it were difficult to fathom. "In the year 2000, I'll be 43. Absolutely ancient."

"Could be worse." Sticky could not compete with Duane intellectually, so he took the low road. "When he's 43, Gebooey'll still be decked out in the dogshit tan, stockin' CGBs, and moppin' up toddler puke."

Experience had taught Duane his best response was silence. Don't take the bait. He held his left hand about eighteen inches from his own face, palm inward. Slowly and deliberately curling inward all fingers except the middle one, which was then thrust, just as slowly and deliberately, six inches toward Sticky's face.

"Gitchy, gitchy ya-ya doo-doo!" Sticky was unfazed. The low road is blissfully free of intellectual roadblocks.

Despite the B's wide-open defroster and wipers on max, traces of Kansas winter were forming on the windscreen. 1977 would come in cold and slick, but if they were at Pogo's, he would be oblivious. The meat market, more cold beer. Drunk girls at midnight, looking for guys to smooch, and then all bets were off. One of his priorities would transport him to the other two.

If he kept going.

If he turned around: recriminating cops; half-drunk gawking onlookers; Duane's dad, in full-throated, "I told you so."

He frowned just thinking about it.

"If you don't see any severed limbs, I can keep going."

All he needed was a hint from Steve that Pogo's trumped this predicament, and he could drop Duane and Danny like hot rocks. It was the kind of decision that never would have been considered, had there been a conscience behind the wheel of the B.

Had Steve not been with him, he likely would have kept going.

Seriously? I knew I'd lost you downtown and wondered what happened to you.

What if someone thought you were their friend but came to realize it was a one-way street? Michael J. hung around with Duane the Man because he respected his intellect. Deep down, beneath the glibness, they felt the same way about living in the moment. And, because Duane tended toward dweeb, Matson felt superior.

All the components of a strong friendship, except the ones that really matter.

"Jesus Tits, he's your friend!"

Despite all the bravado, when a crisis hit, Sticky's humanity surfaced.

"You're the one who gave him the nickname!"

The look on Sticky's face asked, "How is this even a question?"

Michael J. took a deep breath and exhaled audibly.

He slowed, cautiously turned right at Emporia Avenue, then east on the one-way First Street to Washington, and back south to Douglas.

Back to Duane the Man, broken glass, and smashed-up wallpaper samples.

Away from the meat market. Away from his priorities.

Away from his nature.

13.
May 15, 1977

"Michael J., intercom please. Michael J., intercom."

The inflection in Duck's voice gave him the sense this was more than a question about price and availability of IGA-brand Mandarian ornjizz.

"Yo."

The intercoms looked like standard telephone receivers, with a thumb-driven black button that, when depressed, allowed for storewide audio disbursement.

"What's your 20?"

"In the bakery," he said, "helping Lizzie move some massive bags of flour and appropriating the occasional donut."

"Gary D.'s wife is in line on 4. Two deep. You wanna make your way up here and sack for her?"

Mary Ann Denniston was married to Gary, son of Lowell, *aka* Mr. D.

Lowell Denniston's supermarket empire began modestly in his hometown of Cheney, a rural hamlet in the plains country west of Wichita, near the point where the North Fork of the Ninnescah River branches away from the South Fork.

Denniston's expansion paralleled Wichita's postwar growth, which was fueled by the aviation industry. It wasn't a complicated business plan—build supermarkets in areas where people are moving. Mr. D's success allowed him to branch out into broadcasting and commercial real estate, and the humble, small-town grocer became a big deal.

One by one, Mr. D. sold his underperforming stores and

by the late 1970s, the empire consisted of just two huge moneymakers: the Sweetbriar location, and Central Heights at the southwest corner of Central Avenue and Ridge Road, on Wichita's ever-burgeoning west side, where he also built the studios for his radio stations, KEYN AM/FM.

Whether by design or coincidence, the two remaining supermarkets were in closest proximity to Cheney, where it all began.

When Denniston retired, he turned the day-to-day over to his son, Gary, an earnest but emotional man, who lacked his father's confidence and entrepreneurial savvy. Gary had grown up working in his father's supermarkets and, when he took the reins, promoted friends with whom he had come up and relied on for the big decisions.

Gary D.'s man at Sweetbriar was Douglas ("Don't call me Doug") Burchart, who wore neckties with his brown double-knit leisure suits and smoked a pipe with cherry-infused tobacco. When a courtesy boy walked into a cloud of the characteristic, sickening-sweet aroma, he knew Burchart was either coming or going.

"Why me?"

Lizzie was cute, and the donuts were tasty.

"She needs to leave here with a good impression."

Duck knew that Mary Ann Denniston's supermarket visits were more than stocking up on pretzels and pork chops. These were intelligence reconnaissance missions on behalf of her close friend, Mrs. Burchart.

Burchart was going bald, and not in an attractive way. A hair transplant had gone awry, and he tried unsuccessfully to hide a half-dozen closely spaced hair plugs beneath a cheesy comb-over. To make matters worse, a childhood accident robbed the man of a fully formed left eyelid.

To small children and uninitiated courtesy boys, Douglas Burchart was downright scary looking. Despite all these seeming shortcomings, the guy was a ladies' man and could juggle two or three checkout girls at a time.

Mary Ann was in the line of a checker with whom Burchart was having an affair and would be looking for any checkout transgression or perceived slights that might lead to the checker being unceremoniously shown the door.

Duck was aware of Burchart's infidelities and was friends with the checker with whom he was currently involved. In the midst of all this drama, her countervailing mission was to produce a good or at least no-harm-done outcome.

Duck had been in the booth recently with Burchart when his wife stormed in and confronted him. Right there in front of God and the courtesy boys at the express lane (15 items or less). It was messy for all involved, customers included, and she believed strongly that one such episode per supermarket courtesy-booth career was quite sufficient, thanks just the same.

She knew Michael J. had the chops to distract Mary Ann and not make a fool of himself. Duck had also long since learned that, with him, flattery would get you everywhere.

"These doofuses up here now can't pull that off."

"Right on."

He wiped donut-sugared fingers on his flour-splotched dogshit tan apron—this is Mr. D's daughter-in-law, after all.

Later, on break together in the deli, he quizzed Duck for the inside dope.

"The nasty-ass pipe, the hair plugs, what gives?"

Michael J. couldn't imagine how any woman in her right mind would find that the least bit appealing.

"Sometimes women are attracted to power."

Again, Duck with the wisdom.

Most of the checkers had blue-collar husbands who probably appreciated the extra household revenue stream but had mixed feelings about their wives working outside the home. On the job and on break, he had gotten to know these women; had given them flattering nicknames; and had built relationships with them.

Many had kids and grandkids, and these were women whose career aspirations did not include dub-yes-you. They all seemed to like him. Michael J. was not only an efficient and courteous courtesy boy, he could also make them smile or laugh.

Attracted to power?

For the first time, he had begun to think about his place in a system surrounded by people who considered the manager of a supermarket—with a cheesy combover who wore a necktie with a leisure suit—as powerful. There was only fleeting thought of the morality and ethics of the boss sleeping with his employees. He wondered briefly what his mother would think.

Let's put that one in front of the sharing group.

"They're all adults," Duck continued. "I could care less who's doing the horizontal greased-weasel tango around here. My priority is to protect my friend's job."

Since leaving Pleasant Valley, like most subjects which required him to form an opinion, all it took was someone else's good idea and he was on board. Duck's reasoning seemed solid. He framed his thinking around practical ramifications of how the store manager's actions impacted him. As a result, the notion of respect or character didn't even cross Michael J.'s mind.

Burchart is my boss, but he's screwing around. Big deal. Does that make him any less my boss?

Marital infidelity was a non-issue. Michael J. was young and unattached, and he did what every red-blooded courtesy boy did. Lusted after the attractive housewives for whom he carried groceries. Especially that one woman, the one in brushed denim, with feathered hair, and a 1976 white Volvo 245 DL station wagon. She always made eye contact. He would see her in line and maneuver to be there to sack and carry out for her. Small talk in the parking lot. Was that a hint?

Or Mrs. Meacham, who lived down the street from his parents, called him by name, and whose overtures seemed obvious.

Like Jimmy Carter, lust was in his heart, but acting on the thought was a bridge too far. Carter was President of the United States, and his reasons for not acting on the lust in his heart were moral and ethical. Michael J. was scanning the horizon for the next high, and his reasons were driven by fear.

Deviate from my good, true self? Is this the way I was raised? Mom prolly still thinks of me as president of the Pleasant Valley Methodist Youth Fellowship, where we joined hands and sang, "And they'll know we are Christians by our love... "

And they'll know I'm a young man on the move by my newly-found lax attitude toward morality.

The answers were dawning. Layers of naïveté and inexperience were shed for this new knowledge and insight.

"Bunch of us are going to Pogo's tonight," looking at Duck, invitation implied. "Duane the Man and Sticky, Laura Wilson, couple others. Lizzie wants to come."

"It's nickel pitcher night," he added, sweetening the pot and making it an offer she couldn't refuse. "We can get blotto on pocket change."

"I'm in."

14.
August 16, 1977

On his way out, he grabbed what was left of the eight-pack of Miller High Life pony bottles. Six bottles remained, seven, if you counted the one he had just started.

The novelty of eight little seven-ounce bottles of beer drove this purchase. The bottles sat flush with the top of the carton, and it carried differently than a traditional six-pack of 12-ounce bottles. The center of gravity seemed off. It struck him as beer carton design afterthought.

Only when he drank Miller could he actually see the amber liquid as it entered his system. All other beer bottles were brown or green. Transparency provided clarity. His current state of mind was anything but clear, but it was singularly focused.

Where the hell is Laura Wilson and what exactly is she doing?

He dropped the pony bottle carton in the passenger seat, put the top down, and headed west on 21st.

He first tried calling her, a couple of hours earlier, around 7 p.m. No answer then, or from any of the dozen calls since. Earlier that day at Mr. D's she told him she intended to be home tonight, and he suggested maybe they could do something. She was vague and noncommittal, but he tossed that response aside as he Kareem Abdul-Jabbarred an empty pony bottle hook shot crossing the Little are-KAN-zuhz.

He eased the B to a stop, one house down and across the street from the west Wichita home where Laura lived with her parents. A floor lamp in the living room was on, but the house appeared silent and unoccupied. The thought of ringing the doorbell and inquiring of Mom and Dad the specifics of their daughter's whereabouts entered his mind.

Two arguments convinced him otherwise.

First, it looked like no one was home and even if her folks were, once they told him she wasn't, he would be expected to leave.

He preferred to sit in his car, suck on pony bottles of Miller High Life, and wait. If you've got the time, we've got the beer. The high life, enjoyed with friends in good spirits amid lightheartedness and camaraderie after a full day's work fighting fires, shoveling snow, or driving a truck across the country.

Or all by yourself in a cramped sports car in the middle of the night in Wichita, Kansas, obsessing over a girl.

He held his watch under a beam produced by a streetlight: 9:30.

If she's not here by 10, I'm going home.

Laura Wilson had flirted with him shortly after she started working at Mr. D's. She giggled appreciatively the first time she heard one of his intercom bargain calls.

"Attention Mr. D's shoppers. For the next three minutes and three minutes only, we're offering a REAL DEAL on Country Time Lemonade in the 64-ounce canister. Regularly a dollar-seventy-nine a pop... but for the next three minutes and three minutes only... wait for it... TWO canisters... for only ONE DOLLAR! You'll find this timely bargain at the north end of aisle nine. Dehydrated lemonade... just add water! Two 64-ounce canisters for a buck. All because we appreciate your business... AND we like the color of your eyes!"

He had looked directly at Laura on that last line.

Laura's eyes were chocolate brown. When they went on

break together, she used them to make direct contact with his dusty greens, giggled some more, and complimented his ad-libbing.

Her chocolate browns were framed by a Jane Fonda brunette shag. It skewed more 1971 *Klute*/North Vietnamese Communist Sympathizer as opposed to 1977 *Fun with Dick and Jane*/Try to Get Back in Hollywood's Good Graces.

Laura's communication repertoire was verbal and physical. Her sentences typically ended with an up inflection, leaving the impression she was asking a question, even when she was not. This was often accompanied by reaching out to touch some part of an arm, generally shoulder or forearm. Never lingering, just a light, purposeful brush.

The vibe she gave was the one he received. Chaste and demure.

Duck once told him she's only that way with guys and that the women around Mr. D's had sized up and categorized Laura pretty quickly.

You guys are just jealous. Laura's a sweetheart.

Laura struck him as more worldly and intellectually curious than Tracie. She was studying art history at dub-yes-you and talked about things like the adverse environmental impact of the just completed Trans-Alaska pipeline and what she perceived as Jimmy Carter's false piety.

"Don't be so sure about that," he remembered once telling her. "With JC, what you see is what you get."

As the flirting escalated, he had whispered to Duck to call him first, when extra checkout help was needed.

He would maneuver his way to a checkstand adjacent Laura's and the two of them would engage in a nonverbal cash register efficiency competition, exchanging smiles and winks while determining who was faster ringing up groceries.

Laura drove a tan two-door 1974 Plymouth Duster with factory-painted sporty horizontal white stripes on either side. Her father bought it, insured it, kept it fueled and serviced. Batting the big chocolate browns also worked on Daddy, apparently.

Mike arranged his rear-view mirror, so he would see the headlights when she turned onto her street. Even in the dark, he would recognize the Duster grille. Another glance at his watch—now 10:45. He had been there a little more than an hour and three cars had come through. No Dusters.

She said she intended to be home. She's not. Where is she? If she's not here by 11:30, no, let's make it an hour. If she's not here by 11:45, I'm history.

Mike and Laura had become Mike and Laura around Memorial Day. She was going away for the weekend with her parents to their cabin on Grand Lake in Oklahoma and needed to find someone to take care of Molly, her new kitten, barely weaned.

"Look no further," practically bursting with chivalry. "I'm your man."

"Oh, Mike, would you?"

"Would you" stretched out and ended higher in inflection than "Oh, Mike" and came with a light touch on the forearm.

He was by no means an expert in the care and feeding of juvenile domestic felines, but how hard can it be? They're just like dogs, only more neurotic, right?

Here's some Little Friskies, here's a ball of yarn to play with, here's a place to take a dump. Knock yourself out, Mollycat.

He did all the right things, but sometime on Saturday night, Mollycat climbed back in her box perched next to a speaker from the all-in-one, off-the-shelf, rip-off stereo from David's discount store in Sweetbriar and took her last breath.

Dead. Of unknown causes.

Jesus, if I can't keep her cat alive, she'll want nothing to do with me. No more dueling cash registers.

"Laura, Mollycat died."

Brief silence when Laura called that Sunday to check in.

"Oh, no," she said in a tone of voice that was sympathetic, not accusing, as though Molly were his cat. He could almost feel her reaching through the phone line, lightly brushing his forearm.

He fidgeted in the driver's seat of the B and did his best to stretch his legs. If their relationship began with the death of her cat in his custody, and she forgave him, then there was really nowhere to go but up.

He glanced toward the dark window at the corner of the split-level and thought about his first time alone with Laura, in her bedroom of this very house. It was clear that Laura had skills and experience, and it had shattered the chaste and demure façade.

Duck had been right, but it didn't change anything.

The real Laura was the opposite of chaste and demure, but she was still smart and attractive. Even though he lacked the skills and experience to respond to her in a way that would have provided equal footing, it did nothing to dampen the physical and emotional attraction.

It didn't take her long to see that his bravado was bullshit, but she didn't call him on it. With Tracie, he pretty much called the shots, and he thought they both felt comfortable with that. But without ever saying it, or letting on that it was happening, Laura was in charge of this relationship.

He thought back to his chicken-fried-steak-fueled true love inventory with Duane the Man at Kings-X.

Respect and loyalty? We got those.

It never occurred to him that genuine respect and loyalty probably didn't include skulking outside a girl's house in the dark. Deeper than any relationship, so far? Sure. Security? How do you actually define that anyway? He thought there could be a middle ground. You give, I give—that's the way it is supposed to work, right? The way it never worked with his parents.

He talked a good game, but actually playing the game was much harder.

Neil Diamond was right about hot August nights. Where's that south Kansas wind when you need it?

Locusts and crickets. A random hoot from an owl. The only man-made sound was that produced when rubber rolled over pavement from the occasional car drifting by and the clicking on and whirring of central air conditioning units driven by various indoor thermostat levels. They would never say it out loud, but for many westside Wichitans in split-level ranchers, not sweating between the sheets apparently trumped an energy crisis.

Someone next door to the Wilsons peered from behind a curtain into the night, and for the first time, Mike entertained a fleeting thought about how this might look to someone else—a lone young man, a stranger to this quiet residential neighborhood, nursing pony bottles by himself in a foreign sports car at one o'clock in the morning.

He got out, stretched, put the top up on the B, then climbed back in.

Exactly 24 minutes later, he saw another pair of headlights in the rear-view mirror.

That could be a Duster. It's the right size and headlight configuration.

The sporty horizontal white stripe on the passenger's side

seemed to linger in the night air as Laura eased past him, slowed down, and pulled into her parents' driveway.

Her brake lights remained illuminated as she turned off the car, gathered her purse, opened the door, and got out. She was wearing matching blue shorts and a tube top. Bright red nails that caught the glint from the streetlight. Her elevated wedge sandals made her appear taller and the shag played across her bare shoulders.

She turned his way, after hearing the car door close behind him. Mike had four hours to come up with an opening line, but none of that time was spent considering what to do or say when she actually showed up.

"Hi."

"Oh! Hey... how long have you been waiting for me?" Genuinely perplexed, but an automatic transition into upper hand comfort zone.

Not, "What are you doing, spying on me?" or "Why are you parked across from my house in the middle of the night?"

"Less than 30 minutes." He tied to respond breezily. "I was out with Duane the Man."

Given the circumstances, he thought it sounded authentic.

"Where've you been?"

Not "What did you do tonight?" or "I must have misunderstood when we spoke this morning at D's."

"Oh, a group of us got together to study." They were about four feet apart and she took a step toward him. As though she wanted to lightly brush his forearm, elbow, or shoulder.

He wanted to believe her, and he fully expected her to buy his lie that he had only been parked outside her house for less than half an hour.

He had no idea what to do or say next. He thought she

was his girlfriend. He thought they were a couple, he thought they were in love. Reiterating any of those three notions out loud right now would only detract from his belief in them.

"Elvis died today." Changing the subject had proven an effective tactic for Laura in keeping the upper hand. "He radiated sex."

"Well, he was pretty old," Michael J. had heard the news on KEYN and switched over to KFDI, where he learned that mourners were already flooding Graceland with flowers. "Kinda hard to imagine a 42-year-old rock star."

Laura stepped forward and closed the gap between them. "Love me tender?"

It was a soft whisper that ended in an up inflection. Her Yves St. Laurent Opium perfume was a few hours old but still held sway. Holding her close, his three notions fell immediately back into place, right where he thought they should be.

"You were always on my mind," he responded, pulling back for eye contact with her chocolate browns.

She gazed intently at his right dusty green, then his left. "Clearly!"

She glanced at his car, back at him, giggled, then pulled away. She didn't have to acknowledge his obsession to recognize his adoration.

"You wanna go do something?"

Four hours sardined into the B ought to count for something.

"I'm beat. Maybe this weekend."

Another vague non-commitment.

All the Miller pony bottles were empty on the drive back to Woodgate as two thoughts battled for his attention.

She seemed flattered. She obviously thought the notion of me waiting for her to come home was romantic. I'm a goddamn latter-day Romeo.

Parting in her parents' driveway, after we connected in the middle of the night, on the day the King of Rock 'n' Roll died, was such sweet sorrow. Same clumsy center of gravity, but lighter.

15.
September 5, 1977

The business end of the B was up on ramps in the front yard of Inglewood's rental house, where he moved after spending 18 months at the Spartan School of Aeronautics in Tulsa. Inglewood had learned the intricacies of avionics, electronics, and enough ins-and-outs of the emerging computer industry to ensure job security for the rest of his days, but was still in search of that first entry-level position.

The B had been vibrating in a strange way and shifting rough. Over the phone, Mark had diagnosed it as the U-joint and offered to effect repairs.

"You spring for the beer and the parts, and I'll supply the tools and necessary expertise."

It was the essence of their friendship, since Drafting 1 at Heights. It felt good to reconnect.

The house on Perry Street was almost directly in the center of an island of land between the are-KAN-zuhz and the Little are-KAN-zuhz rivers. It was Wichita's geographic heart and two blocks east of Sim Park where, in days gone by, they had partied on the sandbar and threatened to play golf when they grew up and became responsible adults.

There were some assumptions baked into those threats.

"Did you hear Fred Huddleston this morning?"

Inglewood's legs were visible, the rest of him performing automotive surgery, accessing the patient from underneath. Matson couldn't see his face, but the way Mark asked the question made him think he was proud of what he was going to say next.

Elevating the pitch in his voice, Inglewood attempted his best Huddleston.

"20-year-old Mark Inglewood, arrested for grand larceny. He and two accomplices, all employees of Ardan's Catalog Showroom on West 21st Street, are accused of pilfering thousands of dollars' worth of electronic equipment from the store. The trio were booked into the Sedgwick County Jail and each released on bail. Arraignment is set for later this week."

Ardan's sold hardware, electronics, jewelry, housewares, and sporting goods. It was just across the little river from Heads Together, home to Denise Benson's Ciara perfume and disco coiffure talents.

"Huddleston actually used the word, 'pilfering,'" Inglewood grunted. "Hand me the half-inch socket—wait, make it seven-sixteenths."

Huddleston was a fixture on KFH (1330-AM) morning drive and at the cop shops.

He would show up in person, dark and early, at the Wichita Police Department and the Sedgwick County Sheriff's Office, studiously pore over the public docket, take copious notes, bring them back to the station, hammer out the final product on a Royal classic manual typewriter, don the foam rubber headphones, adjust the microphone, and make a public display of the juiciest arrests, in a voice higher than one might expect from a grizzled veteran radio news reporter.

"What the hell, man?!"

Mike struggled with how to react. Inglewood was his best friend, but there had been little contact between the two of them since Mark returned from Tulsa.

"What happened?"

"We were lifting stereo components. We'd move them

near the back door, make sure the coast was clear, and transfer them into our car trunks."

Matson had pitched the question in a broad framework of morality. It was caught in one of practicality.

"The dude that was spozed to be lookout fucked up."

The dude WHO was spozed to be lookout...

He almost said it out loud.

Who is this "we" Inglewood referred to? Did he fall in with a group of Pleasant Valley ruffians and toughs? Did his newfound criminal accomplices talk him into this blatant law-breaking? Was he the ringleader? Did these would-be thieves assess the risks and move ahead regardless?

Matson seemed more worried about the whole thing than the accused. They talked about lawyers, first offenses, prosecution to the fullest extent of the law, plea bargains. All the nomenclature associated with an iteration of their lives that he always considered was kept at arm's-length.

Had Matson been working in the Ardan's storeroom that night, he would have found a way to be Garvey'ing the Ardan's equivalent of $1.59 (not 159¢) on the Ardan's equivalent of gallons of 2 percent milk at the fateful moment. Even had he been aware, Matson would have disavowed any knowledge of his best friend's actions.

If fear kept him out of handcuffs and holding cells, maybe it wasn't such a bad thing.

Bright lines exist for a reason.

His mind went to all they had been through together since Drafting 1. They'd hitchhiked around Colorado and rode motorcycles to Kansas City. On a graduation getaway to Dallas, they had enjoyed more than their fair share of Lone Stars at Arlington Stadium and hollered at Texas Rangers' skipper Billy Martin.

"HEY, BILLY! IS THAT A FLASHLIGHT IN YOUR POCKET, OR DO YOU JUST LOVE THE GAME?"

Matson/Inglewood was his first young adult best friendship. Now the guy's a criminal? Best friends talk to each other regularly. This was only their second in-person encounter in nearly a year.

Was Mark living up to his father? Living down to his father?

He wondered briefly how to maneuver in a world with a best friend who was a criminal. And now, thanks to Fred Huddleston, a known criminal. Was that a reason to cut him loose? If it was, does he come right out and tell Mark he's cutting him loose, or just shut down contact?

Had he stayed in closer contact, maybe Mark wouldn't have fallen in with this shady group. Or maybe it was the opposite—would his best friend have asked him to join the criminal cabal?

Lot of options here. No thought given to how he might be able to help Inglewood during a time of extreme need.

Mike thought about the AM/FM/cassette unit the two of them installed in the B shortly after he bought it. Matson brought the beer, and Inglewood had supplied the tools and expertise. And now that he thought about it, the actual tape deck.

"What about my tape deck?"

The question came out quietly, as though he already knew the answer.

"Ask me no questions, I'll tell you no lies."

U-joint installation complete, Inglewood was wiping his hands on a grease and oil-splotched, red mechanics' shop rag.

"Hey, I have a favor to ask."

Here it comes. He wants me to engage in some criminal activity—

fence some hot Marantz amplifiers, score a dime bag, procure some stardust, kill someone for him, wrap the body in a blanket and heave it into the Mr. D's incinerator.

He imagined standing guard at Ardan's back door, wielding Patty Hearst's M-1 Carbine, ready to gun down any undercover stereo component cartel busting detectives, rent-a-cops, or random do-gooders who stood between them and their criminal enterprise.

"Jennie and I are getting married. How would you feel about standing up for me as my best man?"

"Sure."

No hesitation.

———

Long before Joe Inglewood vanished, little Mark Inglewood and little Jennie Marousek found each other amid the chalkboard dust and safety scissors at Rea Woodman Elementary School in south Wichita. Woodman was a pioneer citizen of Wichita who described herself as possessing an "abounding spirit of adventure."

After Joe vanished and Mark's mom moved the family to Sherwood Glen, Mark and Jennie dated other people, but the torch for each other was never extinguished.

Jennie was a spunky firecracker of a woman, who shared Rea Woodman's adventurous spirit. Once in her inner circle, Jennie held you tight. As her fiancé's best man, Michael J. made it in. He was her beloved's best man, a distinction that set him apart from the run-of-the-mill Ardan's thieves and other Perry Street hangers-on.

Despite his current legal woes, Inglewood had a future. He would get a job in the industry for which he was now trained, find closure—one way or another—to his Ardan's predicament, get married, have kids, and one day describe these times as his "checkered past."

It was as much time as he had spent with Mark since he left Woodgate for Tulsa. It wasn't the same. There was the criminal stuff, plus now he was getting married. It would no longer be just Mike and Mark. No more hitchhiking, motorcycling, or hollering at Billy Martin. It was all a moot point, anyway, because Mark and Jennie were moving to Colorado Springs—a fresh start.

Matson shared James E.'s offer to foot a dub-yes-you bill and said he was considering it. Inglewood knew his best friend and could tell his heart wasn't in it. Mike mentioned big league play-by-play, but in a faraway sort of manner that trailed off.

"You ever thought about tech school?"

Until that moment, he hadn't.

Mark and Jennie were married where they met. There was something innately romantic about exchanging forever vows at Rea Woodman Elementary, in the exact same space where the notion took hold as a childhood fantasy. Matson handed off the rings at the proper moment, walked in and out of the ceremony with Jennie's maid of honor, kissed the bride, offered the first champagne toast at the reception, and boosted a bottle.

Later, the single wedding revelers split themselves into two groups: males and females. The implication was clear that marriage was an end goal for everyone. Matson caught Jennie's garter and slipped it onto the rearview mirror of the B before putting the top down to make his way back to Woodgate.

Still in his tux, he was comforted by the thought of fellow motorists thinking he was coming from a wedding. His best friend's wedding.

He couldn't remember ever seeing Inglewood so genuinely happy.

Jennie is a doll. She loves my best friend, and he loves her.

He wanted to be married, too. With every Ms. Right Now, he could see the promise of Ms. Right. Inglewood had found his. As he passed Parklane Shopping Center, heading north on Oliver, he reached behind his seat, poured some champagne into one of his camouflage cups, and thought about what society expected of him.

He was on track. All he lacked was true love.

A couple of weeks later, pushing 80 on the bypass that ringed Wichita, the drive shaft in the B dropped, just fell out of its housing, which infused some cold, hard doubts about his best friend's auto mechanical prowess.

He thought about calling Inglewood in Colorado Springs, but what good would it do? It's not like the man was going to drop everything, drive all night to Wichita, jack up the B on the side of the bypass and take another crack at U-joint repairs.

Matson sold the B for parts and began the search for his next ride.

His heart said Firebird, Camaro, or pre-1974 Mustang. His supermarket paycheck said wide track 1973 Pontiac LeMans—two-door, fastback, louvered rear windows, in metallic blue. On a sunny day, if you tilted your head and squinted at it from just the right angle, the uninitiated might have mistaken it for a GTO.

It was a step down, image-wise, but the drive shaft stayed where it was supposed to. Two other positives: it would make the 21st Street journey less smelly and, since the LeMans was not a convertible, he might not have to be so vigilant about keeping a McDonald's cup nearby.

16.
October 11, 1977

The backup alarm pierced the pre-sunrise suburban Wichita silence.

BEEP BEEP BEEP BEEP

He stood outside the store's east-facing limestone edifice, narrowing the spread of his arms to help the driver gauge the distance between the back of the truck and the limestone veneer. Matson craned to glance in the cab's side-view mirror to get a sense of what his next hour would be like. Two truck drivers would alternate these twice-a-week perishables deliveries.

Billy was a nice guy. Bobby was a pain in the ass.

He caught a glimpse of the driver's face.

Great.

The trucks emanated from the Fleming Foods Distribution Warehouse in north Wichita and served IGA supermarkets throughout the Great Plains.

When he got the promotion, he viewed this task as a vital function in the vast supermarket cog and embraced it with zeal. As the newly-minted Frozen Foods Manager, the promotion from courtesy boy meant more money, more responsibility, and the duty that came with the territory as low man on the next rung up on the flow chart. Unloading the truck at oh-dark-thirty. Since the demotion, he sang a different tune.

No longer middle management, but I still have to unload their goddamn truck.

It was no longer "our" goddamn truck.

"Hold your arms up higher next time," Bobby growled as he unlatched the door, slid it up and hopped into the truck. "I damn near hit the building."

Open your eyes, old man.

"My mistake."

Michael J. was operating on about two hours sleep. "Happy Trails" at midnight, a couple other bars that stayed open until 2 a.m., chicken-fried steak at Kings-X.

This deep into the high life, he knew the formula for survival. Slam a cup of coffee and a handful of Excedrin, don the dogshit tan apron, pull on some work gloves, get the blood flowing with the physical exercise that came with unloading the truck, and in no time, good as new.

At 19, one tends to bounce back quickly.

The drivers would unload cases of Kraft Cracker Barrel Extra Sharp Cheddar (small and liable to fall off the skate-wheel conveyor), huge boxes of Toddler Size Quilted Pampers that would fall to either side if he were not Johnny-on-the-spot to keep up and guide them down. One man in the truck pushing the boxes down the conveyor. One man in the store pulling them off.

Billy would work with him, match his pace. He would let Michael J. decide the unloading order, depending on his daily receiving space logistics. They developed a rhythm. Bobby would launch the boxes down willy-nilly, at his own pace, oblivious to anything beyond his immediate confines, kid in the dogshit tan apron and work gloves included.

Often, Bobby would see Matson down there, humping boxes, desperate to keep up and quicken his pace. Just because he could.

The worst were the 50-pound boxes of frozen "bull meat" the butchers would grind up for hamburger. All the other boxes, even the frozen ones, had some "give" in them, and effective courtesy boys-cum-frozen foods managers learned to stack, tie, and otherwise organize.

Bobby would rocket those frozen slabs down one right after another, forcing Matson to wrestle them off the belt before they'd slam into the unprotected cases of Yoplait yogurt at belt's end or wobble off, careening into a tied-in five-foot stack of Totino's pizza, frozen pepperoni slices scattering like orange poker chips across the concrete floor.

The 50-pounders were frozen solid in whatever shape they entered the freezer and so not conducive to stacking or rolling on the skate-wheel belt. Ideally, they'd need to be babied down one at a time. This lesson had been learned the hard way.

When they finished, Billy would often hop down from the truck and help him stack and stow whatever stopgap workarounds he had devised in order to keep up. They would share a quick cup of coffee, shake hands, and move on with the remains of their days.

Bobby would grunt, slam the truck door and split. Mike would wave goodbye with his middle finger.

The man Matson succeeded as frozen foods manager had landed a gig selling noodles.

He would find the grocery-buying manager at each of dozens of supermarkets, build a relationship, explain why Martha Gooch elbow macaroni was superior to American Beauty elbow macaroni and therefore worthy of more shelf space, cut deals, and leave them with enough Martha Gooch product until he returned next week.

Effective grocery managers knew their profit margins,

shelf space, and customers. Most of them knew which salesmen they could trust and which ones to hold at arm's length. Recently-promoted courtesy boys had negligible experience and zero training. Their transactional experience was limited to cars, girls, and beer.

The fringe benefits associated with the title bump did not include a requisite infusion of judgment.

As frozen foods manager, his duties were to order quantities of frozen food sufficient to keep the customers satisfied, ensure a steady stock between deliveries, deal with the specialty salesmen/vendors, stock the frozen food, and keep the storage freezer orderly.

The Rich's salesmen took one look at the new guy and saw opportunity.

Thirty cases of Rich's Coffee Rich. Twenty-four 16-ounce containers to a case. Seven hundred-twenty individual containers of frozen non-dairy coffee creamer.

What he did not know was that Rich's Coffee Rich was among the worst performers in the entire frozen food inventory. Only when they didn't sell did he begin to get a sense of the folly of his purchase. Even if he sold one a day, his stock wouldn't run out until sometime in 1980.

He literally could not give it away. Tried using it as a throw-in to the ad-libbed 3-minute intercom specials.

"... and a free 16-ounce container of Rich's Coffee Rich! Clouds in your coffee? Make your way to the end of aisle 4!"

The product itself was strange. Frozen coffee creamer? It required extra levels of thought and action and assumed an element of time the consumer was unwilling to invest. What was he going to do, stand by the freezer case and buttonhole every housewife who rolled by?

Well, first, you let it thaw...

Rich's Coffee Rich simply could not compete with the ease and convenience of a fresh carton of Steffen's half-and-half or a jar of Coffee-Mate.

Thirty cases also took up valuable space in the storage freezer. He had to move them so many times to make way for frozen food that people actually wanted to buy, the cases became worn and torn.

Gary D. left the decision to Burchart, who cornered Matson between the Cool Whip and the 12-ounce Minute Maid Orange-Grapefruit Juice Concentrate.

"As frozen foods manager, you make a damn fine courtesy boy." Burchart chuckled at his own cleverness.

Michael J. was stripped of his ordering responsibilities, which were given to the dairy manager, who had a dozen years on him and could apparently spot a charlatan salesman at twenty paces.

He thought about running to Duck for a rescue, but then remembered how irritated she got when he lost sight of customer service priorities, icily intoning—with em-FOSS-us—for all the store to hear, "FROZEN FOODS MANAGER, courtesy help up front, please."

No longer frozen foods manager, just another garden-variety frozen foods stocker.

A truck unloader at oh-dark-thirty.

A monkey can do this.

Until the demotion, the thought of making a career out of supermarket work had crept in. Or maybe supermarket-related work. An actual career in a supermarket didn't hold much allure, but when he looked around, he saw some possibilities.

Martha Gooch. Tony's Pizza. The specialty vendors. The guys who stocked the housewares aisle and the magazines. These guys were professionals. You couldn't pigeonhole them as white-collar management, but they wore neckties, drove nice cars, or at least nice panel delivery vans. They didn't have to schlep 10-pound bags of ice all over creation. They didn't have to block and tackle 50-pound boxes of frozen bull meat hurtling at top speeds toward vulnerable strawberry yogurt, while simultaneously pushing back against a hangover.

Unlike the poor blue-collar schmoes who humped the full cases of Coke, Pepsi and 7UP in, and the empty bottles out. Not like that miserable bastard up in the truck, zooming the ice-cold cases of Swanson Meat Loaf in Tomato Sauce TV dinners and the greasy boxes of Rainbow animal fat margarine at him so fast he could barely keep up.

The feeling had not yet reached the level where you could call it ambition. But more than once, he thought he couldn't stay out until 3 a.m. and go to work at 6 a.m. forever.

The Martha Gooch guy didn't lift a noodle until 8 in the morning.

17.
October 28, 1977

In the silence, he wanted to tell Malea how much he was falling for her, but chickened out.

If she feels that way, she'll say something first.

He thought back to their initial encounter.

"Have you met the new checker?" Duck started the conversation.

"Uh, no."

"You know who she is, right?" Pretty clear Duck wanted him to have this data.

"Melissa something?"

"Malea Sisk, daughter of Junell Winfield, who used to be Junell Denniston. Junell's the younger sister of Gary D. and daughter of Mr. D., so that makes Malea... "

"Mr. D.'s granddaughter, I get it."

He was still a little pissed about the demotion.

"You don't have to spell it out. I didn't just roll into town on the frozen coffee creamer wagon."

"Just warning you."

Even without the title or portfolio, Duck was an effective manager. She knew the tendency of the rank and file to disparage the brass and sought to arm them with information.

Everyone loved Mr. D., but since he retired, was rarely around. No one knew Junell—she lived in Minnesota—but there was no shortage of opinions about Gary D., not all of them flattering.

After his experience with Laura, he was just fine fishing

for Ms. Right Now on weekends at Pogo's. But it also wouldn't hurt to stay on the good side of all the various Dennistons. So, early that evening, he waited for her customer line to wind down.

"Hi! Mike Matson, they call me Michael J."

She took his extended right hand.

"Really nice to meet you. I'm Malea... " She paused. "It's a Hawaiian name. It means calm or gentle waters... " She was used to explaining her first name. "Sisk."

Her makeup looked like it was done by a pro. Wedge brunette. Dimples. She always seemed to look down, after making direct eye contact.

He toyed with the notion of a princess-related nickname, after all, she was Denniston royalty. But Malea desperately wanted to be one of the crowd and even joined in some of the milder forms of Gary D. disparagement.

One-on-one, Duck shared some additional intel.

Malea is Junell's daughter by her first marriage, to some lowlife from Butler County, long since out of the picture. Junell's now married to a hotshot businessman in the Twin Cities. Two cars, two snowmobiles in the garage, collection of expensive Hummel figurines. Pomeranian named Misty. The picture of suburban domesticity. Malea has two brothers—one older, one younger—from the same lowlife. Malea graduated from Wayzata High School, class of 1977.

In addition to an effective supermarket manager, Duck would have made a damned good detective.

At the end of their shift, a handful of courtesy boys and checkers were gathered in the deli. Coffee cups, ashtrays, soft drink cups scattered across a couple of tables.

Malea sidled up like she'd been working there for six years, taking a chair next to Matson.

"Are you guys going to Pogo's tonight?"

Duck was not the only one who had done some intel gathering.

Depending on how one viewed time, it was either very late or very early when they got to the cabin. He and Malea had worked the day shift and had been up since early the previous morning. Same with Lindsay, only she was on vacation. Duane the Man didn't get off until 10 p.m. By the time they got the car loaded, it was close to midnight.

They were all a little punchy.

Bill Walty's fishing cabin at Fall River Lake was an hour and a half due east of Wichita. Bedroom, living room, kitchen, and bathroom, small and sparse. Walty had no need for frills, he used it strictly for its intended purpose and made sure the boys were aware of these characteristics before committing to the loan.

The four of them didn't really have a purpose, other than spending time together partying at a lake.

Since they were now a couple, Mike and Malea got the bedroom. No formal conversation, it just happened. Duane and Lindsay barely knew each other and were relieved when assumptions proved true. Each of them staked out separate living room floor space and unrolled separate sleeping bags.

Lindsay Griffin was Malea's best friend from Minnesota, down for an extended visit. It was easy to see how the two had become friends. Lindsay's time and energy in high school was spent mastering the nuances of lateral quickness and the dribble-drive, while Malea concentrated on soft foundations and shimmer eye shadow.

Lindsay helped Malea with confidence and Malea

reciprocated with image.

They took Malea's car, a 1976 Ford Gran Torino Elite, since it was nicer than the LeMans and the Z had no back seat. Matson drove, Malea rode shotgun, each harboring the assumption that Duane and Lindsay together in the back seat equals ideal "getting to know you" time. Didn't work out that way, with the backseat conversation directed forward.

On the living room floor, the ice cracked a little as punchiness and a few beers took hold.

"There seems to be an unspoken indication that any attempt on my part to lessen the distance between our respective slumber receptacles would be met with resistance," Duane projected loud enough for Mike and Malea to hear him in the bedroom.

"Slumber receptacles!" Malea laughed out loud.

"You got that right, Duane the Man." Lindsay drew the bright line early.

"This existing scenario could logically end one of two ways. Romance, or 'zip up and go to sleep.' The latter will come naturally, regardless."

Duane the Man was on a roll.

"For the former to succeed, there needs to be, at the very least, a hint, an inkling, if you will, of potential reciprocity with respect to the notion."

"If you will," Malea repeated, "I'll bet she won't."

Lindsay reached down, and in one swift motion, pulled the zipper up tight around her neck.

"No inklings outa this sleeping bag, bud."

Duane had recently started taking flying lessons and the romance-probing banter de-escalated into a conversation about the joys and freedom felt watching Kansas unfold below while clipping along in the clouds at 140 miles per hour. When it became clear he was not a threat, Lindsay relaxed.

"So, I gotta know," still snugly cocooned, she rolled over on her side. A four-way conversation in the dark. "Why do they call you Duane the Man?"

"You wanna take this one?" A bounce pass in the lane.

Matson thought about it a second before responding. Rare for him.

"He is clearly smarter than the average bear and he understands what motivates people. He'd never tell you this, because it would shatter his carefully constructed self-image as 'above it all,' but if you needed it, and your blood types were compatible, Duane would give you his left kidney. In every respect, Duane William Smith is the man."

Easy layup. Silence for a few beats. Duane said quietly, "Aw, shucks."

The girls giggled. Somewhere outside the cabin, high in a tree very near Fall River Lake, an owl hooted.

Michael J. thought about altruism and quickly reached the conclusion that when kidney-crunch time came, he would find a way to hang on to his—both of them.

Even if the blood types were compatible.

The sound of ice hitting the bottom of an empty cooler roused the other three. Lindsay was first up, already scrambling eggs, frying bacon, and preparing the day's liquid refreshment. While stocking up on provisions before leaving Wichita, she had insisted on Pabst Blue Ribbon. Matson thought, "gopher piss" and snagged a few sixes of Coors.

Eyebrows raised, he looked at Duane the Man, who answered with an almost imperceptible head shake.

Kitchen bound, Duane said, "Hey Lindsay, can I help you

with anything in here?"

She relinquished beer icing duty and turned all of her attention to breakfast prep. Mike grabbed a sleeping bag and commenced rolling, while Malea attacked the other one.

"Teamwork makes the dream work." Coach Lindsay.

18.
November 14, 1977

Michael J. and Duck would take turns carpooling to their second job, waiting tables during the weekday 10 a.m. to 2 p.m. lunch shift at the Wichita Club, a swanky, downtown private club.

The radio in the LeMans was tuned to 103.7 FM, their default station. Out of a spot set, directly into a fast-paced jingle, female vocals, engineered specifically to reach deep into their target demographic heart and gut.

"The Rock... of Wichita, K-E-Y YYY-N."

Before the jingle faded, Don Hall started the record, 45 revolutions per minute. Exactly 14 seconds of instrumental lead-in before the vocal hit. Hall's smooth, natural patter ad-libbed to the start of the vocal, perfectly timed:

"Sunny skies, fifty-eight degrees in the Air Capital... expect the overnight low around 48... a gorgeous fall weekend headed our way, Wichita. It's the stuff of Dreams. From the L-P *Rumours*... Fleetwood Mac on K-E-Y-N."

The Stevie Nicks vocal hit instantly.

It wasn't hero worship as much as genuine respect, admiration, and connection to a voice on the radio that was literally helping define their era, time and place. Don Hall's voice on the radio, solid, steady, and comfortable. He never sounded like he was actually working. Hip, casual, with-it, glib, witty. Wichita's Sherpa to rock 'n' roll nirvana. The personification of cool.

"*Rumours* is not *Dark Side of the Moon*, but I'll tell you this…" Duck reached over and turned down the volume.

At a red light at First and Broadway, he swung out and punched it, bound for the Wichita Public Library, a few blocks away. The 'right on red after a full stop' law was only a couple of years old in Kansas, but he never paid much attention to the last part.

"…Nicks and Buckingham moved those guys from the fringes of obscurity."

Duck had become Wichita's one-woman Fleetwood Mac proselytizer, going so far as convincing a friend to name her newborn daughter, Rhiannon.

The Wichita Club was lodged in the top two floors of the Vickers/Kansas State Bank & Trust Building on Market Street, a sky blue and beige-paneled structure with a massive time and temperature lighted display perched on the roof. As a kid, that's how he told time when he would take the city bus downtown to the library or ride his bicycle to Wichita Aeros games at Lawrence Stadium. Prior to the recent construction of the nearby Holiday Inn Plaza, the Vickers/KSB&T was the tallest building in Kansas.

"They're a mess, though," said Duck. "John and Christie are splitsville, Buckingham and Nicks, too."

Twenty hours a week downtown, plus their 40-45 at Mr. D's and they were pocketing good money. Duck had been working two jobs since graduating high school. She had preceded him at the Wichita Club by six months, and arranged everything, including locking in his full-time courtesy boy job to evenings, after the demotion from Frozen Foods Manager.

"Word is Stevie's hooked up with Mick." Duck was on her second copy of the vinyl LP and had given Matson a cassette version, shortly after MGB hot tape deck installation, which had since been transferred to the LeMans. "Every one of them is all coked up, but it's damn fine music."

She reached over and cranked the volume back up.

They parked on the west side, in a pay-as-you-park lot governed by the honor system. Pull into a numbered slot, find the corresponding number on a massive bank with individual slots for each parking spot, fold up a couple bucks and slip them in.

It didn't take Mike long to notice protruding corners of dollar bills not fully inserted in various slots, so he'd grab a corner, pull and redistribute the cash to the slot corresponding with his parking space. When she saw him do this, Duck would frown, but never verbalize her objections.

The honor system was only as good as the honor of its participants.

A grand, curved, white carpeted staircase connected the 18th and 19th floors of the Wichita Club. The bar and informal gathering spaces made up the 18th floor, with the serious dining on the top floor. Two big dining sections, with assorted separate rooms of various size and configuration for the private luncheon meetings to cut the big deals.

Club members were oilmen, bankers, real estate developers. Men who wore charcoal pinstripe, gray glen plaid and solid navy-blue business suits, starched-white collars and polished black wingtips. Neckties designed to pull out a thread color of the suit, with the occasional primary color splash. Men of substance and purpose who officed in downtown Wichita and took humble pride in being able to tell their secretaries, "Two for lunch, Thursday at the club."

As a private club, they could make up their own rules, which complemented their culture and demeanor. Men only for lunch, though wives and families were more than welcome for dinner.

Steep annual membership fees and a membership committee which served as the final arbiter of who got in. The Wichita Club wasn't a secret, but there was also no need for public relations. The public was not invited.

Lunch was designed to be efficient. Important men to whom time is money. The food was not fancy, soup and sandwiches. Get in. Conduct the vital business. Eat lunch. Dab the corners of your mouth with a white linen napkin. Get out.

No tips, that was also written into the membership agreement. Michael J., Duck and the other waitstaff earned the same amount, regardless of the quality of their service. The waitstaff tended toward nice, polite, and deferential to men in power, for two reasons: That's the way they were raised, and if they happened not to be nice, polite, and deferential, there's the door.

Waiters wore black pants, polished black leather shoes, white shirts with white jackets, and a black clip-on bowtie. Similar uniforms for the waitresses. A short-sleeved black dress with crisp white collar and sleeve ends, black hose (no fishnets), and black heels. And as if to put them in their place, a black apron with white borders replaced the white jacket.

When pouring coffee, servers were instructed to place a saucer between diner and cup, to ward off the inadvertent hot splash on a man in power.

At the library, he pulled into the only open slot in the south side metered parking lot.

"Back in a flash."

He did not feed the meter. Maybe the Wichita Public Library Parking Lot Police already knew he wasn't honorable.

"Leave the car running, I'll wait here," Duck said. "If the

meter maid comes along, I'll do a song and dance."

He hustled to the research desk, quickly determined he'd not been there since his high school term paper on manifest destiny, and asked the lady if she had a volume that listed all the broadcasting technical schools in the country.

"I do, in fact."

Fifty-something, graying around the temples. Reading glasses dangling around her neck. She was the kind of reference librarian who recognized that young people learning how to access vital information was just as important as the actual information.

"Wait right here, son."

Son?

He leaned over a nearby table, but did not sit down, Duck was still waiting. He found what he was looking for and ran his finger down the list:

Md.: Maryland School of Broadcasting, Baltimore.
Mass.: Wentworth Institute of Technology, Boston.
Mich.: Lawrence Tech, Southfield.
Minn.: Brown Institute, Minneapolis.

He grabbed a piece of scratch paper and a yellow #2 lead pencil from the community stash. On a break that afternoon at Mr. D's, careful to charge the call to his home phone, he had another component of the plan.

He hadn't yet shared it with anyone, but the framework was emerging. Quit the grocery biz, learn the basics of a new industry, stick with Malea, launch a professional radio career. Align all these stars and parlay it all into a gig deejaying at KEYN.

Mr. D, Lowell Denniston, owned KEYN. Malea was his granddaughter. Boy meets girl, girl tells Gramps that boy is the next Don Hall.

≡

Junell Winfield was using the spine of a table knife to slide excess mayonnaise from a measuring cup to ensure accuracy, and as a consequence, consistency, while fixing lunch in her mother's kitchen. Leona "Lonie" Denniston was Lowell's first wife and the mother of his two offspring.

Mike couldn't help but compare Junell to her brother. If Gary D. was nervous and unsure, his younger sister was his polar opposite, poised and confident.

Lonie lived in a high-end luxury duplex adjacent to Sweetbriar, bought and paid for by Mr. D. when he grew weary of being married to her. Lonie adored her children and grandchildren and missed all the glamour that came with being Mrs. D.

Junell was back home from the Twin Cities for a family visit. Two items on her agenda: checking in on Lonie and sizing up her daughter's new beau.

They were four for lunch. The menu included sliced cucumbers and onions marinated in vinegar, potato salad slathered in mayonnaise, and ham sandwiches on white bread spread with your choice of mayo or pale-yellow margarine. An optional stack of individually wrapped processed American cheese food product slices rested on a melamine plate within easy reach.

"How old are you, Mike?" Junell smiled as she passed him the white Pyrex bowl of cukes.

He took a generous slotted spoonful, careful to hold the spoon against the inside of the Pyrex bowl, to drain excess vinegar before placing the cukes on his plate.

"I'll be 20 next month."

It was a casual lunch, but he wanted to leave a good impression. He hadn't really had many formal meals since leaving Pleasant Valley, but he'd seen how the big boys behaved at the Wichita Club. They were using paper napkins, but he made certain to unfold one and put it in his lap before the meal.

When she dined alone, Lonie's lunch was often liquid, and she was usually in the bag by noon. Junell knew this about her mother, and if it bothered her, she did not let on. Tall, slender, with a dark complexion, Junell Denniston had been 1955 homecoming queen at Cheney High about the time her father was getting his supermarket foothold in Wichita.

Perhaps seeking company in her luxurious misery, Lonie reached into her fridge, pulled out a gold foil-topped brown bottle of Michelob, deftly unscrewed the cap, and placed it at two o'clock adjacent to Mike's plate. His diagonally cut ham sandwich seemed to be pointing at it.

"Thanks, no," wondering if this was some sort of test. "I have to be at work in a couple of hours."

It was the first time in his nearly 20 years he had ever turned down a beer. Lonie shrugged, picked up the bottle and took a long pull, still standing. Junell kept smiling the homecoming queen smile.

"Do you have a life plan?"

Jesus, a life plan? You gonna sell me some term?

His eyes shifted from Junell to her daughter. Malea's eyes met his briefly, before diving into the potato salad.

"I do. I intend to get into broadcasting. I've been looking into some technical schools... "

Not, I want to, I 'intend' to.

If lunch was a test, he felt like he came through. Young man with a "life plan" in love with your daughter. Earnest and ambitious. Maybe he was going after the wrong Denniston. Maybe the life plan needed another sub-point. Maybe Junell can whisper in Daddy's ear and encourage him to open some radio station doors.

"That went well, I thought." Malea raised her eyebrows as though it was a question, as they slid into the Gran Torino Elite. When she smiled, he could see glimmers of the 1955 Cheney High homecoming queen.

"I'm pretty good with mothers."

He was also pretty good with grandfathers. He wondered if he should just come right out and ask her to arrange a one-on-one.

It's a pleasure to meet you formally, sir. I've long admired your success. Two things. I'm crazy about your granddaughter, and Don Hall needs a protégé. Look no further!

How else is he gonna know?

THE CITIES

19.
January 4, 1978

"Double-you—C—C—Oh... F-M One—Oh—Three... "

This is the big leagues.

The Acapulco radio station jingle on "CCO," as the locals called it, filled him with a new sense of pride and ownership. He created the nickname the first time he heard the term, *a capella.*

This is now my radio station. The Twin Cities, 'the Cities,' as the locals called them, *are now my cities.*

The radio commercials advertised the same goods sold in Wichita, but the vehicles delivering them were new and different: Musicland records. Red Owl supermarket. Dayton's department store.

Light snow was falling as he headed east on Lake Street. Glancing up, he saw a billboard reading: "Mike Marshall Saves at the Met." Marshall was a screwball-pitching relief ace for the Minnesota Twins at Metropolitan Stadium in Bloomington, a cities' suburb.

Tech school started Monday. Before then, he needed to find a job and a place to live. Mike spent the previous evening on a rollaway guest bed in Malea's family's basement in Wayzata, but her mother's husband's (she couldn't bring herself to call John Winfield her stepfather) non-verbal communications were easy to translate and he was determined not to wear out his welcome.

Brown Institute was a full-service trade school and kept an up-to-date list of apartments, rooms to let, and other student housing. Between Brown and the until very recently cloistered University of St. Thomas Catholic college just across the Mississippi in St. Paul, rental property owners in south Minneapolis and west St. Paul were fed a steady stream of paying tenants.

He took the southeast bedroom on the second story of a three-story Victorian near Powderhorn Park in south Minneapolis. The landlady and her family occupied the first floor, self-contained and separated from the riffraff in the two floors above.

The riffraff occupied six separate bedrooms with a shared kitchen and bathroom. He caught on early that it paid to be the first one up; the hot water lasted long enough for about half a shower. Access by way of a separate rickety staircase tacked onto the back of the house, opening to the kitchen, ensured riffraff/landlady's family separation.

There was one telephone, for all six guys, included in the rent. Make all the collect calls you want, but the first long distance call that shows up on the bill and the phone comes out. No visitors, especially girls. No parties. No loud music.

A long time ago, this house was a south Minneapolis showcase. Knowledge gleaned in Drafting 3 gave him a sense of what he was getting into. The elaborate 12-inch dark mahogany baseboards were very early 20th century. He didn't know specifically how old, until the landlady handed him his room key after shaking hands to seal the deal.

A skeleton key. She had to show him how it worked.

This Victorian was the anti-Woodgate. No pool. No central air. No tennis courts. No bikini-clad friends. That's okay. He had a girlfriend. In the outer ring of the suburbs. He would trade "single young courtesy boy with Ms. Right Now," for "studious young future broadcast professional with a steady girlfriend."

Both iterations were hungry, but the end game goals were tweaked.

Within five years, maybe three, he would be a popular deejay on WCCO-FM, ad-libbing weather forecasts on the heels of Acapulco jingles. The voice of Musicland records, Red Owl supermarkets, or Dayton's department stores. He and Malea would be married, and he would be the up-and-coming radio pro, featured in the Sunday insert of the *Minneapolis Star-Tribune*, in which he would regale his humble start in the Cities. The skeleton key would add a nice touch of color to the story.

Mike was schlepping his all-in-one, off-the-shelf rip-off stereo from David's discount store in Sweetbriar up the rickety stairs when he was met at the landing outside the kitchen by another of the riffraff, offering to lend a hand.

"I got it, thanks." Squeezing past, forcing his fellow riffraff to take a step backward.

Leave me alone, complete stranger. I had a tight circle of intimate friends in Wichita, but I traded them all for one person, my girlfriend in the suburbs. She is all I need and I've neither the interest nor inclination to make friends with the likes of you.

He would gradually and eventually reach a riffraff rapprochement. Mike wanted none of them as friends, but they could be tolerated as roommates or neighbors. All six were in similar circumstances. In fact, three were fellow Brownies, one was recently divorced, tossed from suburban home life, and one was a do-nothing criminal wannabe, in and out of trouble with the cops and the Hennepin County criminal justice system.

The riffraff had two things in common, three, if you counted the fact they were all guys. They were all a paycheck away from poverty, and—beer.

Beer now came in handy new 12-packs and one brand or another was often on sale at the corner liquor store. They became such good customers that they built a first-name relationship with the proprietor, who meshed their loyalty with their financial dire straits and gave them the sale price on the new 12-packs, regardless.

These guys were never going to be friends in the Duck, Duane the Man, or Inglewood manner. He would pound a few beers with them around the kitchen table, but never as a specific event, always to or from his time with Malea.

He had no credit cards and only enough money for a week if he ate light. His expense inventory amounted to rent, tuition, car payment, Malea, and beer. Those last two became the essentials. Fuel for the LeMans to and from Wayzata and dinner, movies, disco cover charges, and other assorted expenses that come with the territory when trading in all your relationships for one person.

It brought to mind a Bill Walty truism, shared over coffee in the Mr. D's deli during a break the Sunday before he left Wichita: When your outgo exceeds your income, your upkeep will be your downfall.

A job was an absolute necessity.

Mike had identified three supermarkets in the general area. He intended to cold call them all, armed with his resume, such as it was, at age 20. Using carbon paper, he had a half-dozen copies, typed up last night on Junell's IBM Selectric. A year-and-a-half as a busboy/dishwasher at Angelo's, two-and-a-half years at Mr. D's where he did it all, sack, carry out, check, stock. Even a short stint in supermarket middle management as frozen foods manager at the tender age of 19.

Using the Drafting 3 block lettering, he added the phone number he now shared with five other guys and made a mental note to introduce himself to the riffraff.

I don't have to break bread with my riffraff brethren, but at least they need to know my name so they can take a phone message.

"Mr. D's, huh?"

Ray Westergaard looked at his resume, then back at him, clearly visualizing some dinky mom-and-pop corner store in the Great Plains sticks, frequented by hayseed farmers in overalls more interested in kicking dirt clods while shooting the shit than in spending money on groceries. Certainly not the level of this state-of-the-art operation he was managing in the heart of the Cities.

The SuperValu on the northwest corner of Hiawatha Avenue and Lake Street was the latest in the chain and among the newest supermarkets in the Cities.

Not so fast, there, Sven. I was Michael J., the frozen foods manager of a major metropolitan supermarket, with serious responsibilities, thank you very much. Whether it was fantasizing about the attractive housewives after carrying out their groceries or ordering 30 cases of 16-ounce Rich's Coffee Rich, the buck stopped with me.

"Yes. It's a family-owned IGA chain in Wichita."

Within a half-hour of entering the SuperValu, an anchor store in the Minnehaha Mall, he had a job as a dairy stocker. Westergaard made it clear that everyone in his supermarket had very defined roles. Sackers sack, checkers check, and dairy stockers stock dairy. Period.

Twenty-five hours a week. Six a.m. to 2 p.m. both days one weekend, 2 p.m. to 10 p.m. both days the next. The other nine hours would be picked up on weekday afternoons or evenings.

"And don't come running to me with your problems," he added. "Kerry Andersen will be your boss, but I'm his boss."

Between a two-handled cart loaded six-high and two-across with milk crates, a long-haired guy was bobbing up and down, transferring gallons of SuperValu whole milk from crate to dairy case. White short-sleeved shirt, royal blue apron covering a green and blue striped necktie, bushy mustache, dingo boots, wide leather watchband, blue jeans.

The milk gallons at Mr. D's were plastic jugs. These gallons were made from the same plastic-coated paperboard as the half-gallons back home. Each was topped with a plastic loop handle for convenience. A second cart loaded with unstocked half-gallons and quarts of SuperValu 2 percent and skim, and a host of sizes of dairy one offs: chocolate milk, half-and-half, and whipping cream, loomed nearby.

Seeing Kerry in blue jeans elevated his first impression of SuperValu. At Mr. D's, dress slacks were the expected norm.

"Kerry?" No way was he gonna call this guy "Mr. Andersen."

"Yeah?"

Andersen's first glance gave off: "Who's this yahoo and why's he bothering me? I'm shorthanded and I gotta get these fluid ounces on the shelf, doncha know?"

"My name's Mike Matson," extending his right hand. "Ray Westergaard sent me back. I'm your new part-timer."

Like throwing a switch, "leave me alone" became "Ah, my new best friend."

"Pleasure," standing up from his crouch to shake his hand. "When do you start?"

"Right now. I'm here until 10 p.m."

"That's what I wanted to hear. You finish up these fluid

ounces, then come find me and I'll give you the lay of the land. Do you know how to work a Garvey?"

Do I know how to work a Garvey? These gallons are $1.69, not 169¢. I didn't just roll into the Cities on the unpasteurized, unhomogenized milk wagon.

"Sure do."

Kerry twirled his Garvey like a six-shooter and handed it over, handle first.

Mike finished stocking the milk and went in search of his new boss. Found him smoking a cigarette on the loading dock. Kerry Andersen was in his late 20s, destined to be a SuperValu lifer and perfectly at peace with it.

There, but for the grace of Brown Institute, go I.

Two things struck him as Kerry gave him the store's walking tour once-over. The space for dairy products was roughly three times as big as the dairy space at D's, but the store itself was not that much bigger. Twice as much milk and cheese, an entire section of yogurt, which Kerry called "yogi." Had he encountered a fellow lingo appropriator? Yogi? Fluid ounces? He considered sharing that he was the one who came up with CGBs and WKC but bit his tongue.

I should get to know him better, first.

Because sackers sack, checkers check, and dairy stockers stock dairy, the SuperValu silos prevented the kind of relationship building that the courtesy-boys-do-everything mentality fostered at Mr. D's. As a result, he knew the names of his fellow dairy stockers, Westergaard, (whom he rarely saw), and Kerry.

He also had considerably less customer interaction than at Mr. D's and did not get near an intercom. More businesslike, less screwing around. He liked it that way. The silos complemented his new persona.

Don't need to be friends with these people, or even try to impress them. I have a friend, a girlfriend, in fact. In the suburbs.

When he compared his supermarket employers, he registered the biggest difference in his own dairy stocking work. Back home, the margarine to butter space allotment ratio was 95/5. Just the opposite up here.

He did bring this up with Kerry.

"Butter comes from a cow, while yer margarine is basically vegetable oil on a stick." Kerry looked at him and smiled. "Lotta dairy farms here in Minnesota." It came out minney-SO-duh. "We Scandahoovians love our lactose."

Did Kansans consider butter an expensive extravagance and that's why they opted to spread vegetable oil from a pale-yellow stick on their white bread toast? Or maybe their unrefined Great Plains palates couldn't discern the difference.

He was also enthralled and paying rapt attention as they walked by the beer cooler on their way back to the dairy. Some familiar names and seeming prominence up here for brands that were an afterthought back home: Pabst Blue Ribbon, Hamm's, Old Milwaukee. So many brands he had never heard of before. Blatz, Grain Belt, Schmidt, Special Export, and the one that would become his Minnesota go-to, Heileman's Old Style.

An entire new range of suds to be explored. He could not wait to sample them all.

Mike learned the phone call protocol from Kerry ("local calls only and keep 'em short"), and on a break at 5:30, he called Malea. As he was dialing, he wondered briefly whether the outer ring of the suburbs was a local call but quit wondering when she answered.

"Guess what?" He tried to undersell his excitement. "I got a place to live and a job."

He had left her house right after lunch. Junell, always leading the way with exotic lunch options, had served grilled Velveeta sandwiches. Real butter on the white bread, now that he thought of it.

"That's soooo great!" Her excitement for him was palpable. Exactly what he wanted. He would low-key the news, she'd respond with how significant of an accomplishment it was. "Wow, you only left here, like four hours ago!"

"Yeah, well, modesty prevents me from bragging, but I am a studious young future broadcast professional with a steady girlfriend."

She laughed.

He was not slated to work again until Friday. They made Thursday plans. He would drive to the outer ring of the suburbs, bring her back into the Cities and retrace his housing and employment successes.

20.
April 3, 1978

On a matchmade-double date with Lindsay, the four of them ended up at Mitch Burns' apartment, where he fired up his multi-component stereo, receiver tuned to CCO. Burns led with his voice, playing deejay.

"The Bee Gees, from the motion picture, *Saturday Night Fever*, on Double-you-C-C-Oh-F-M-one-oh-three, asking the time-honored question: How deep is your love?"

Burns paused a beat and looked directly at Lindsay.

"About six inches, eight, when I'm around Lindsay."

Lindsay rolled her eyes, wondered if this was Duane the Man slumber receptacles redux, moved a bit further from Burns and shot Malea and Mike the "let's get out of here" look.

Subtlety was not a Mitch Burns strength.

From LaCrosse, Wisconsin, Burns was a ladies' man, and the ladies knew it, which said something about his conquests. Burns lived alone in a one-bedroom apartment in Minneapolis, which along with food, gasoline, and other essentials, were paid for by Mom and Dad back in LaCrosse. Matson envied the apartment, the voice, the financial flexibility borne from parental subsidization, but not the umbilical.

The original plan was dinner and disco. Mama Rosa's, an Italian joint in the West Bank neighborhood, then downtown to Scottie's on Seventh, which landed just north of Pogo's but south of Studio 54 in the informal disco sophistication rankings lodged in his brain. He had never been to Studio 54 or New York City. In fact, the Cities marked the furthest east he had ever traveled in his two decades, but that did not stop him from fantasizing and drawing conclusions about such things.

Over spaghetti and meatballs, he suggested an alternative plan.

"Hey, the Oscars are tonight. Travolta's up for Best Actor," he had already cleared this notion with Burns. "How 'bout we go to Mitch's and watch it?"

Lindsay and Malea were noncommittal. They had invested considerable time and effort to look good Rollercoastering, Hustling, and Bus Stopping at Scottie's on Seventh. Burns played his part with Oscar-worthy poise.

"Great idea!" His eyes lit up at the thought. One less logistic for his game plan, as he lapsed back into announcer mode.

"LIVE from the Dorothy Chandler Pavilion in Hollywood, it's Oscar's golden anniversary… "

"Besides, it's Monday," Matson bolstered the argument. "Scottie's'll be dead."

Each generation has a few iconic film stars to call their very own. Someone their age, with whom they identify. That's the inherent value of art.

John Travolta's compelling portrayal of Tony Manero in *Saturday Night Fever* was an emotional connection. A deep one. One performance connected to a specific point in time that was a mirror reflection of their lives. The movie justified their culture, and it followed naturally that Travolta would define their era.

Girls in waist-length rabbit fur jackets, guys who worked for an hour on their feathered hair. Their lives right up there on the big screen. A movie with a soundtrack as important as the script. Travolta's dancing as important as his acting.

Saturday Night Fever was just good enough to make you wish it was better.

As last year's Best Actor winner, the duty fell to Sylvester Stallone. The four of them sat riveted to Burns' new parentally-subsidized RCA XL 100 13-inch portable color set, tuned to Channel 9, KMSP-TV, the Cities' ABC affiliate.

"Tonight's nominees for an outstanding performance in a lead role are... " The teleprompter operator was apparently not fast enough for Stallone, because then he got pissed, waved the envelope containing the Oscar winner's name and spat out, "Want me to do it by memory?"

"That's what actors do, you prima donna," Burns sneered at the screen. "Bush league move."

"Woody Allen in *Annie Hall*," Stallone shifted his eyes as the camera stayed on him. Woody was not in the house. "Richard Burton in *Equus*." A tight shot of Burton, affecting a pose somewhere between humble and bored, leaning toward bored.

Mitch got up, reached around behind the TV, and fiddled with the horizontal hold. The image rolled a couple of times before stabilizing.

"Richard Dreyfuss in *Goodbye Girl*," Stallone's voice over a live shot of Dreyfuss, wearing a goofy smile.

"Dreyfuss is not sure how he's supposed to act," Matson pointed his right index finger at the TV, holding a can of Old Style.

"He's not yet mastered the Richard Burton nonchalance."

"Marcello Mastroianni, *A Special Day*," who looked rigid and tense, visibly blowing out a deep breath.

"...and John Travolta in *Saturday Night Fevah*." Cut to

Travolta, wearing a white scarf around his neck, accenting his jet-black tux, looking the way you're supposed to look in such circumstances: nervous. The director of the Oscars telecast punched up a shot with Stallone in the middle, framed by the four live shots of the nominees and a grainy black-and-white still of Woody Allen.

"... and the winner is... and new heavyweight champ... RICHARD DREYFUSS!"

Malea and Lindsay groaned in unison as Dreyfuss made his way to the stage and said all the right things. Nothing against Dreyfuss, but Mike felt his Oscar-worthy performance came two years earlier in *Jaws*, a couple of cocktails deep in the galley of the *Orca*, comparing battle scars with Robert Shaw. He remembered Cinemas East, Ben Gardner's head, and Nancy Ellis clinging to his arm for dear life.

"Travolta was robbed," Matson said, dismissing the whole thing with a wave of his arm. Enough of a cue for Burns to turn off the TV and get on with the rest of the evening.

At 30, Dreyfuss became the youngest-ever Best Actor Oscar winner. Still in Travolta's generation and arguably on the fringes of theirs. If *Saturday Night Fever* mirrored their culture, *The Goodbye Girl*, a Neil Simon formulaic romantic comedy, was their parents' idea of Hollywood. If the torch was going to be passed, they would have preferred a cleaner break.

They talked about Travolta's next big picture—to be released in the summer—playing Danny Zuko to Olivia Newton-John's Sandy Olsson in the motion picture adaptation of the Broadway smash, *Grease*.

"You guys wanna make plans to see it together?" Malea's eyes shifted between Lindsay and Mitch, apparently missing Lindsay's non-verbals.

"Think I'm gonna be busy that night," Lindsay responded

quickly, before Mitch could. "Lots of important things to do, pretty much every evening all the way through to the holidays."

Burns moved closer to Lindsay on the couch, so she got up, walked across the room, and sat on the arm of the chair where Matson was parked.

"I already have one asshole in my pants," looking directly at Mitch. "What makes you think I need another?"

The problem was, Lindsay's brushoffs, though heartfelt and purposeful, were often accompanied by nervous giggles, which Burns interpreted as "She really doesn't mean what she's saying."

On their way home, Lindsay leaned forward from the backseat.

"No offense, Michael J., I know he's your friend, but I'm done with that guy," controlling her anger. "He has a one-track mind."

"I'll go see *Grease* with you guys this summer," Lindsay said, leaning back. "But just the three of us. No more fixing me up."

He couldn't bring himself to apologize because he could not recognize the problem. Duane and Mitch were just doing what came naturally. He had made up his mind about the kind of girl Lindsay was, even with a complete lack of evidence to support his notions. The thought that Lindsay might find their behavior rude or even potentially dangerous, never entered his mind.

The pop culture mirror reflection of their lives was not a direct reflection.

Life does not always imitate art.

21.
June 13, 1978

"Don't get too comfortable with the Cities." Burns waved his arm in the general direction of Brown Institute, right next door.

"If this works the way it's supposed to, you'll soon be in Bumfuck, North Dakota."

Donna Hansen chimed in, "Or Nowhere, Minnesota."

"West Overshoe, Wisconsin," Kenny Johnston added, between bites of an Egg McMuffin.

The four of them had become a clique. The Brown Institute morning broadcasting section was comprised of roughly forty students. Many had tried their hand at the upper Midwest equivalent of dub-yes-you and found it wanting. Or, truth be told, found their ability to succeed there wanting.

Their ambition and talent levels were as wide and varied as any group of forty such human beings, but all forty shared a motivation to launch a career in broadcasting.

Nearly all were from the upper Midwest and possessed some semblance of northern plains dialect. Yooper English from the upper peninsula of Michigan, Iron Range English from the Bemidji-International Falls-Duluth region north of the Cities, and a generic minnie-SO-duh accent from everyone else.

The young man who, up until very recently, was known as Michael J., was the geographic and linguistic outlier. His voice lacked the flat, nasal twang so prevalent in the Great Plains and leaned just a skosh toward the tenor side of the baritone range.

When his fellow students heard his broadcast voice, free of generations of Scandinavian genetics, they immediately pigeonholed him as from "the south."

Kansas is smack in the middle of the country, can't you guys read a damn map? Well—I guess it is south of here.

Real good, then.

The four gathered each morning before class at McDonald's on Lake Street next door to the school. As a play on a Brown diction exercise, Mike called it, "The arches which are, were, and shall ever be golden," and it stuck. Since money was tight, his culinary selections were consistent. Cinnamon danish, the cheapest item on the menu, and a large black coffee, which could and would be brought next door, to class.

Johnston, a tall, skinny drink of water, possessed an innate grasp of the underlying electronics which actually allowed for the broadcasting. Since he was headed for the technical side of the biz, and the other three were bound for Bumfuck/Nowhere/West Overshoe on-air glory, Kenny was not shy about reminding his chums of some fundamental broadcasting truth.

"Without my efforts, all your records and dulcet tones disappear into the ether," Johnston said, while lifting his arm and wiggling his fingers. He already grasped radio station pecking order. Talent gets the glory, technicians get taken for granted, until something breaks.

"Without me, you guys are just pissing in the wind."

Donna wore high-heeled boots, tight jeans, a blonde pageboy, and her feelings on the sleeve of a rabbit fur jacket. A small-town girl from Arlington, South Dakota, she had started on the four-year plan at South Dakota State University in nearby Brookings. Impatience brought her to the Cities.

The three boys were in love with the one girl, in that

nature-takes-its-course way when 20-year-olds with common interests find themselves in close proximity. Donna was naturally genuine and heartfelt, and her demeanor was often misinterpreted as a romance-oriented act. She had been fending off unwanted advances since puberty and had developed the skills to maintain relationships at the platonic level.

Rising to levels of closeness to wisdom and true beauty, and eventually, union with the truth.

She preferred to think of the four of them as the four of them. Friends, not with benefits, but with a common cause. Mike had considered making a move and harbored no illusions about how he would react had those intentions proven reciprocal. If he thought about the fact that he was already in a meaningful monogamous relationship bent on marriage, he did not think about it for very long.

They didn't want to say it out loud, but the four thought of themselves as better than the other 36. Four like-minded fledgling radio professionals, together on their sleek sailboat charting a course to success in a raging sea of mediocrity.

Cinnamon danish today. Club sandwiches in Bumfuck. Filet mignon when they hit the bigtime.

Other classmates who saw the four as the four wanted in, but no one made the cut.

At Brown, he was not shy about sharing his dream to become a Major League Baseball play-by-play announcer. Six months in, Bruce Browning, in whose class students learned the ins and outs of a radio station control room, took him next door, bought him a quarter-pounder with cheese and a Coke, and let him down easy.

"Don't limit yourself strictly to big league baseball." Browning knew lessons learned over a burger and fries at McDonalds were every bit as valuable as those offered in the studio or lecture hall. The radio station in Bumfuck did not need the next Curt Gowdy. They needed a solid announcer who was versatile.

"If you're that good, play-by-play'll happen. Most guys are not that good."

No blowing smoke up his ass. Honest, direct, real truth.

College was scattershot. Brown Institute was a cruise missile. Four hours a day, 50 weeks out of the year, Brown taught announcing, diction, pace and pronunciation, the rudiments of journalism, sports play-by-play, commercial production, advertising and airtime sales. Most importantly, the Brown curriculum brought interconnectivity of each disparate part that made the whole of a successful small-market radio station.

Take people with drive, ambition, and at least a modicum of talent, infuse them with technical knowledge, shine them up, and offer them to radio and television stations. Those in the Brown pipeline were eager to spill out of it, at entry-level, into the real world.

"Am I that good?" Mike put what was left of the burger back in its yellow Styrofoam pod.

"Don't know yet." Browning softened his gaze and smiled. "You clearly have talent, you're smart. You'll get a job in radio, I'm confident."

If the Brown Institute experience led to some character molding beneath the arches which are, were, and shall ever be golden, then gravy.

"A good part of your success, though, won't come in doing the actual work, deejaying or calling a basketball game,"

Browning leaned back. "It'll be how you approach it with your head and your heart."

The Brown instructors were broadcast pros, each with a specialty niche. Some preferred the economic security of a teaching gig, some were natural-born educators, others had radio or television careers and moonlighted at Brown for some extra scratch. All of them genuinely cared about passing along their knowledge and experience.

"It's rare for these stations to hire a guy with a singular focus right out of Brown. Get your foot in the door." Browning was making sense and for once, Mike was actually listening.

"Most of these stations that hire Brown grads don't have just one guy who does only sports play-by-play. You'll do a board shift and call the high school football game."

Without coming right out and saying it, the man was describing the real world of entry-level broadcasting jobs in an effort to motivate and provide direction.

"And you will likely be asked to sell the commercial airtime during the football game."

Browning wanted to say, "You will probably also empty the trash and sweep the floors," but recognized the fine line between encouragement and hard cold reality. The fledgling broadcasters would find out soon enough about "other duties as assigned."

Everything at Brown was practical and pointed toward job placement, so they honed their sparkling personalities, direct eye contact, firm handshakes, and audition tapes.

Mike had settled into a comfortable routine. Ignore the riffraff, cinnamon danish and coffee with the clique, class in the morning, yogi, fluid ounces, and the wall of butter in the afternoon and on weekends.

Malea got all the rest of the time, spent either in the outer ring of the suburbs or be-bopping around the Cities in search of entertainment. She worked at a daycare center, wiping the noses and kissing the owies of outer-ring suburban Gen Xers. Since it compartmentalized neatly into his long-range perception of himself, he was not afraid when they talked openly of marriage.

It fulfilled a societal expectation, fit nicely into his young-broadcast-professional-on-the-move perception, and offered a sense of security.

The ambition that emerged late in 1977 had evolved into a driving force. He was learning an industry, paying attention, honing his skills, acing the tests. Technical school had depth and meaning. He got it. He could become a sports announcer or a deejay. He wasn't as good as Donna or Burns, but he was sure better than the others in his class.

For the first time in his life, he thought differently about his father's short-tempered sermons regarding potential. James E. was not particularly good at communicating it without anger, so it never really stuck. Until now. His father was right. He did have potential. He could see it. When he worked on his audition tape, he could hear it. He could visualize the rough framework of a life's direction.

Marry Malea, have a couple of kids, succeed professionally. Six months in the boonies, spinning records and calling Friday night high school football.

Welcome friends, to what will doubtless prove to be an evening of exciting gridiron action here on WBFK as our beloved Bumfuck Margarine Eschewers play host to their arch-rival West Overshoe Snow Shovelers.

Then onto a medium market, Madison, Sioux Falls, or Des Moines, and back to the Cities within three years. Or St. Louis, Milwaukee, Kansas City, or Chicago. A starter house in the first ring of the 'burbs, with the implication of an eventual forever house in the outer ring.

If you had talent, you could get a job. If you had ambition and drive, you could get your foot in the door. He had all three, and the trend line of the latter two was in ascendancy.

22.
August 23, 1978

Donna's blue eyes widened as she slid tight next to him in the lecture hall, excited and nearly breathless.

"Mike, have you heard the new Gerry Rafferty song, 'Baker Street?'"

He was glad he had abandoned "Michael J." when he got to the Cities. When he thought about the possibility of Donna calling him "Michael J.," an extra layer of explanation was needed, which now seemed a little juvenile.

Ya see, there were three courtesy boys named Mike at Mr. D's, and my friend, Duck, with whom I had a platonic relationship, not unlike the one you and I seem to have, by the way. Well, she gave me this nickname, to set me apart. It also sounded cool when she called me by that name on the intercom...

"Yeah, it's his first solo shot since splitting Stealers Wheel, right?"

"Correct. And it'll be perfect for your middle song."

The audition tape was just that, a 5-minute sample of you. The key that would unlock the door to that first job. You were selling a voice, the knack to ad lib, ability to change inflections and tone purposefully but seamlessly and naturally. He knew he could do all those things.

Attention Mr. D's shoppers...

The tape was an audio snapshot. The announcer's voice introducing records, reading a weather forecast without sounding like you were reading, promoting other station programs, all in short snippets over the instrumental lead-ins to popular songs of the day.

Female disc jockeys were somewhat of a novelty in 1978, but Donna didn't care about breaking ground or glass ceilings. She had been planning to talk on the radio since childhood. Donna understood music at a deep level and was fluent on the day's rock scene. Her smooth patter was not a bedroom voice, not a know-it-all, more of a knowledgeable, cheery sister/best friend.

There was no shortage of sharp elbow-throwing, jockeying, and jealousy among the guys. To a man, they all thought they were better than each other. Not Donna. She stood alone. Everyone knew Donna Hansen would go far in this business.

Donna looked over the list of records he was considering and talked about the need to start strong, with a positive first impression.

"The 17-second intro in Nicolette Larson's 'Lotta Love' is perfect," Donna coached. "The synthesized sax is distinctive enough that it will complement your voice. The sax is upper register, your voice is lower."

Radio studios had two turntables, to allow seamless music transitions. Deejays would place a 45-RPM record on one, drop the stylus, manually rotate the record until the first note of the song is heard, then rotate it back about a half inch. This was done "in cue" over an internal studio speaker.

Success came in timing. Throwing the turntable toggle switch, the words spoken over the song's intro, talking right up to the first vocal without stepping on it.

"As Nicolette fades, pot her down and punch Eddie Money," Donna said. "Another 17-second talk-up ramp, this one with drums and guitars, very clearly defined."

"Pot" is short for potentiometer, a three-terminal resistor, used to control volume on a radio station control board. One did not turn down the volume, one would pot down the volume.

"The beats are easy to follow," Donna said. "Gives you the chance to intersperse pithy announcer couplets."

Donna left it up to him to discern the pith.

Recorded on reel-to-reel and produced with a grease pencil, razor blade, splicing block and splicing tape in a studio, then dubbed to a 5-minute cassette. State-of-the-art, literal cutting-edge technology.

Since they were designed to open the entry-level door, they were not real airchecks but audition tapes, in the true meaning of the word, scripted and engineered to precision.

He chose KDWB as his call letters—one of his favorite stations in the Cities—not out of any allegiance, but because he liked the way the phonetics of the letters sounded as they flowed out of his mouth.

His second record had a cold close, meaning the song did not fade but ended abruptly with Eddie Money crooning "hold on," which would lead directly into Baker Street.

"There are 59 seconds before the vocal hits, but there's a natural 25 second intro leading to a saxophone bridge that is perfect for an extended announcer riff," she counseled. "That can be the heart of your tape."

Donna knew using all 59 seconds would be overkill, that the station manager in Bumfuck listening to the tape would agree, quit listening, and move to the next tape in his stack. Out of Rafferty, directly into six seconds of harp arpeggio before Gloria Gaynor communicates that, at first she was afraid, she was petrified.

"Call letters and time. That's it."

It's seven-twenty in the morning on kay-dee-double-you-bee.

His initial intent was simply to pick out five records he liked, but Donna knew better. Mix it up, female vocalists, groups, male voices. Listen closely to the instrumentals and mix them up, too.

"It's a harp in a disco song," he said.

Donna nodded in agreement, two young up-and-coming broadcast professionals, on the same wavelength.

"You're right. It doesn't get more distinctive."

She was not coaching anyone else on their audition tape. She did not slide tight next to Burns or Johnston at breakfast, she was slid tight next to him right now. These were the things that were so easy to misinterpret and led him to at least entertain the thought of making a move.

He took solace in their friendship.

It can be like me and Duck.

Except he was not physically attracted to Duck the way he was to Donna. Gloria Gaynor was not the only one who was afraid and petrified.

He started over so many times, the stylus on the Brown Institute studio turntables degraded the talk-up ramps on his first set of vinyl records, resulting in a staticky-scratchy sound that made the whole project sound like amateur hour. Aiming for perfection, he ended up buying a second round of his five 45s.

His tape ended with the steady bass undertones of "Love Will Find a Way" by Pablo Cruise. Five minutes of consistent rhythm.

Donna had learned the most valuable lesson in deejaying. Less is more. Shut the fuck up, already. Too many deejay-wannabes, and actual professional deejays, wanted nothing more than to impress their listeners, using every second of musical intro by blathering verbal word vomit that had no relevance or meaning. When they do that, she argued, they are digging a hole and losing listeners.

"Think about it." Donna clearly had. "It's the easiest thing in the world for a listener to literally turn you off. Everything you do, every utterance that leaves your mouth, should be carefully planned and designed to prevent that."

"You're an actor," she said. "You're putting on a performance."

23.
September 16, 1978

The second hand swept north, bound for the 12 at the top. The song was fading fast, and Mitch Burns was ad-libbing a promo about a weekend bake sale, benefitting the St. Olaf Choir.

"...the premier *a capella* choir in the nation. Mutual News is next. Clear skies, sixty-seven degrees at ten o'clock on K-Y-M-N, Northfield."

To be officially and formally identified, the call letters needed to be verbalized, followed immediately by the city in which the radio station was officially licensed with the Federal Communications Commission. You could say whatever you wanted before and after, but regulators required that legal ID at the top of every hour.

The federal regulatory expectations had been hammered into them at Brown, though the consequences of not adhering, remained murky.

"It's Acapulco." Matson said it with a straight face, as he leaned on the countertop opposite the control board.

Mitch's foot in this door was secured purely by his voice. The KYMN general manager needed a weekend part-timer yesterday, called a friend who taught at Brown, who pulled Burns out of class and put him on the phone right then. That very weekend, Mitch was on the air, pimping the bake sales and nailing the station IDs. Everything seemed to come easy for him.

"What?" Burns, flushing red, fearful he had just

committed an on-air screwup.

"You said '*a capella*,'" Matson kept a poker face. "It's pronounced ah-kuh-PULL-koh."

Make the man for whom everything comes easy squirm a little.

"Horseshit, it's ah-kuh-PELL-uh," Burns said, missing the humor entirely. "It means they sing without instruments."

"I know what it means, genius," feeling the need to take Burns by the hand. "It's a play on words."

The unspoken competition among the Brown Institute radio announcer-wannabes seemed more pronounced between these two. Burns had more raw, natural talent, Matson had the edge in imagination and smarts. Each looked for ways to lead with their strengths.

Add a real deejay job at a real radio station to the list of things Mike envied about Burns.

Mitch signed his name and time on the KYMN logbook, relieving himself of the federal regulatory responsibility for what was left of Saturday night.

An hour due south of the Cities, Northfield was home to a pair of liberal arts oases in the heart of farm country: Carleton College and St. Olaf College.

For generations in southern Minnesota, Catholics and their deeds-driven notion of salvation jostled for supremacy with Lutherans, who believed faith alone would turn the trick. By 1978, the zeal for Martin Luther's reformation long since fizzled, Northfield's goings-on manifested themselves in a comfortable, predictable pattern with little desire—much less expectation—for change, regardless of one's denominational persuasion.

The bake sale succeeded last year, didn't it? Why, the choir traveled to such far-flung exotic locales as Omaha and Fargo.

"This place may be Bumfuck, but it's not without its advantages," Burns said over his shoulder as they entered the bar, met by a wave of Charlie perfume in a sea of halter tops and bell bottom blue jeans. Burns wore a down-filled vest and tight jeans. It was still summer, but Mitch liked the look. Matson was togged out in his standard Saturday night uniform: polyester shirt and Levi button-fly's.

Entering a bar always required at least a little pregame planning. Entering a bar in a college town where meat market rules were in effect required extra thought. Burns led the way, smiling at girls, gathered in groups of two or three, making eye contact and mental notes about the ones who smiled back.

They'll think I'm his coat holder, for Chrissakes.

"Where's Malea tonight? You two are normally inseparable."

Until now, he had never really considered how he had compartmentalized the people in his life. Mitch, Donna, Kenny, and Mike were a hermetically-sealed foursome at Brown and for breakfast at the arches which are, were, and shall ever be golden. He was usually good for one Special Export beer at the bar across Lake Street after the Friday tests, then off to meet Malea.

"She's doing something with her family." Nine months into their relationship and this was actually the first time he and Burns had done something together, just the two of them.

At least he thought she was doing something with her family. He had no reason to suspect otherwise.

"Watch and learn," standing up, grabbing his bottle of Old Style by the neck, and making his way directly to two of the girls who smiled at him on the way in, all before Matson had a chance to settle in, achieve a buzz, or even get the lay of the land.

"Hi there, my name's Mitch." Lots of teeth, tilt of the head, natural deep baritone radio voice. "Perhaps you've heard me on the radio? Mitch Burns, K-Y-M-N, Northfield."

My God, he actually used that line out loud?

Nothing made him more uncomfortable than being by himself in a crowded place where social discourse with one or more fellow human beings is the accepted norm. Especially in a bar filled with college girls. At Pogo's, when he found himself alone, he could always get up, walk around, go to the game room, fetch more pitchers from the bar. Anything to kill the time until his table mates returned.

He felt everyone was watching him, drawing conclusions. He slugged down his bottle of Old Style, providing a reason to get up from the table where he was sitting alone. Oh, he's getting another beer, everyone would think. He visited the men's room. Oh, he had to take a leak, everyone would think.

After exhausting his tried-and-true perception-management tactics, and with Mitch now zeroing in on his target, Mike chose the nuclear option.

If I'm not there, they won't think I'm a loser at a table in a bar all by myself with no friends.

As he sidled up, before Mitch had the chance to introduce his new friends, Matson said, "I'm headed back to the Cities, man." He wasn't due at SuperValu until 2 p.m. the next day but wanted to leave a loftier impression. "Got a late date."

He didn't, but Burns would buy it. It was important the two girls did, too. Two girls he had not met and would never see again.

"I'll be right back, girls," Mitch smiled at one girl, then the other. "I gotta give my friend some advice." Again, with the one-upsmanhip.

They had driven separately to the bar, in case of this very contingency.

"Thirty seconds. Clock me." Broadcasting technical school habits. Practicing precision any chance they could.

"Listen, quit sweating placement, you're gonna get a few offers." Placement. Fully assimilated to Brown lingo.

"They'll all be in Bumfuck, so pick the best one."

Why does he think I'm worried about not getting a job offer? Does he just assume he's more talented than me?

"Get thee to a college town," looking around the bar, in his element. "It's a veritable smorgasbord and you'll be a big fish in a small pond."

Veritable?

He glanced over Mitch's shoulder at the two girls. Clapton blasted from the corner jukebox—something about trying all night long to talk to Sally after encouraging her into the supine position.

"Plus, you're twenty years old. Too damn young to get married. Don't you see how I operate? Be like Burns!"

"Twenty-nine seconds, exactly," Matson said, extending his right hand. "Thanks, Mitch. Seeya Monday morning at the arches which are, were, and shall ever be golden."

He did see how Burns operated, and as much as he envied the voice and the material things, he preferred the peace of mind that came with monogamy. He thought of Lindsay's reaction on Oscar night. Mitch's approach was not aimed at peace of mind. It was pure, unadulterated wham, bam, thank you, ma'am.

"Hey Mike, wait!" as Matson reached the door. Loud enough now for newfound female friends to hear, "You think they sing *a capella* in Acapulco?"

The bastard boosted my line.

"Hard to say."

Sometimes it's just easier to surrender. Still, as he drove back to the Cities, he worried about what the dozen or so total strangers within earshot of his response thought of him.

Only if the trumpets and marimbas give out. That's what I shoulda said.

24.
September 17, 1978

"Mike, this is Tony. Tony, this is Mike."

It was as though Malea thought this could be civilized. When she had called earlier that morning and said they were coming by, he harbored a sneaking suspicion it was not her idea.

His first impression was, "This guy is trying too hard to be Rocky Balboa." Leather jacket, even the black stubby fedora. The only things missing were the fingerless gloves and a heart. If you had a vivid imagination and an open mind, you could sort of see indications of Stallone. Matson felt a vibe that, like Rocky, Tony was used to violence.

"Sit down." It was not a request.

Fuck you. I'll stand.

They were on the landing leading into the shared kitchen.

"Stay away from her," Tony was apparently not inclined toward small talk. "Or you won't have any teeth to broadcast with."

Clearly, the man had formulated this line and plan of attack. Probably stayed up all night working on it, honing it, practicing in front of a mirror. From all outward appearances, it would have taken him that long. Malea was standing a good two feet behind Tony, looking pained.

"Listen, motherfucker," Tony leaned in and grabbed a handful of his shirt, which included a couple of fingerfuls of skin. "She's made it clear to me that... "

"No, YOU listen."

From below, he brought his right arm up with force. Tony lost his grip while simultaneously rocking back on his heels. Matson could feel his heart racing, fist clenching, and feet inching forward. If it came to it, the skeleton key in his right front pocket could do some damage.

He was not sure exactly what he wanted him to listen to. He considered reason and intellect, but two things held him back. He was not confident he could pull it off. And he assumed, based on his first 15 seconds of relationship building, that Tony's listening skills trended low.

At that moment, he remembered how Duane the Man responded to Sticky's taunts. "Never get into a battle of wits with an unarmed man."

The hook may be six inches in front of your eyes. Don't take the bait.

What he really wanted was for Malea to listen. He looked directly at her, his gaze somewhere between longing for her and antagonism for Tony. Her eyes met his briefly before she looked away. Part of him was still in denial.

You're trading me, for—this?

He wanted to see if this really was splitsville. He could feel the loss welling up in his gut and heading north. He was desperate to know if she felt it, too. If she did, he wanted both of them to sense it, together. No ground would be given to the usurper, but he wanted Malea to know that whatever was wrong between them could be fixed, that he still loved her.

That's a lot to communicate without opening your mouth.

"Let's go, Tony." Malea pulled on his other arm. She saw the bloody future and wanted to avoid it.

Yeah, let's go—Tony. Greasy Neanderthal shitferbrains.

The story he told himself was she sounded sad. He had been with her long enough to know it was not an act. The foundation on which all of the assumptions of a future together were based, was crumbling.

The enormity of the events unfolding right in front of him were ahead of his ability to process them. He did not know it yet, but he was already living in the past. It would be their own, individual, separate loss.

He stood his ground as Malea and Tony descended the staircase, breathing no easier. He waited for Tony to glance back up. When he did, scowling, Matson returned the scowl and raised his right arm, the same one that fended off Tony's handful of shirt and skin. Fist now unclenched; middle finger unfurled, trained on Tony's egress from the back yard to the car, like crosshairs in a rifle scope.

I got the last word, asshole. Without even opening my mouth.
I. Win.

Except Tony was leaving with the girl. His girl. Except he could not remember ever feeling like this. His physical intimidation skills were nonexistent. Anger was uncharted territory. He inherited James E.'s impatience, but not his short temper. He sat down on the outdoor bench, hands and knees still trembling.

Maybe it wasn't anger, after all. Maybe it was fear. Maybe it was sadness. It all cratered rapidly into a knot of confusion. She was everything. What would he do now?

No way he would have prevailed in a fight, and even if he had, aided by a skeleton key jammed into Tony's eye, then what? The asshole was right about one thing. He did need those teeth to broadcast with.

So, yeah, he won. What a victory.

A couple of riffraffers watched the drama unfold from the kitchen window. While they shared a kitchen, a toilet, and a shower, Matson had zero interest in sharing a near-fight postmortem.

"You had him all the way, man."

"Nice flourish with the bird, man."

Anyone witnessing the confrontation saw the outcome. The other guy left with the girl. His girl. He felt compelled to save as much face as possible.

"Done with her anyway," muttering on his way to the fridge, heart set on a few Old Styles, settling for the remnants of a Blatz 12-pack. He thought Blatz tasted like badger piss, but once he had three or four in him, it wouldn't matter.

"I'm taking the rest of these." It was not a request.

He slammed the door to his room, not because he was angry, but because he wanted the riffraff to think he was angry. He may have lost the girl, but he is pissed off about it and in there plotting revenge. The truth was he was perilously close to losing it, and he sure as hell did not want them to see or hear him lose it. It was none of their goddamn business.

His grandmother's frieze upholstered swivel rocker had made the trek north, without the swivel/rocker mechanism. He plopped into it, cracked a Blatz, spiraled down and obsessed. He viewed Malea's choices as a reflection on him.

What, in God's name, would she find attractive about that moron? She thinks violence and brainless is better than charm, good looks, and quick wit?

Maybe she wanted more.

As much as she said otherwise, maybe she didn't like the notion of being married to an underpaid/overworked radio deejay in West Overshoe, Wisconsin. He would either be programming that station within five years or moving on to a medium market. But maybe she couldn't see that far into the future.

Maybe she just wanted to stay in the Cities. And No

Ambition Tony would give her that.

Or was he too needy? Too clingy?

Like many young women of the era, Malea smoked. She came by the habit naturally. Her mother smoked Mores, slender, 120-millimeter cigarettes wrapped in dark brown paper, cocooned in a bright red pack, taller and skinnier than all others.

When the two of them were together, their smoking would enable and feed off each other. Anyone within proximity tended to worry about their own pulmonary well-being. The result was everything around Malea and her mother smelled like an ashtray. Hair, clothes, car, breath, skin, Misty, the family's Pomeranian.

By 1978, the carcinogenic cat was out of the bag, so ad agencies threw all the marketing ideas on the wall, good and bad.

"More smooth, mild, satisfying taste."

"And because More lasts longer, you may find yourself going through fewer packs and saving more money."

Malea smoked Benson & Hedges 100's Lights. Gold pack.

"Who could make light of themselves better?"

Well, her boyfriend, for starters. He was constantly on her, complaining about how her smoking impacted the smell of his clothes, his hair, his skin. It was his lone connection with John Winfield, but unlike Winfield, who had charged this hill only to retreat and surrender, Matson kept charging.

"Quit trying to change me," after the most recent volley. It was as angry as she had ever been with him. "Why can't you just love me for who I am?"

He desperately needed reassurance and wanted to talk to someone, but quickly talked himself out of the logical options. Donna, Mitch, and Kenny were friends, but really more like junior professional colleagues. He thought about Duck or Duane the Man. Inglewood crossed his mind. He worried they would think he was an emotional wreck.

He was, but they didn't need to know it.

Malea had always filled this role. When he had something on his mind, she would say all the right things and never question his choices. If anything, it seemed like he was always giving her life advice.

You can hit the daycare center up for a raise but line up your arguments. Yes, your butt does look big in that swimsuit. I know Winfield's a prick, so when he goads you, don't take the bait.

He thought back to that time Malea got into it with Winfield and wanted out of the house in Wayzata. She stayed in Mike's room for eight hours, during his SuperValu shift. With the landlady's "no girls" edict in mind, he told her to keep the door closed, pretend like no one was there, and ignore the entreaties and pleadings of the riffraff.

He thought all this was agreed to, mutual consent. When she had the questions, he had the answers. Could it be she actually had a mind of her own and had her own answers on how to manage her own time while he was yogi and fluid ounces-occupied?

During their year together, he failed to recognize how tenuous the connection was. It was not love leading to marriage. It was emotional dependency leading, inevitably, to this.

Besides having no one to talk to, he had a more practical problem. The community phone was on a shelf next to the bathroom within easy earshot of the riffraffers in the kitchen.

The remnants of the Blatz twelver were gone. He looked at his watch: 10:45 a.m. He did not have to be at work until 2 p.m. Matt's Bar, a local watering hole known for their Juicy Lucy, a cheese-infused burger, opened at 11. It was just a few blocks away; he would be there when the doors opened.

After a burger and draft Old Style in a tall pilsner glass, he reached Lindsay from the pay phone near the pool table. The morning's drama was news to her, so whatever insight she could have shared would have involved breaking confidences and, as much as she admired him, Lindsay would not cross that line.

"Michael J., I don't know."

His nickname when they met. Fall River Lake with Duane the Man. Slumber receptacles zipped to the neck. Four states away and twelve months ago. Everything was shiny back then. They circled with a few more desultory, inconclusive platitudes, when Lindsay signaled an end to the conversation.

"Hang in there, buddy."

If Michael J. turned out only to be her best friend's 1978 version of Mr. Right, Lindsay had no doubt where her long-term allegiances would lie.

He felt no better. In fact, as the losses compounded, he felt worse. In addition to losing Malea, he had lost her family, the grilled Velveeta sandwiches, the snowmobiling, the KEYN-through-her-grandfather dream, and now Lindsay.

Within a couple of days, the confusion sorted itself out. No anger or resentment. He was overwhelmed by sadness. Even if he wanted to, he was too consumed by it to unpack it. Even if he wanted to, he had no skills to unpack it. If he did, he would have come to realize it wasn't sadness as much as it was false pride, which was nothing but pure, unadulterated fear.

Later that week, in class, he overheard Kenny engaged in a hushed tone conversation with Donna.

"Jesus, what's with Matson? He's like—morose."

"I think he got dumped."

Kenny buttonholed him after a studio session in which they practiced enunciating the letter "W." Not dubya, double-you.

"Yo! Wanna grab some lunch at the arches which are, were, and shall ever be golden? On me. Fine dining for breakfast and lunch!"

Matson waved him off and walked away, saying, "Can't get a beer at McDonald's."

Johnston raised his eyebrows, shrugged, and made his way to the exit.

The list of current small market entry-level job openings was updated weekly and posted on the bulletin board in the Brown Institute lobby. They didn't pay much attention to it during their first six months, but as graduation drew nigh, they would huddle around it like bears inspecting a beehive. Matson made his way over to the list, grudgingly seeing Bumfuck in his future. This week, a half dozen:

KBEW-AM Blue Earth, Minn.: Announcer
WMFG-AM Hibbing, Minn.: Evening board shift/sports
KNDK-AM/FM Langdon, No. Dak.: Announcer
WCLO-AM: Janesville, Wisc.: Announcer/production
KIJV-AM Huron, So. Dak.: Board operator/news/sports
KAKE-TV Wichita, Kan.: Broadcast technician

Through the darkness, a glimmer.

25.
September 24, 1978

Streaming through the east window, the sunshine took the form of luminous parallelograms on the floor, with just enough ancillary brightness to roust him.

As he slipped on his glasses and reached for his watch, he wondered why he hadn't pulled down the window shade. He always pulled down the shade. Can't sleep otherwise. It was quickly consumed by a second thought, which carried so much fear, and consequently, power, it would stay with him for the rest of his life.

How did I get here?

The axe plowed into his forehead as he sat upright. He paused a beat, played through the pain, and slid into the jeans hanging over the bed's footboard.

I do not remember taking off my jeans and hanging them there.

Barefoot and shirtless, he stumbled into the hall, through the kitchen, and past one of the riffraff eating white bread toast with real butter, deep into the *Star-Tribune* sports page box scores.

"Pauly Molly went oh for four but stole a base. His 29th."

He and this riffraffer had connected over baseball. A native of Stevens Point, Wisconsin, the guy's passion for the Milwaukee Brewers and Paul Molitor bordered on obsession.

"Replogle went the distance and the Twinks only got three hits. Their offense is pathetic!"

"Hm," bare acknowledgement as Mike made his way out the door and down the rickety stairs.

The LeMans was parked on 36th Street facing east toward St. Paul, like always. As he walked around the car looking for damage or, God forbid, blood, his heart quit pounding so hard. His head did not.

"I'm goin' to the Met today. Caldwell versus Erickson."

Riffraffer picked up the conversation as Matson made his way back up and through the kitchen as if he'd sat down, slathered his own white bread toast with real butter, and talked baseball.

"Wanna come with?"

"Can't man, gotta work." He stopped long enough to grab an Old Style from the fridge.

"Sorry."

I must have driven myself. There is no other explanation. Why can't I remember?

Back in his room, he fumbled his bottle of Excedrin, shook out four and swilled them down with a sudsy slug.

Old Style is just right for sadness.

A flash of memory.

Did I say that? Sounds like something I would say. Did I think it? Did someone else say it?

The last thing he remembered was being at Kerry's party. Last night. He checked the day and date on his watch to make sure. Earlier in the day, while stocking yogi, Kerry had noticed his mood and questioned him about it. It was none of Kerry's business, he could handle it himself, but since the man asked, he reluctantly shared the Tony story.

"Man, you need some fun in your life." Kerry grabbed a nearby Dannon vendor receipt, scribbled something on the back, and handed it over. "I'm having a party tonight. I want you to come."

Apart from the principals involved in the breakup, Kerry was the first person who knew the truth. Everyone else got the sanitized version. On the receipt, Kerry had scribbled 5736 W 25½, SLP.

St. Louis Park was in the first ring of suburbs. He had driven through it dozens of times on his way to the outer ring. He had not departed south Minneapolis since Tony. A full week ago.

He left SuperValu at 7 p.m., went home, changed into clean clothes, then sat in the LeMans debating whether to go to the party. He studied his foldable, laminated Twin Cities street map to find 5736 West 25½ Street in St. Louis Park.

He imagined the embarrassment of the city planning genius who ended up with an extra street between 25th and 26th. Thinking like a radio professional, he wondered how to properly pronounce it. Was it twenty-five-and-a-halfth-street or twenty-fifth-and-a-half-street?

First ring suburb nomenclature problems.

Pulling away from the curb, he ventured three blocks east on 36th to Cedar.

As he waited at the stoplight to turn left, it struck him this would be his first social engagement in the Cities as a single man. First time venturing out as a dumpee.

Twelve blocks north to the Hiawatha Avenue/55 Highway expressway. In the loop that fed the expressway he punched it. With 350 cubic inches and a V-8 engine, the LeMans responded. The only thing he remembered from summer school Drivers Ed with Inglewood at Heights was freeway on-ramps are designed specifically for acceleration to freeway speed.

He wondered how Inglewood and Jennie were getting along. He missed them in a gloomy sort of way that was framed in a thought of happy couples, since he was no longer part of one. If he told Inglewood his tale of woe, would Mark commiserate? Isn't that the unspoken given in the groom/best man relationship?

Dipping into a tunnel, bound north by northwest, he checked to make sure his headlights were on. Out of the tunnel, he eased left and punched it again, quickly merging into oncoming traffic on Interstate 94.

Now westbound, he was paralleling Interstate 35W for a stretch. He glanced to his right and caught the IDS Tower, at 792 feet, the tallest building in Minnesota. He remembered surprising Malea with a birthday dinner in July at a fancy restaurant on the top floor, the lights of the Cities spread out below them.

That date was one more way he sought to portray "studious young future broadcast professional with a steady girlfriend." No longer a waiter in the Wichita Club, these waiters were waiting on him. He smelled the cork and sampled the wine like he owned the place. That dinner had wiped him out financially, but it was worth it.

He had implemented Plan B to remain nourished when the paychecks didn't stretch. Slip into the SuperValu storage freezer right before the end of his shift, ease a package of frozen Stouffer's Cream Chipped Beef down his pants and walk out as nonchalantly as one could with an ice-cold brick of shit on a shingle in one's nether regions.

His pilfered meal choices were not without variety. Occasionally Swedish Meatballs and Fettuccine or Mac and Beef, but mostly Cream Chipped Beef. He'd contemplated shoving a Swanson Hungry-Man down his pants, but the box was pretty big, and people might think he really loved leaving work. Besides, they tasted like sawdust. Always Stouffer's. It was the most expensive, and if you're gonna steal your meals, why not boost the best?

The IDS Tower and all of downtown disappeared as he curved northwest and sped directly into the Lowry Hill tunnel. Not quite a half mile underground, then back on the surface of the planet, now heading due north. The Basilica of St. Mary just on the other side of the freeway to the east was his visual cue to merge right.

He let his foot off the gas, the LeMans decelerated to allow him to negotiate the one-80 on yet another freeway ramp to access Interstate 394 heading west. After nine months in the Cities, he felt proficient at freeway negotiation.

So far, he was on the same path he took every pre-Tony day to the outer ring of the suburbs. Tonight, he was bound for the first ring. When he exited south to access the Minnesota Highway 100 freeway, it felt new and untested. Not uncharted, he'd visualized this route with the laminated map, he'd simply never been here before.

Merge right and exit at Minnetonka Boulevard and he was deposited directly onto the mean streets of St. Louis Park. Backtracking north to get to 25½th Street and Kerry's party, he contemplated the socio-economic difference between first ring and outer ring suburbs. John Winfield in Wayzata is a successful business owner. Kerry Andersen in St. Louis Park is a supermarket dairy manager.

Winfield's an asshole. I won't miss him. Kerry's the closest thing I have right now to a real friend. He wants me to come to his party. He used those exact words.

West on Minnetonka to Xenwood Avenue, then back north, four-and-a-half blocks until Xenwood ends at 25½. Hang a Louie and start looking for house numbers. Mike knew he was in the right place when he saw several cars parked near a house with Kerry's taxicab-yellow-orange 1978 AMC Javelin in the driveway.

Kerry was drunk or high. Maybe drunk and high. Red eyes, slurred speech, the mellowest man in St. Louis Park, Minnesota. Sitting on a tree stump, smoking a cigarette, surrounded by two nameless girls he recognized from SuperValu and some guy he'd never seen before. Happy to see him, but too wasted to make any formal introductions, or shepherd him through a sea of heretofore siloed strangers.

Mike was on his own.

Hi, you don't know me, but I stock dairy. Cheese, yogi, fluid ounces, and butter. Not a lot of margarine, but tons o' butter. You Scandahoovians sure love your lactose. I realize that at SuperValu, sackers sack, checkers check, and dairy stockers stock dairy, yet you all seem to know each other pretty well.

It would appear I used Westergaard's silos as a rationalization not to make friends with you guys. You see, I have a girlfriend in Wayzata— uh, I mean I used to.

The party was a backyard affair, and Kerry's stretched into a wooded area which had been partially cleared. A redwood picnic table was loaded with chips and dip. Three more people he did not recognize were huddled around a small square mirror with lines of stardust. A dozen or 15 lawn chairs, clearly brought by partygoers. Kerry said nothing about bringing a lawn chair, not that it would have made a difference.

He had no lawn chair.

Spotting the kegs, he made his way through a gaggle of pot smokers, inhaling. One keg was Old Style. He thought they both were. The other was something called Olde English 800. Similar names, no label, just a tag near the spigot.

The cups were translucent, emblazoned with the Old Style logo. Probably a throw-in with the kegs. After downing a half dozen cups in rapid succession, tapped from the Olde English keg, he was feeling better. He had never associated getting drunk with an effort to purposefully achieve the feeling produced by alcohol. It just happened, naturally.

A few more cups and his inhibitions were lowered just enough to allow him to move to the periphery of small clumps of siloed partygoers, but still not enough to engage. So, rather than talk, he drank. His sadness moved to the back, displaced by the familiar brain-tingling light-headedness.

He remembered nothing after that.

Twelve hours ago.

Clad in a Brewers cap, riffraffer knocked on his door, offering one last chance to blow off work in favor of Pauly Molly and the Twins' pathetic offense, Rod Carew and Bombo Rivera notwithstanding. He politely begged off, sat on the floor, back against the bed, facing the closet, feeling sorry for himself. His stereo was tuned to KS95.

Christ, those were complex logistics stone cold sober. How do you travel 12 miles, negotiate a half-dozen freeway exchanges, two tunnels, another dozen traffic lights—at night—while being that much under the influence and not remember it?

If you're that hammered, how do you manage a 30-minute journey behind the wheel of a 350-cubic inch, V-8 engine, when your default is to drive fast anyway, and not remember any of it?

Old Style is just right for sadness.

He still could not remember who said it, but now wondered if it was one of the siloed SuperValuers at the party. That thought made him cringe. So much for his ability to put up a brave front. My God, if Kerry noticed it, if those people noticed it and they don't even know me, it must be obvious.

There's no damage to the car, and no blood, but how do I know I didn't run over a little kid or smack into a little old lady or knock them far enough away to keep the blood off the car but spilled it all over the street?

Maybe all the injuries were internal. Maybe my victim was thrown in a ditch and remains there right now, unable to be seen by passing motorists, with a faint but shallowing pulse.

The KS95 newscasts came on at 10 minutes before and 20 minutes after each hour. He shuddered and listened intently, fully expecting to hear:

"Authorities are investigating an early morning hit-and-run accident in St. Louis Park/Golden Valley/Minneapolis that resulted in the death of a five-year-old child/78-year-old woman. Witnesses report seeing an early '70s metallic blue Pontiac GTO or LeMans with Kansas plates. Anyone seeing a vehicle fitting this description is encouraged to contact the St. Louis Park/Golden Valley/Minneapolis police department. More news in 60 seconds on K-S-95, after this word from Olde English 800 Malt Liquor..."

He breathed a little easier when he did not hear it and felt a desperate need to talk to someone, but there was no one to call. Kerry was not an option, what would he think? Even though they already knew it, his pride had not allowed him to tell Mitch, Kenny, or Donna that he had even been dumped.

At 1:30 p.m., the axe in his forehead now reduced to a steak knife, he showered, shaved, got dressed, shook out four more Excedrin, cracked open another brew, and drove ever so carefully to the Minnehaha Mall.

More Old Style has to be just right for more sadness.

Because it did absolutely nothing for the fear.

KAKELAND

26.
October 12, 1978

On the biggest television monitor, Fred McMurray was unpacking his actions, after plunging hard for Barbara Stanwyck.

The job was the epitome of behind the scenes and the antithesis of a big fish in a small pond. The movies were on actual 16-millimeter celluloid film held secure within reels the size of a manhole cover. He would thread *Double Indemnity* through behemoth film projectors, which projected into a video camera through a series of mirrors.

Film noir washed over insomniacs in living rooms, basements, and bedrooms throughout Wichita and the central Great Plains.

The commercials, advertising Niemann's of Attica, "a revolutionary new concept in furniture buying," were on 2-inch videotape, contained in individual hard, red plastic cartridges, roughly the size of a pint milk carton. Mike would load them in the chronological order they were to air, into a state-of-the-art conveyor belt carousel videotape player so large it took up an entire wall.

"Ol' Flick" was the on-camera, local star of *Nightwatch*. Jim Erickson, eccentric dub-yes-you English professor and classic movie aficionado, created the character and would introduce each movie in schlock bits, offering pearls of cinematic history specific to each film, seemingly from memory. Erickson was pre-recorded on 2-inch videotape reels. Toward the end of each movie, Matson would hustle back to the tape machine and fire it up to ensure it was "at speed" when it was time to roll Ol' Flick.

If the tape was not at speed when it was rolled, Erickson's voice would sound deep, thick, and distorted, as though he had taken too many Valium.

Then Mike would plop down in an upholstered chair on casters at Master Control, exactly what the name implies, a Wurlitzer organ-esque array of flashing buttons, knobs, faders, levers, and a bank of smaller television monitors which allowed him to choreograph McMurray, Stanwyck, Ol' Flick, the bumper slide, and the commercials.

I feel like Lt. Sulu at the helm of the Enterprise. Steady as she goes.

His overnight shift was bookended by lunch pail-carrying lifer technicians who reminded him of the Fleming truck drivers. There he sat in his polyester and platform heels.

My God, I don't want to be like these guys when I'm that age.

He got the job back home in Wichita after two separate telephone conversations—one informal, one formal—with Dave Morris, second in command of KAKE-TV engineering, human-resourced by a phalanx of lunch pail-carrying lifer technicians who were really good at keeping the electronics functioning optimally and ensuring the analog television signal was being transmitted at 195 megahertz on the Very High Frequency Band III, to be received when those in the Wichita Direct Market Area tuned their Panasonic Quintrix and General Electric Performance television sets to Channel 10.

"I've never hired anyone solely from a telephone interview, but I have a good feeling about you."

Damn skippy.

Morris was tech: first, last, and always. Matson was talent, demeaning himself for a tech job. The Malea dump changed everything, starting with his priorities. After she cut him loose in the Cities, he was singularly focused on getting back home to the bosom of his friends and the life he left, only nine months ago. Deejaying could wait. Bumfuck wasn't going anywhere. Now, he needed stability.

Thanks to Brown, he had the requisite First Class Radio-Telephone Operator's License, a regulatory vestige, seemingly since Marconi. He remembered Kenny Johnston's pecking order, read Morris' mind about his pressingly urgent human resources need, and said all the right things to land the job, including a promise to be there, at Master Control, in one short week.

Within the span of those seven days, he quizzed out of the final three-month term at Brown, where placement was always king, negotiated a deal with the landlady to break the lease, schlepped his grandmother's orange frieze upholstered swivel rocker, sans swivel/rocker mechanism, and the all-in-one, off-the-shelf rip-off stereo from David's discount store in Sweetbriar down the rickety stairs and into the LeMans. By now, the riffraff knew better than to even offer to lend a hand.

At SuperValu, he felt bad about leaving Kerry in the lurch. Andersen waved him off, saying something about having been left in lurches before and genuinely wishing him well.

"Goin' back to Mr. D's, huh?" Ray Westergaard cackled when Matson broke the news that his two-week notice would actually be a one-week notice.

No, asshole. I am bound for the promised land of pale-yellow vegetable oil margarine. I can't get away from your wall of butter fast enough.

"No, I actually have a job in broadcasting, which is why I came up here in the first place."

≡

When Dave Morris hired the young whippersnapper to man his overnight Master Control, KAKE-TV was preparing to celebrate its silver season. Twenty-five years of creativity and innovation elevated KAKE-TV as the unchallenged leader in Kansas television broadcasting.

KAKE's visionary general manager, Martin Umansky (you-MAN-skee), took seriously the broadcasters' charge to serve the community, and in the process, turned a tidy profit. In the '50s and '60s, while other medium-sized market television stations stayed dark in the daytime, Umansky cornered the market, with locally produced daytime children's programming that included Bill McLean as Cap'n Bill, and Henry Harvey as Freddy Fudd and Santa Claus, with his sidekick, Toy Boy.

Local news is where KAKE-TV really shined. Umansky leaned on his newsroom to perform, do more, cover the community. In the mid-'70s, Umansky and his news director convinced the local health department to allow KAKE-TV mini-cams to go along on routine restaurant inspections. The results—complete with infestations of rats, cockroaches, and other assorted vermin—made for great TV and resulted in a restaurant rating system adopted by many local health departments.

An "A" rating reflected a clean bill of health, dine with confidence and peace of mind. Uneasy diners in "B" rated restaurants always had the rat and cockroach images in the backs of their minds as they slathered their lettuce and tomato side salads with Thousand Island dressing. Restaurants earning a dreaded "C" rating were rearranging the deck chairs on the Titanic.

Everything about KAKE was on the leading edge of an exciting industry entering adolescence and nothing was off limits.

It was the height of Dennis Rader's murder spree. The self-professed BTK (Bind-Torture-Kill) toyed with the cops and sought attention by sending missives containing cryptic clues to the *Wichita Eagle* and also to KAKE-TV. Even serial killers knew which TV station had the juice.

The business model was as effective as its simplicity. A generation earlier, the government granted frequency bandwidth and licenses to television broadcasters who promised to serve their communities. Most broadcasters paid lip service to the promise, taking comfort in the riches earned from the novelty of new technology.

Umansky actually served the community. The community returned the favor by watching his television station and spending money on the goods and services of his advertisers.

"Ratings should never be the sole means of judging a buy," Umansky once told a trade publication. "The station that is closely integrated with the community is the one that will produce the greatest results for its advertisers."

In the '70s, Wichita was one of the smallest markets in the U.S. to boast three standalone stations, each affiliated with a national network, so the competition was fierce. By building a business model grounded in community service, Umansky created KAKEland, a place visited in the imagination where television viewers and radio listeners could see themselves or their neighbors in the community service-driven programming and connect with the on-air personalities who hosted it.

Earlier in the decade, Umansky struck a deal to acquire the movie library of King Brothers Productions in Hollywood, a massive collection of hundreds of vintage motion pictures. Those films became the feature for the late afternoon *Cash Calls Movie*, hosted by Gene Rump, the talented young morning deejay and program director for KAKE Radio, a broadcaster who had mastered the art of swinging both ways (radio and television).

Three times per movie, Rump would fire up a ping-pong ball blowing machine, then using a complicated Umansky-inspired formula, would select two balls for a local exchange prefix (9 and 4 for WHitehall, 8 and 3 for TEmple, 6 and 8 for MUrray), followed by five more balls blown at random to create a phone number.

Rump would dial the number on-air and introduce himself as the host of KAKE-TV's *Cash Calls*. If the recipient of the call could identify that day's movie, they got the cash. If not, if no one answered, or he got a busy signal, ten more bucks in the pot.

Imagine the KAKEland housewife, just returned home to the split-level rancher from the supermarket where her groceries were carried to her wood-paneled Ford LTD station wagon by a charming and witty courtesy boy.

She turns on the Magnavox Three-Way Console (color TV, radio, record player), clunks the selector over to Channel 10, setting out newly purchased Chips Ahoy and Mr. D's whole milk as the kids return home from school. Ignoring the kids as they attack the cookies and repair to the backyard to roll a doobie, she is glued to her television set, fighting back the tears as young socialite Bette Davis, dying from an inoperable brain tumor, falls for her doctor, played by George Brent.

The banana yellow rotary dial telephone on the wall in the kitchen clangs. Now sobbing, she would take Rump's call, correctly identify *Dark Victory* as today's movie, and pocket that day's pot of cash.

Tears of sadness mingle with tears of joy. In the service of community, all the buttons were pushed in KAKEland.

When KAKE started a local 5 p.m. newscast, the *Cash Calls* movies were bumped to even earlier in the afternoon. By the time Matson returned to KAKEland, the movie collection had become the centerpiece for *Nightwatch*.

He may have been working an entry-level broadcasting tech job in the middle of the night, but he was doing it in a medium-sized market for one of the glossiest, most successful and well-respected television stations in the country.

His foot was in the door.

27.
November 30, 1978

He still pined for Malea, though a brand-new beer helped dull the pain. Shortly after returning to Wichita, through a highly controlled experiment, he reached the inescapable conclusion that if Miller Lite tasted great and was less filling, the new silver canned Coors Light tasted even better and was even less filling.

Woodgate-era Wichita was Olympia. The Cities were Old Style. This time around, Wichita would be Coors Light.

One of his first calls upon returning was to Duane the Man, and they quickly agreed to room together, signing a six-month lease on a two-bedroom place in the Indian Hills apartment complex on West 13th Street, about halfway between KAKE and the are-KAN-zuhz. Indian Hills was much like Woodgate, with a smaller footprint and done up in faux-New England Colonial, red brick buildings with white trim.

Since every man got a bedroom, no doorknob socks were needed. Duane's time was now split between his aeronautical engineering studies at dub-yes-you, and a new job selling caskets and cemetery plots, so he wasn't around much.

"It's a racket," indicating how he viewed the job. "The prices are exorbitant and to make a sale I gotta get the would-be buyer all worked up emotionally."

He also missed Donna, Mitch, and Kenny more than he thought he would. Every time he passed a McDonald's.

The arches which are, were, and shall ever be golden.

Donna's Nowhere was Oelwein, Iowa. Her foot in the

door was at a country music station, completely out of her pop-rock wheelhouse. The two of them would take turns calling each other late at night, bitching about the entry level.

Ida Lupino, Robert Mitchum, and Mike in Wichita. Kenny Rogers, Crystal Gayle, and Donna—in Oelwein.

"If God were to perform an enema on the Earth," Donna lamented, "Oelwein, Iowa, would be the point of entry."

By then, enough time had lapsed since he split the Cities in such a hurry, he was able to share with Donna the truth about being dumped. Not being an idiot, she had long since pieced it together. She understood his motivation in taking the TV tech job, not because he wanted it, because he wanted to go home. Even if Mike didn't yet realize it, Donna knew it was a stopgap.

"You trained for radio and you're so good at it." Donna reverted comfortably to audition tape coach. "Do a six-month dance with Joan Crawford and Veronica Lake and get into radio. Christ, there's a radio station right fucking there!"

Donna read the trades, kept up on industry trends, and realized exactly what Mike had in KAKEland, even if he didn't. Most Brown grads would have given a pinky toe and signed a promissory note on a spleen to be in his position. Foot-in-the-door job right out of tech school in the top-rated television station in a medium-sized market? With an equally successful, self-contained, fully functional, turnkey radio station connected at its hip?

Donna was right, not once, but twice. Deejaying was more fitting of his self-image. He was "talent," not a lunch pail-carrying lifer technician. And there was a radio station right fucking there.

He walked by it every night.

He didn't set out to hijack *Nightwatch News*, but that's what happened.

After each movie, before Ol' Flick would debrief the film that just aired and preview the one on deck, the KAKE-TV programmers were convinced the community could best be served by offering two or three minutes of news. Insomniacs care about world and local goings-on as much as sound sleepers, after all.

The idea was simple. The all-night deejay at KAKE Radio would rip some wire copy, record it, and deliver it to the tech on a "cart," a loop of audio tape in a cartridge that in appearance, resembled an 8-track tape. Through heavy eyelids, viewers clad in flannel jammies watched a static orange-over-black *Nightwatch* bumper slide, depicting the Wichita skyline, and listened to the newscast.

Or they fixed another sandwich.

The deejay was supposed to record fresh wire copy to air after each movie, based on the premise of immediacy—broadcast journalism's inherent advantage over the *Wichita Eagle* which was put to bed hours before it hit the front porch early in the morning.

The news in the *Wichita Beacon* was already at least a half-day old when it hit the porch in the late afternoon and it had to compete with KAKE-TV's flashy 6 p.m. newscast, going live from the Century II civic center to cover the ongoing dispute over whether James Rosati's freeform sculpture called the *Tripodal* was, in fact, art.

If the Iran hostage crisis was resolved during the time it took Bogey to reunite with Bacall in Key Largo after dealing with Edward G. Robinson, the insomniacs throughout greater KAKEland would be the first to know.

One more community service.

Sometimes the overnight KAKE Radio deejay would forget, forcing the playing of an earlier recording a second time. Astute insomniacs no doubt caught on.

"Wait a minute," casting a wary eye at the static *Nightwatch* slide while getting up from the La-Z-Boy to fetch a fresh bag of Sta-Krisp potato chips, being sure to hang on to the greasy plastic blue disc at the bottom of the bag, good for free rides at Joyland.

"Still no meltdown at Three Mile Island?"

Matson was not supposed to leave Master Control, but he did. Film segments were timed to the second, so he would pick the longest segment in the movie, usually 15 or 20 minutes, start a stopwatch, descend the stairs, and network with the only other human being in the building, Jack Oliver, the all-night deejay at the radio station Matson walked by every night.

This networking proved valuable right away, for it was in building this relationship that Matson learned Jack's heart was all-in for deejaying, but he viewed the recording of *Nightwatch News* as a gold-plated pain in his ass.

"Why don't you do it?" Jack knew of Mike's radio ambitions and didn't have to ask twice. One man's scut work is another man's opportunity.

"Think it'll be okay?" Matson harbored entry-level worries about unseen hierarchy and unspoken expectations.

"Sometimes it's better to ask forgiveness than to ask permission," Jack said.

It was a perfect storm of big organizational compartmentalization. The TV programming department had emotional ownership in Ol' Flick and the vintage movie collection. TV News cared deeply about all the journalism that went into *TV-10 News* at 5, 6, and 10. KAKE Radio News took pride in their hourly newscasts, live mobile capabilities, and fledgling statewide radio news network. Engineering owned Master Control, the film projectors, tape machines, and the transmitter.

As with most afterthoughts, no one component of the system claimed *Nightwatch News*. As long as there was a professional voice offering up-to-the minute news, the community was served, and no one gave much of a shit. It was the middle of the night.

Of the three or four movies that would air each night, Mike was lucky if one of them was worth watching, so he'd search for ways to combat boredom.

The editing, compiling, recording, and presentation of *Nightwatch News* became a professional, creative challenge. He remembered from Brown that news on the radio—or in this case radio news on TV—should be short, to the point. Written for the ear. Put yourself in the shoes of a listener. They are not reading a newspaper, they are not hanging on your every word, they're listening passively.

What came hard for most people, even those in the business, came easy for him. He had a knack for linguistics. Foreign words and names that flummoxed the most talented broadcasters, rolled off his tongue.

Abolhassan Bani-Sadr (ah-bowl-HOSS-un bonnie-SOD-er)

Sadegh Ghotbzadeh (SAW-deck goat-buh-ZAHD-ay).

Ayatollah Ruhollah Khomeini (eye-uh-TOLL-uh roo-HOLLA koh-MAIN-ee).

Wojciech Jaruzelski (VOY-check yahr-oo-ZELL-skee).

Lech Walesa (LECK vuh-WENN-zuh).

It wasn't eye-RAN, it was ear-AWN. It wasn't eye-RAIN-ee-uhn, it was ear-AWN-ee-uhn.

He prowled the TV newsroom wire machines at night and

found the perfect product: Associated Press international, national, and Kansas headlines. He would scrounge around the KAKE Radio newsroom for local news and often hit paydirt. Local news stories, complete with actualities—short snippets of newsmaker voices recorded either in person or over the phone.

Each two-minute segment was finished with a one-line weather forecast.

"Look for Wednesday's weather in KAKEland to be mostly cloudy... slight chance for rain... with a high of 75. That's *Nightwatch News.*" Purposeful pause. "This is Mike Matson."

He went in search of other ways to ward off boredom. To jazz up the between movies on-air look, he would often set up shop in the adjacent television production control room, fire up an even bigger Wurlitzer with a state-of-the-art character generator, type the word NEWS in a font, color, and special effect complimenting the *Nightwatch* slide, and superimpose it during the playing of the audio recording.

KAKE-TV had a live announcer's booth, a vestige of the '50s and '60s. He figured out how it worked and rigged a way to go live with *Nightwatch News.* On-the-ball insomniacs would catch on when he would give the exact time before signing off.

One night, Jack shared the news of his promotion to evenings, creating an all-night deejay opening.

"Slide down this way after your shift." Jack had heard and even critiqued his audition tape. "I'll introduce you to Gene Rump."

28.
December 5, 1978

It had taken him more than two months to get the gang back together again. In the nine months since his departure, he was not the only one who made life decisions that had an ancillary consequence of breaking up the band.

The event was to mark his 21st birthday. Not Pogo's or the taverns. This was not a meat-market night. Pat O'Brien's, a high-end club on East Kellogg, attracted a classier, more genteel clientele. It was the kind of place they had always talked about as an aspiration.

Duck, who traditionally would have taken charge and organized such gatherings, preferred being a participant, along with Duane the Man, Sticky Steve, and a couple of others from the Mr. D's heyday.

Twenty-one years old. It seemed sort of anti-climactic and somewhat of a disappointment.

"Cutty and water," as though he'd been ordering cocktails all his life. He would have preferred a beer, but appearances matter. He didn't like Scotch any more than bourbon, vodka, or gin. But he was now 21 and needed to look and act like it.

Something had changed. Before, he was Michael J., leader of courtesy boys. Live fast, die young, leave a good-looking corpse. Now, he was a broadcast professional. Same charm, good looks, and wit, but no longer leading.

No one was following.

"At the tender age of 19, I was the frozen foods manager of the anchor supermarket in what used to be a chain of supermarkets throughout the are-KAN-zuhz River Valley of south-central Kansas, I'll have you know."

The Cutty acted quicker than Coors Light.

"Yeah, that chain is now down to two," Duck chimed in.

"And Gary D. is selling Central Heights."

Something was off. Maybe it was the Cutty. Maybe you can't force aspirations. Maybe aspirations are perishable, with a defined shelf life.

"Why, I quizzed out of an entire term in broadcasting tech school," with Cutty-and-water-elevated volume.

Duane the Man, his friend, gave no ground.

"Yeah, but that was only because you were a goddamn basket case after getting dumped and wanted to retreat back home, tail between your legs."

"Bullshit." He said it aloud while squirming and could not make eye contact.

A couple of tables over, he saw two young women glancing his way. Maybe it was a meat market-night.

Be like Burns.

Hi there. You look as though you may be insomniacs who while away the wee hours watching vintage motion pictures on the top-rated television station in the market. Perhaps you've heard me on Nightwatch News? I'm the one who pronounces a mean Abolhassan Bani-Sadr.

He came back from a bathroom break to an empty table.

"Your friends said you'd take care of this," their waitress, in black pants and a starched white blouse buttoned all the way to the neck, handed him a brown leather folder with the night's damage. He looked down and tried desperately not to freak out. $125.86. Before the tip.

Happy Birthday, Michael J. Welcome to being legal.

By the time he got to Indian Hills, Duane the Man had already crashed, snoring behind a closed door. The confrontation over the stiffed Pat O'Brien's tab would have to wait. He dug out his wallet, plopped down in Grandma's orange frieze swivel rocker sans swivel/rocking mechanism, cracked open a Coors Light, and took a hard, close look at Wes Gordon's draft card, now faded and frayed.

He hadn't used it since 1975, when he turned 18, three years ago tonight. But in the two years before that, it ensured a steady, if illicit, supply of 3.2 beer. Miller Lite, Inglewood's rhinoceros piss Budweiser, Olympia, Miller High Life pony bottles, pitchers of Coors at Pogo's, Blatz, Old Style, et al, ad infinitum. Now that he was 21, he could walk into any liquor store in Wichita and buy a bottle of Cutty, or any other hard stuff, for that matter.

It was a hollow victory since he didn't like the taste of hard stuff and loved the taste of beer. One good thing, though. As of tomorrow, he could and would switch over to 6 percent Coors Light, available at any of those same liquor stores in Wichita.

Tasted even better. Even less filling. Twice the alcohol content.

He drained the suds, rolled up the draft card like it was a doobie, and stuffed it into the empty beer can.

You're a real boy, now, Pinocchio.

29.
October 7, 1979

"You are looking LIVE... at sold out Giants Stadium in East Rutherford, New Jersey. The amazing, unbeaten Tampa Bay Buccaneers are going to try to make it six and oh against a New York team which will start rookie passer Phil Simms in an attempt to get victory number one... "

Brent Musburger opening the *NFL Today* pregame show Sunday mornings on rival KTVH, Channel 12, was his cue. That meant it was 11 a.m. The first game would kick off at noon, the late game at 3 p.m. A one-hour pregame show was sufficient justification to start an afternoon of drinking.

He had reached the point where a purposeful errand was required every Friday and Saturday to stock up on beer, to secure enough for the entire weekend, since Sunday beer sales in Kansas were not allowed. His home state only crawled out of prohibition thirty years ago, and the temperance culture dies hard. This often meant the purchase of two 12-packs of Coors Light, a case of beer, every weekend. A dozen for Saturday, a dozen for Sunday.

On the rare weekend he would forget to stock up, he generally just white-knuckled it. Occasionally he would make his way to a bar and pound down a few. He loathed doing that alone, though, because of the perception of a 21-year-old young man entering a bar by himself. To drink by himself.

By the end of their six-month lease at Indian Hills, Duane the Man couldn't sleep at night after spending the day working a would-be funeral package customer into a death panic, lost the job, and was forced, reluctantly, to move back home with his parents.

Matson could not swing the two bedrooms by himself, and with no potential roommates on the horizon, he took a one-bedroom apartment at Amidon Place, between 26th and 27th Streets on Amidon, six blocks north of Sweetbriar, on the fringes of Pleasant Valley.

The new place was directly across the street from Angelo's, where he bussed tables and scrubbed lasagna tins in high school. Three blocks from Pleasant Valley United Methodist Church, where he sang "Kum Ba Yah" and did not contemplate Points B through Y.

Less than a mile from his parents' home.

When Inglewood called from Colorado Springs to alert his erstwhile best man that he and Jennie were preggers, Matson shared the news of his new place. His former best friend pointed out that since departing the Cities, with each move, he seemed to be edging closer in proximity back to James E. He was back to within a mile of ground zero.

It's clearly not by design. Must be some subconscious bullshit.

If Woodgate was shiny and Indian Hills colonial classy, Amidon Place was neither. It was a visible, tangible step down. Mostly blue collar, no covered parking, and Mike saw more cops there than the other two complexes combined.

Three long, two-story buildings, with each apartment front door opening directly to the elements. Red brick veneer on the ground floor, where Matson lived. Plywood siding trimmed with strips of 1 x 3 lumber evenly spaced every 24 inches on the upper, painted avocado green.

Indian Hills was named for the middle-class neighborhood that surrounded it. There was an actual decorative wooden gate at the entrance of Woodgate. Amidon

Place was a place on Amidon Avenue. It was as though the developers knew a classier name would have been construed as putting lipstick on a pig.

Inside, a cheap Berber carpet, compared to Woodgate's plush shag, and low pile at Indian Hills. A hollow front door, painted red, with the lock in the doorknob, no deadbolt. He often thought of it as Soviet housing.

No parties, no barbecues, no clubhouse. There was a pool, but like everything at Amidon Place, the bikini-clad women paled in comparison to their Woodgate counterparts. Often, literally. No one came to visit, for a pretty logical reason as it turned out. No invitations were extended. If he thought Amidon Place was beneath him, he sure as hell didn't need anyone else coming over to confirm it. So, he kept to himself. Alone.

Jayne Kennedy wrapped up her perfunctory NFL human-interest feature.

She's so good-looking, CBS should just put her on set, spotlight her in a tight shot, and ask her to stare at the camera for ten minutes.

Hell, he'd watch, and he'd buy the beer that sponsored it. Jayne tossed it back to Brent, who teased a preview of the late afternoon Cowboys-Vikings matchup.

Then came a commercial for Michelob Light. He was glued to it, mesmerized, just like he was to Jayne Kennedy. The spot ended with a shot of a frosted glass tankard imprinted with the Michelob Light logo, suds spilling over the top and a male announcer intoning:

"...good taste runs in the family... "

Every time he saw a beer commercial, regardless of the brand, he would make his way to the fridge and bust open a fresh Coors Light. Speaking of subconscious bullshit. What's the sweet spot between beer marketing and addiction?

Tick tick tick tick tick...

He awoke to the sound of an Aristo stopwatch.

"... I'm Harry Reasoner. I'm Morley Safer. I'm Ed Bradley. Those stories and more, tonight on *60 Minutes*."

He hadn't moved very far in the roughly seven hours his General Electric Performance Television was tuned to CBS and KTVH, Channel 12.

The Giants did pull off the upset against Tampa Bay. He remembered that. In his first start, Giant's halfback Billy Taylor rushed for 148 yards, while in his first start, Simms was an inauspicious 6 out of 12 passing, for a paltry 37 yards. Taking a page from the Bucs' playbook, New York's three four defense kept Tampa Bay bottled up.

He also recalled knocking back the requisite four Excedrin at halftime of the first game. Experience had taught him it was the most effective way to proactively short circuit a hangover.

He remembered Tony Dorsett scoring two touchdowns for Dallas early in the second game and then he must have fallen asleep.

Getting up slowly, to gauge the ferocity of the hangover—another workaround lesson gleaned from experience—he moved from the orange frieze chair to the bedroom. A built-in bookshelf, painted white, extended from the west wall, separating bedroom from living room. No door, just an open space between the end of the bookshelf and the back of the kitchen wall. Hence, no doorknob on which to hang a sock.

Even for old time's sake.

No need for privacy when you live alone.

He had been working nights for the better part of a year,

and his mind and body had still not adjusted. He wanted to go to bed when he got off work, around sunrise, sleep six or eight hours, and have most of the afternoon and evening free before going to the station about 10:30 p.m.

Two problems with that. First, sunrise. He simply could not sleep when it was light outside. He tried blackout curtains and a blackout sleeping mask. No luck.

The second reason was more practical. Most of the world does business between 8 and 5. Doctors, dentists, cable guys, any routine appointment was scheduled when he should have been asleep. Mike was never much of a catnapper. The result was a discombobulated biorhythm. He would often run out of gas at just about the exact time he needed to be on the air, projecting charming and happy.

What was it that Donna said? You're putting on a performance.

Liquor stores also screwed up his inner clock. They were not yet open when he got off work in the morning, so he often stopped by a QuikTrip for his daily 12-pack. 3.2 percent beer is better than no beer.

"Little early, ain't it?" The clerk cast him a sideways glance, after one such pop-in.

What business is it of yours?

"I work overnights. I just got off."

He did most of his business at a liquor store in the Sweetbriar parking lot, but when he thought that clerk was silently judging him, he began to spread his business around. Wichita had many liquor stores.

30.
October 12, 1979

He found himself rooting for the Pittsburgh Pirates. Part of it was their pillbox ballcaps and interchangeable gold, black, and white uniforms. Major League Baseball had broken away from the traditional home whites/road grays and the Pirates were on the cutting edge.

A big part of it was his admiration for serendipity. He suspected neither Sister Sledge nor the Pirates' brass of purposefully planning the adoption of a disco number as their 1979 theme song. It just happened, organically. That seemed like the best way to impact hearts and minds.

Part of it was weariness of Earl Weaver. He'd been watching Weaver manage the Baltimore Orioles in the postseason since they lost the World Series to the Mets a decade ago.

Familiarity breeds contempt.

He was in the kitchen of Frank Dunn's immaculate west Wichita home, sucking on a bottle of Heineken. It tasted like a skunk smelled, but in a good way. Frank was Martin Umansky's hand-picked general manager of KAKE Radio and the executive responsible for the station's recent success. The party was being thrown to celebrate another successful billing year. Frank served top of the line libations. Chivas Regal instead of Cutty Sark, Ancient Age over Wild Turkey, Heineken, not Coors Light.

Al Michaels, Don Drysdale, and Howard Cosell calling the World Series for ABC Sports on a portable Panasonic color

TV perched atop Frank's refrigerator.

Three fellow partygoers joined him around the kitchen table. The husband of the radio station accountant, a shy, quiet young lady who worked in traffic, and her equally shy, quiet date. The couple gave the distinct vibe they would be there only long enough to make an appearance and then escape to some place where they could be shy and quiet by themselves.

He bonded with the accountant's husband over baseball. With one down and the bases loaded in the 8th inning, Pirates' skipper Chuck Tanner brought in his submarining relief ace Kent Tekulve to face the Birds' right-handed hitting Gary Roenicke.

"Watch," said the accountant's husband, nursing a Chivas and soda. "Weaver will pinch-hit Lowenstein for Roenicke." He did, Lowenstein slammed a 2-run double, and Baltimore went on to win the game.

Matson felt compelled to point out to those at the table, that when John Lowenstein played for the Wichita Aeros in 1971, he and a buddy rode their bicycles from Pleasant Valley to Lawrence Stadium and witnessed Lowenstein hit a ball over the right field wall where it bounced on McLean Boulevard and rolled into the are-KAN-zuhz River.

"How could you see the ball hit the street and roll into the river from inside the ballpark?" It seemed like a logical question.

"Well, I didn't actually see it," he took a long Heineken swig. "That was the story Aeros' play-by-play man Jack Munley told the next day on KWBB."

He thought about following with the career tidbit that listening to Munley call Aeros' games inspired him to get into radio, but no one at the table seemed very interested.

All the important people, the daytime deejays, the women

from traffic and continuity, the account execs and all their assorted plus-ones, were clustered in small groups in Frank's living and family rooms. The atmosphere was social and friendly, as existing relationships were nurtured and strengthened.

He was one of them, officially and formally, now six months ensconced as the all-night deejay on the top-rated radio station in the market. But unofficially and informally make the world go 'round, and in those realms, he was "the overnight guy" or "the kid." Either way, the outlier.

How can I be expected to get chummy with my colleagues when I never see them? When I'm at the station, they're all sawing logs.

The early luster of the gig had worn off. There were days, it seemed, that his most important role at KAKE Radio was to serve as Gene Rump's alarm clock, to make certain the talent around which so much of KAKE's success rode, made it to work on time.

"Gene, good morning, it's 5 a.m.!"

"Hrglmphz."

"Great! See you soon!"

RumpInTheMorning was morning drive radio programming that worked. Adult contemporary music, happy voice, interaction with listeners, and a good sidekick. Longtime KAKE meteorologist Jim O'Donnell was the perfect straight man. Ed McMahon to Rump's Carson.

As program director and Umansky acolyte, Rump originated a St. Patrick's Day city parade with the Irish O'Donnell as front man. Fourth of July fireworks shows at dub-yes-you's Cessna Stadium, which came to be known as Concerts in the Sky, were also Rump's brainchild.

KAKE Radio had Kansas City Royals baseball and acquired the rights for dub-yes-you football and basketball. Bill

McLean, now aging gracefully, brought his Cap'n Bill character from TV to mid-days on the radio, and afternoon drive was held down by the dynamic John "Hooter" Myers.

The result was success. KAKE Radio, at 1240 on the AM dial, became the top-rated station in the market, billing $1 million.

If KAKE-TV was the soul of KAKEland, KAKE Radio was its heart.

On TV, after the movies shifted overnight to Ol' Flick, Rump took over and turned around a moribund noon talk show. *Kaleidoscope* started as a local daily live variety/talk show from Towne East Mall but migrated to the KAKE-TV studios.

Rump brought in Mogie Langston, a former Miss Wichita, as co-host and the show took off. Every Labor Day, Rump would host the local cut-ins of the Jerry Lewis Muscular Dystrophy Telethon, and, like Jerry, loosen the bowtie of his tuxedo in about the 22nd hour, when they were bringing it home.

When Oliver first introduced Matson to Rump, he held out little hope of getting the all-night deejay gig. With a grand total of zero professional radio experience, he believed what had been drummed into him at Brown: Getting your first job in a market that big is unheard of. It just doesn't happen.

Because of *Nightwatch News*, Mike was a known commodity to those in the KAKEland hierarchy who mattered, and he wanted the job. But most importantly, he was handy. He worked right upstairs. Same overnight hours. During his formal interview in Rump's office, when it became clear he had the job, Matson expressed concern about leaving Dave Morris in the lurch.

"Watch this." Rump picked up the receiver, scanned the station directory, found Morris' extension and punched three numbers.

"Dave, Gene Rump here. I just extended Mike Matson an offer to be our overnight deejay. He's accepted and I wonder if you'd mind letting him go now, so we can get him squared away down here?"

Silence as Morris responded with words that made it clear he understood the pecking order. Rump looked at Mike, smiled and nodded.

"Gosh, thanks, Dave. Really appreciate your flexibility."

Talent gets the glory. Technicians get taken for granted. Peace is kept in the KAKEland family.

Rump hung up the phone, extended his right hand and said, "Take a couple days off, you can work alongside Jack for a night or two, then you'll be on the air Monday night."

31.
November 13, 1979

At the point of entry in Oelwein, Donna Hansen had become Donna Kasey. She toyed with Donna Winter at Brown, as sort of a blonde-haired, blue-eyed yang to Donna Summer's yin, but quickly abandoned it when she realized how hard her northeast Iowa country music listeners would have to work to catch on.

"I don't have their attention for that long," Donna told him in one of their late-night mutual gripe fests. "They'll say, 'shut up already and gimme the hog markets.'"

As a tech, Kenny didn't need an air name. Mitch Burns kept his real name at KYMN, mostly because he had no intention of staying in Northfield. It was a part-time weekend job while going to school. For his career, Mitch played around with Mitchell Brooks or Mitch Bryant.

All night television master controllers didn't have to worry about an air name, but all-night radio deejays sure did.

He had one. Michael J., or Michael Jay. Problem was, there was already one in the market. Michael J. Elston had made a name for himself reading radio news on KLEO.

There were really no objections with his real name. When he would introduce himself, people would often hear "Matt" first. He could not count the number of times, upon meeting someone for the first time, he would get back, "Nice to meet you, Matt," so why not lead with what people actually hear?

Donna's admonition about putting yourself in the listener's position. Think about the receiving end of all your brilliance. He considered Matt Michaels. Matt Michaelson. Matthew Michaelson. Matthew J. Michaelson. Seemed like a lotta suh-LOB-uls.

Reading *Nightwatch News*, he felt he had to use his real name. Another Brown lesson. If the person delivering the news is pretending to be someone else, how can you trust them? Goes to credibility. And community service.

In the end, he landed on the obvious. He was already "... that's *Nightwatch News...* (purposeful pause...) this is Mike Matson" on KAKE-TV. He'd be the same guy on KAKE Radio.

No alternative air name. No more nicknames. No more differing interpretations of reality to hide behind.

To his fellow announcers, he was an afterthought. Nothing of consequence ever happened overnight. They were glad he had the job so they wouldn't have to fill in.

The girls in traffic, who juggled programming and commercials and were responsible for the daily generation of broadcast logs, saw him as eligible, but the disparity in hours actually spent awake, put the brakes on any action. When they were available, he was trying to sleep and vice versa.

Mike looked at the salesmen and saw Herb Tarlek. To them, overnights were worthless. They couldn't give away that airtime, so what few commercials that did air were throw-ins to larger deals.

The newsroom denizens saw themselves as above the fray, what with journalism being a higher calling than spinning records. They turned up their collective noses at his *Nightwatch News* prowess. He wasn't gathering or writing news. He was just pronouncing it.

Of all the systems at the radio station, the young ladies in continuity genuinely appreciated him. Their job was to take the creative copy sent by the ad agencies, get it produced and on the air. This meant assigning commercial copy to the announcers. All the advertisers wanted Rump, McLean, and Myers. But everyone needed to be wary of overkill, too much of one voice.

To them, he was a ready, new voice on a commercial. While they would have to beg, cajole, and bribe the big boys to produce a spot, Matson took them all willingly and asked for more.

But to Roxanne Reynolds, he was a project.

"Smoking or non-smoking?" The hostess said it with a smile as she clutched a pair of oversized laminated menus. It was clear she took her cheeriness seriously.

As an ex-smoker, Roxanne had become extremely prejudicial, bordering on militant, in her non-smoking.

"A non-smoking section in a restaurant is like having a non-peeing section in a swimming pool," over her shoulder to him, as the two of them were led through a visible second-hand haze to a part of the restaurant ostensibly carcinogen-free.

Roxanne Reynolds was in her early 40s, and as executive assistant to Frank Dunn, the go-to at KAKE Radio for anything vital.

"Do NOT call me a secretary."

Divorced and childless, those two attributes alone had the wolves lining up. She wore form-fitting dresses accessorized with color-coordinated jewelry. While many women in her peer group sought Farrah Fawcett-Majors, Roxanne leaned Jaclyn Smith.

His air shift ended at 6 a.m. when *RumpInTheMorning* started, but his commercial production often kept him at the station until 8 or 9. Roxanne stopped him earlier that day on his way out.

"Meet me for lunch. Applegate's Landing. 12:30. Don't be late."

It was not a request.

He had seen her fending off the wolves and something in the back of his mind made him wonder whether she was turning the tables and he was now the prey. She was old enough to be his mother, and he'd never really considered her that way before.

"You're what? 21 years old?"

"Yes."

It took him through the salad before catching on to her motivation. His assumptions were dead wrong, and he felt like a heel. Maybe now that he was a professional it was time to change the way he approached relationships with women.

"Do you wanna be a radio disc jockey at age 50?"

He thought about it for a minute then realized she was waiting for an answer.

"Well, until very recently I thought I wanted to be a Major League Baseball play-by-play announcer."

"What changed?"

It was the first time he'd ever really verbalized these thoughts with another person.

"For starters, there are only 26 of those big-league jobs on the planet, and I haven't even called an American Legion game."

He told her about yearbook class and Drafting 3 at Heights, about Mr. D's, about Brown Institute, Malea and Tony, the wall of butter, and the riffraff. He actually used the words, "sufficiently chagrined," in describing his return to Wichita.

"Sounds to me like you got a whiff, dropped everything, and followed the girl to Minneapolis."

Roxanne took about a dozen dainty bites of her pasta primavera and then put her silverware at 4 o'clock on her plate. When the waitress asked if she could take her plate, Roxanne glanced up, smiled, and said, "Yes, please."

He'd never really considered that perspective. The story he always told himself was a year in tech school and then launch his career, a year ahead of everyone else in the class of 1975 on the four-year plan. That's exactly what he had done.

"Some of these guys are driven by ego, some by sheer talent," Roxanne pressed her point. "Some of the ones driven by ego haven't the first clue that is what drives them."

"Look at Gene, he's arguably the most famous person in Wichita—and he's well-liked. You think that's by accident? There are other morning guys on other radio stations in Wichita. Who even knows their names?"

"Yeah, but it's also because he's on TV." Matson's salad was gone, garlic bread and ravioli half gone. "I would argue his radio gig just bolsters his TV gig."

"Could not agree more," Roxanne said, "because he knows his audience."

She was right. Gene came across as modest and self-effacing—reflective of the Kansas culture—with an added layer of show biz that only enhanced his appeal.

"Some guys are great at timing, some have great voices but zero talent, skill, or knack. Some have a heart of gold, but that doesn't work on the radio. Others are pros at production."

She had seen the way he acted around the station.

"Do you want to be a yes-man all your life? Those people

get no respect."

"But—but—I'm a courtesy boy!" The two "but's" were on purpose. He was aiming for a chuckle. Roxanne didn't crack a smile.

Earlier that day, the station's music director had chastised him for shoddy quarter-hour maintenance and airing songs not on the playlist, admonishing that the playlist exists for a reason.

Rating surveys counted listeners each quarter-hour if they were tuned in for at least five minutes. KAKE and nearly every other station in the market would "hot track" the quarter hour with a hit song from the playlist, to retain the listener until they were counted.

Deep breaths, Ace. Couple things. It's the middle of the night. You can count my listeners on two hands.

Also, when I play Richard Harris' MacArthur Park (7:21), it gives me time to book it across West Street to Denny's to fetch my pre ordered cheeseburger and fries. Provided I haul ass and don't get hit by a truck.

"Yes, sir. Won't happen again."

Even though he had yet to admit it to himself, much less her, Roxanne saw that he, too, was driven by ego. She also saw the talent and the skill. The potential.

"Now is the time to decide not only what you want to be, but how you are going to be."

Roxanne saw that her tactic was working. He was genuinely listening.

"Develop an edge. You don't have to be an asshole about it, but you also don't always have to defer to authority, and you definitely don't always have to be the smartest guy in the room."

"*Moi?*" He looked at her with feigned indignation. "You got the wrong man, lady."

She smiled but wasn't about to tell him she found him charming, in a wise-ass little brother way.

Mike reached instinctively for the check because he thought that's what guys were supposed to do. Roxanne snatched it out of his hands.

"I invited you. I'm paying," imparting another valuable lesson.

"One more thing. You are in the 'look at me' business. Is that really what you want? What will you do with that fame?"

He thought of his glossy 18 by 24 headshot hung prominently on the wall in the station lobby, right under similar shots of Rump, McLean, Myers, and other KAKEland personalities.

"You will have a career where people will know who you are, recognize you. Look around you, it's already begun."

Outside, she put on her sunglasses. Now she really looked like Jaclyn Smith.

"Thanks, Roxanne."

He offered his hand down low, as if he expected her to give him five. With an exasperated sigh, she reached down and pulled his hand into a traditional firm handshake. Another lesson.

"For the lunch and the advice."

"It's my pleasure," she removed her sunglasses and made intense, direct eye contact, as though words alone were insufficient to carry the message.

"Decide what you want to be, then be it," turning to walk away, then stopping to face him again, shades back on. "You need to know these things."

32.
December 31, 1979

As the second hand swept toward 1980, he thought about the coming decade. Not with trepidation, but also not with a lot of confidence. Job, fine. Love life dwindling to nonexistence. He could not be like Burns. He had tried and could not pull it off.

Mike had spent some time trying to think of something pithy to say on the air when the clock struck midnight, something at least semi-profound. He assumed that otherwise passive listeners might be paying a little more attention to the radio as a new decade rang in.

But all the cool kids would not be listening to the radio at midnight New Year's Eve. They'd be at Pogo's, at the bars with live bands, at intimate parties with noisemakers in the homes of close friends. Who's listening to Linda Ronstadt or Air Supply on an AM radio station at midnight on New Year's Eve?

Those poor, lonely miserable souls home alone, or others like him—working. Cops, cabbies, truck drivers. Maybe a waitress or grill man at Kings-X. Provided they had a radio. Provided it was turned on. Provided it was tuned to 1240-AM. Provided they were actually listening.

In the end he decided it was foolhardy to try and script profundity. Plus, he didn't really want to work that hard.

"Mere seconds away from a new decade... Mike Matson with you on KAKE Radio... clear skies, 34 degrees. Happy New Year, KAKEland. It's January first, 19-80 on 12-40, K-A-K-E, Wichita."

During the top-of-the-hour news from the ABC Radio Network, he remembered New Year's Eve 1976. Duane the Man plowing the Z through plate glass. When he hung the nickname on him, it was designed to be cynical, ironic. Matson had no idea how Duane would actually grow into it.

He remembered Duane's distress. He did not think about his own instinct that night to leave him there. Three years is sufficient to take the sharp edges off trauma and morph the memory into something more worthwhile.

The lead story on the network newscast was American reaction to the Soviet invasion of Afghanistan, now a week old.

Carter's gonna screw this up just like he did the hostage crisis.

There was already talk of American involvement, of reinstating the draft. Escape to Canada? He's all alone. What's keeping him here? For the first time, he knew how the older demographic wave of baby boomers felt. The notion of Vietnam all over again scared him.

He was unsure what the 1980s would bring. He was comfortable with the '70s. He was a child of the '70s. These were his times. When he thought about it, which was not very often, he would define himself through his professional success, and then he would stop thinking.

Times were changing. Could the '80s be his times, too? He had no way of knowing the coming years would define the way he thought and approached life's circumstances. No way of knowing the coming years would define him.

His normal M.O. was to get off work and crack a Coors Light. *I deserve it after a hard night's work,* had evolved into, *It helps me sleep.*

For the first time, a new feeling washed over him. He wanted that drink now. Right now. This minute. Like the radio station that surrounded him, he was becoming a man of immediacy.

We'll drink a cup of kindness, yet.

A glance at the clock. Fifteen minutes into the new decade.

It was still six long hours until right now.

He didn't know it at the time, but Matson found himself on the cusp of an industry trend that would smudge some of the shine associated with local radio and TV.

KAKEland was for sale.

Channel 10 went to a concern that owned television stations in San Francisco and Omaha. The radio station was purchased by some Wichita businessmen who had made their millions in the oilfield supply game. Astute businessmen, but their knowledge of broadcasting started and stopped with the perceived show biz luster it would bring to their otherwise mundane Kansas business portfolio.

Martin Umansky's business model had sprung from the birth of an industry. The government first allocated the amplitude modulated frequencies on the radio spectrum to broadcasters who promised to serve their community well and faithfully. Umansky considered himself as a steward of that trust first, businessman second.

The new owners leapfrogged right over steward. Among the changes ushered in was to replace the overnight adult contemporary music with a talk format, programming the new *Larry King Show* from the Mutual Broadcasting System, an overnight live gabfest based in Washington, D.C. featuring the Brooklyn-born King, who had made a name for himself basically inventing the talk radio genre in Miami.

For Matson, it meant no more creativity. No music meant

no need to script or ad lib, to plan and time his words carefully right up until the vocal hits. No need to do the arithmetic to backtime records and commercials to hit the top of the hour newscast. He was no longer jockeying discs. He was now simply a board operator.

A monkey can do this.

King turned him on to Sinatra and Nat King Cole—the culture of his parents' generation. Just in time for Ronald and Nancy Reagan.

Somewhere, John Francis Endler was smiling.

In the spring of 1980, a lifeboat emerged. The new owners shuffled some deejay staff and Matson was moved to the evening shift. He was now "on the air" from 6 p.m. to 11 p.m., a better fit for his biorhythms but a lateral move for his ambitions. Instead of pushing buttons for Larry King, he was now pushing buttons during baseball game broadcasts. The Royals were a powerhouse that year, winning seemingly every night led by George Brett flirting with a .400 batting average.

At least now he could sleep when it was dark and start to feel more like a normal human and not an outlying creature of the night. The optics of his addiction were more appealing. No one would look askance at putting away a few beers after getting off work at 11 p.m. The same was not true at 7 a.m.

The evening shift also robbed him of *Nightwatch News*, and he began to think about Roxanne's advice. Still a disc jockey at age 50? He was already reduced to glorified button-pusher at age 21. The notion of radio news seemed to linger. He'd seen and heard enough of the KAKE radio newscasters to have at least a ballpark sense of what they do.

No one leans into Bani-Sadr, Ghotbzadeh, and Jaruzelski like me.

"I don't want to be just another voice in a raging sea of mediocrity," he cried on Roxanne's shoulder. "Crappy deejays are a dime a dozen."

"You may be too serious to be a successful high-level deejay," Roxanne's influence was beginning to surface. A few days after this conversation, she flagged him down.

"I talked to Keith Williams. He's expecting your call."

"Thanks, Rox." He was excited and nervous at the same time. "What should I say to him?"

"Frame it up. Start with Brown, then *Nightwatch News*, deejay, then talk about your aspirations." She lifted a finger as she ticked off each point. "Just be yourself."

"Should I tell Gene?"

She shook her head slightly, gave him a half-smile and a four-finger wave off. Roxanne didn't tell him, but Gene was already clued in. She had covered that base herself.

He rolled down the driver's and passenger's side windows on the LeMans and headed for Amidon Square, stopping at Mr. D's to fetch his nightly Coors Light twelver. There was hardly anyone left from the glory days but walking in still filled him with a warm sensation of comfort and familiarity.

When he worked there, he was the one called upon to serve the VIP customers, the issuer of nicknames, the instigator of courtesy boy lingo, the winker/nodder with attractive housewives in their Oldsmobile Custom Cruiser station wagons.

He had manipulated and controlled his immediate environment to suit his needs to a point where he knew exactly what to expect. It was his stagecraft. As much as any place these days, Mr. D's still felt like home.

A girl he didn't recognize in the booth made an intercom call for courtesy help up front. The next iteration of Duck, a logical chronological successor. Did this girl's power and authority over courtesy boys stem from her ability to mold and influence personal relationships or had Gary D.'s thinking about human resources evolved? Was this girl now standing on Duck's shoulders as a full-fledged assistant manager?

A high schooler in a spotless dogshit tan apron was stocking dairy, hauling ass. He watched as the kid holstered his Garvey, moved his milk-laden cart away from the case to allow shoppers' access, and made his way up front.

Must have just passed 90-day muster.

Matson stepped over to the dairy cooler to inspect his work.

Steffen's whole milk gallons. 159¢.

He shook his head, let out a sigh, clutched the twelver to his breast, and headed for a checkstand, thinking about his aspirations.

Even before the stations were sold, KAKEland featured two distinct and separate newsrooms: TV and radio. Keith Williams was the News Director for KAKE Radio, which prided itself on real journalism, and helped position the station as a ratings leader in the market. *RumpInTheMorning* was escapism. KAKE Radio News was reality. A full-service radio station, meeting all your emotional needs.

The radio newsroom featured reporters, most of whom doubled as news anchors who, armed with cassette tape recorders and microphones, would cover spot news like fires and multi-vehicle pileups that snarled traffic, but also regular beats like city government and the cop shop. These journalists would develop and nurture sources and often dig deep into certain news stories with extended "mini-docs;" 3-minute self-contained packages of enterprise broadcast journalism which often piggybacked the local radio newscast.

Williams was also the force behind the creation of a new statewide radio news network, made up of about 60 radio stations in communities across Kansas. From KAKEland via satellite, the network offered 5-minute broadcasts featuring Kansas-centric news at the bottom of every hour.

The network's news content—the actual journalism— came from the KAKE Radio newscasters, staffers at the 60-stations, and a two-person reporter crew in the Kansas Statehouse in Topeka, covering state government.

Surely, within this vast milieu of broadcasting, with all these bodies running around gathering, writing, producing, and anchoring radio news, would be found an opportunity for a bright, young, eager Kansas broadcaster. If he could pronounce Abolhassan Bani-Sadr, Sadegh Ghotbzadeh, and Wojciech Jaruzelski, then Wabaunsee (wah-BUN-see), Arkansas (are-KAN-zuhz), and Marais des Cygne (mare-uh-duh-ZEEN) would be a breeze.

"Have you ever interviewed anyone?"

"Well, I got to ask Marie Osmond a few questions when she swung by here before her concert a couple months ago."

Williams smiled at this, thinking, "About what I expected."

The truth was Marie was interviewed by Gene Rump during morning drive and before Rump shooed him out of the studio, Matson's two off-air questions consisted of, "May I take your coat?" and, "Would you like some coffee?" He remembered Marie's gleaming smile, fire engine red-lacquered fingernails, and her polite "No, thank you" to each of his penetrating queries.

"Have you ever written a news story?"

"Uh—no, but I've ad-libbed around stories others have written when I produced and anchored *Nightwatch News.*"

"Produced" and "anchored" were purposeful choices, as it began to dawn on him what he considered a full-blown job interview was to Williams, merely a professional courtesy, a favor to Roxanne Reynolds.

Williams kept it short, with no sugar coating. To work in radio news in a market the size of Wichita required actual radio news experience. Journalism, not just pronunciation.

Williams was saying the same thing Bruce Browning told him two years earlier over lunch at the arches which are, were, and shall ever be golden. Get your foot in the door.

Advice, it turns out, is universal.

He was gonna have to go to Bumfuck, after all.

BUMFUCK

33.
October 14, 1980

When the upstairs neighbors' leftover spaghetti came up through his kitchen sink, he was done.

Hays was a college town and he got there a month after the fall semester had started. The best rental housing had been snapped up, and he ended up in a dank, musty basement apartment with limited amenities. The landlord promised to install a fiberglass shower stall if Matson signed a six-month lease. Otherwise, it was sponge baths and an extra dab of Hai Karate.

Citing the plumbing deficiencies, Matson negotiated a month-to-month deal. When the spaghetti made its appearance three weeks later, he was gone the next day, to a two-bedroom apartment. It was more space than he needed, it stretched his finances, but it was shiny, clean, and the neighbors' noodles went where they were intended. The new place was close to the radio station, not that it mattered. You could get from one end of Hays to the other in 10 minutes.

KAYS was like KAKEland, Jr. on the High Plains. A television station and accompanying AM radio station built and nurtured to success by Kansas broadcasting pioneers Ross Beach and Bob Schmidt, like Umansky, tuning the resonant frequency and finding the bandwidth balance between serving the community and earning profits. The riches really rolled in when they acquired the cable TV franchise.

Matson was hired to write, produce, and anchor radio news on KAYS-AM, operating at 1400 kilohertz broadcasting music, local news, sports, and farm markets in a coverage footprint bound by Holdrege, Nebraska on the north, Salina to the east, south to Greensburg, and west as far as Colby.

Roxanne had whispered in Frank Dunn's ear, Frank picked up the phone and called his good friend BoB Templeton (that's how he spelled his first name), general manager of KAYS Radio, and within days, Matson found himself in Hays, dodging used pasta.

Management had just cleaned house in the newsroom. The reasons were a little fuzzy, but warm bodies were needed, yesterday. Broadcasting had always featured a revolving door aspect for entry-level newsroom jobs, especially in small and medium markets. Get your experience and move up. Hard work, long hours, little pay.

With a large, seemingly limitless pool of "talent" eager to break into broadcasting, management had struck on a business model that worked.

When Matson arrived in Hays, all that was left was a guy who anchored the TV news but did no gathering, writing, or reporting, and a local jack-of-all-trades know-it-all with good instincts but shaky camera presence and lousy social skills.

When the newsroom was fully built out, there would be four of them. One spot was reserved for what could only be described as a token female. She would enterprise human interest feature stories and serve as "TV weather girl" at six and 10. The token female when Matson arrived was married to a minor league ballplayer in the New York Mets farm system and was off to Port St. Lucie when spring training rolled around.

They were responsible for gathering, writing, and

producing news for morning, noon, and evening drive-time hourly radio newscasts, and news, weather, and sports for two half-hour television newscasts at six and 10 p.m. The "six strip" or "ten strip" lingo was a vestige of early industry scheduling, when programming would appear as a strip, straight across the weekly calendar.

While each had certain specific duties, they cannonballed into the deep end of the work and shared the load. When Matson was reporting a TV news story, one of the others would run the camera and vice-versa. Another would dub the audio from the videotape, for use in the radio newscasts. Literal on-the-job training.

At home, the Thursday night of his first week in the scuzzoid basement apartment, he tuned his General Electric Performance Television to KCKT-TV, Channel 2, Great Bend, the only station in the area that could even remotely be considered competition.

Game 1 of the 1980 World Series. Joe Garagiola, Tony Kubek, and Tom Seaver calling the action. After three years of failing, the Royals, now his KAKE Radio control board Royals, had finally made it past the Yankees in the American League playoffs and were in the fall classic.

Earlier that day, he learned the meaning of "other duties as assigned."

"Where's this new guy—Madison?" The bellowing voice came from a bull in a china shop barreling down the hallway, bound for the newsroom, poking his head in various production studios along the way.

"That's Bernie Brown," local jack-of-all-trades with shaky camera presence said. "He manages the TV side. Before TV, he was a barber."

"Are you Madison?"

Eager to please, he jumped up and extended his right hand. "It's Matson—Mike. It's a pleasure to... "

"Get a haircut," Brown interrupted, ignoring the outstretched hand. "You're anchoring the TV news on Saturday. Sunday, too."

He remembered last year's World Series at Frank Dunn's party. Sister Sledge and we are fam-a-lee. Then, the overlooked all night deejay at the kitchen table, wanting desperately to be in the living room with the cool kids.

What a difference a year makes. He was going from being an entertainer who could count his listeners on two hands and maybe a foot, to an informer of the masses. Frivolous to serious. Ignored to being paid attention to. It was now his job to inform all these people living in the High Plains of the goings-on relevant to their lives on radio and TV. Every day.

A journalist. A broadcast journalist. Gonna be on TV this weekend.

Pecking order-wise, the four grunts were separated from the KAYS stars. The six and 10 strip news anchor was strictly TV, and Bob Davis was strictly radio.

Matson connected right away with Davis, who would later become a household name as the Voice of the Kansas Jayhawks and on Royals' broadcasts. At KAYS, Davis called play-by-play for local high schools, Fort Hays State University football and basketball, and the occasional American Legion baseball game.

Davis would saunter nonchalantly into the newsroom 30 seconds before his sportscast was to air, grab some wire copy off a nail in the wall, make his way to a microphone while "carefully editing and compiling at the High Plains Sports Desk," blow right past the headphones, hold his finger to his ear to feel the vibration of his voice on his skull, and deliver a flawless sportscast.

Mike came to admire Davis' talent, but even more, his cynicism, grounded in experience. Davis did nothing to hide his disdain for the television side of the operation, often detouring into the newsroom to select a newspaper or magazine, *en route* to the facilities, telegraphing his intentions to the four of them by intoning, "I'm gonna go take a television."

Davis was hip to Mike's now fading big league baseball play-by-play aspirations and buttonholed him one summer weekend for a road trip to nearby Russell and allowed Mike to call a couple of innings of Legion baseball on the air. Seated next to a real pro in a makeshift broadcast booth in Russell, Kansas, watching Bob Davis in action, put the final nail in that coffin. News was his future. He would cast his lot with broadcast journalism.

The opportunities to build real friendships seemed scarce. Davis was a dozen years older and married. Local jack-of-all-trades was third tier. Hays had its share of night spots, including a club called The Home, where college kids and the college-aged gathered as a throng to drink beer and dance.

Matson went a few times and couldn't help but compare it, unfavorably, to Pogo's. There was a disco ball and a half-ass strobe, but he could not bring himself to call it a disco since it had no lighted dance floor.

Lots of feathered hair. A few rabbit fur waist length jackets had even made their way to Hays. But there was no Hustle or Bus Stop. No four-on-the-floor. No Duane the Man. No postgame chicken-fried steak at Kings-X.

No goddamn subculture.

Mitch Burns and Roxanne Reynolds were right. Big fish, small pond. Waist deep in the "look at me" business, by choice, but he struggled to find the sweet spot between people actually recognizing him and feeling comfortable with it.

34.
June 14, 1981

"Raw hamburger? Jesus Christ, I don't want to get food poisoning!" Jim Larkin screwed his face into a question mark as the delicacy was placed on their table, accompanied by a stack of saltines.

"I know. I thought the same thing," Matson reached for a table knife and spread some of the concoction on a cracker. "Then, I tried it."

Lean ground beef mixed with onion, tabasco, garlic, and other goodies was a fixture at Mary Kay's, a watering hole that carried on the traditions of the Volga Germans who settled in the area in the 1870s.

Vestiges of the culture were everywhere. Devout Roman Catholicism featuring ornate, hand-crafted limestone churches with towering spires in the villages surrounding Hays. A community-wide Oktoberfest, which Matson interpreted as an excuse to get drunk in the daytime. Many old-timers still clung to the old country dialects, and the name of their community came out as "Hayce."

"Plus, when you wash it down with enough of these puppies," Mike said, lifting a frosted globe of red beer, "whatever bacteria remains crawling around in your gut, are neutralized." A brief pause. "IS neutralized. Is 'bacteria' singular or plural?"

Broadcast journalists gotta know these things.

"After a few of these," Larkin reached for his globe, prioritizing, "who gives a shit?"

"Happy days." Matson hoisted his globe toward his new friend, who returned the gesture and the toast.

A native of Longmont, Colorado, Larkin was four years younger. Like him, Jim sought experience. He wanted a career in television production and KAYS-TV was his foot in that door. While Matson skewed disco, Larkin leaned cowboy.

They connected over sports. Jim worshipped the Denver Broncos and the New York Yankees. On Matson's 25th birthday, Larkin took him to Mile High Stadium for his first in-person NFL game. The Broncos succumbed to a second half comeback by the Atlanta Falcons, and the boys drowned their sorrows all the way back to Hays, their empties littering the median and shoulders of I-70 eastbound.

A couple of months earlier, their Coors Light-fueled boisterousness prompted complaints from neighbors as they chose sides in the 1982 World Series. A traditionalist, Larkin preferred the St. Louis Cardinals while Matson hitched his star to skipper Harvey Kuenn's slugging Milwaukee Brewers, nicknamed Harvey's Wallbangers.

The next summer, Larkin rounded up a half-dozen KAYS chums, declared himself commissioner, and formed a Statis Pro baseball league, a board game precursor to online fantasy baseball.

Matson's team, the Hays Haze, donned home whites trimmed in maroon and sky blue. On the road, they wore sky blue unis, with a maroon jersey/white pants combo reserved for Sunday afternoons.

Steve Carlton on the mound, Terry Kennedy behind the plate, Julio "Won't You Take Me on a Sea" Cruz at second, Jack Clark in left, and a reserve outfielder named Thad Bosley, selected solely because Sharon Kent, the most recent of the token females in the newsroom, had a cat named Thad and

Matson wanted the talking point.

The Haze played their games in the 70,000-seat Hazedome, and when a Haze player homered, strategically placed fog machines would emit clouds of haze that would rise to ceiling vents for atmospheric disbursement, while scoreboards and the public address announcer would scream the team's mantra.

"The fog has lifted!"

When he sized up his relationship with Larkin, Matson drew comparisons to Inglewood and Duane the Man.

In Colorado Springs, Inglewood's marriage to Jennie was on the rocks. When he visited, he spent time with each of them, separately. Jennie seemed easier to talk to than Mark, and he worried not only about what happened to the marriage, but more importantly, what had changed in their friendship, now ten years since they met in high school.

He thought about that day at Rea Woodman Elementary, when he stood next to his best friend and handed over the rings that symbolized eternal love, a forever commitment. Two cars later, Jennie's garter still hung from his rear-view mirror. Shortly after he got to Hays, Matson traded the LeMans for a 1981 Toyota Corolla. His first new car. Five-speed manual, sunroof, no air conditioning.

It was different with Duane. Maybe because the two of them had never declared themselves best friends, the pressure was off. They'd touch base occasionally on the phone and then forget about each other until the next phone call.

He considered Jim his best friend, but the guy code prevented it from being verbalized. He was Inglewood's best man, but now, they never communicate. Maybe there should have been more verbalization. Maybe the guy code was flawed.

Just before moving from Longmont, Jim had tied the knot with his high school sweetheart, and when Mike and Sharon became Mike and Sharon, the four of them were often inseparable. Jim's wife, Tammy, was a mother without children, and Mike and Tammy developed a schtick. He would call her "Mom." She returned the favor with "Son."

In a particularly rowdy round of Statis Pro playoffs, Larkin's 17th Street Bombers eked out a sketchy victory over a team fielded by a colleague. A Bomber had stolen home with the winning run. But differing interpretations of the rules led to a disagreement, which became heated. Larkin assumed his commissioner's mantle and made a unilateral ruling in favor of the Bombers. It ended the evening's competition, and as it turned out, the Statis Pro season.

"Fuck 'em." After the others left, the two of them decamped to the front porch of Larkin's rental house on 17th Street, coincidentally, just a block east of the house Matson's great-grandfather Fred Bemis built after moving the family to town when the Bemis Pool began to churn out the wealth forty years earlier on the banks of the Saline River, north of Hays.

"My game, my house, my rules." Jim was determined not to let the victory be anything but sweet.

The only relief from the western Kansas summertime humidity came at night, and then only marginally. They dragged the remnants of an iced cooler to the front porch. Some Coors Light and a few cans of rhino piss brought by the Statis Pro player on the short end of the commissioner's ruling.

"Yeah, he was just nursing that can of Bud," Larkin fired up a Marlboro and cracked open a fresh Coors Light, in that order.

"Nursing seems counterintuitive to the whole notion of drinking," Matson shunned the smoke, but joined him in the beer can cracking.

Neither of them said much for a while. The only sounds were cicadas and the rustling of the occasional south breeze, momentary and fleeting. Their friendship had evolved to the point where neither felt compelled to fill in the occasional gaps of silence.

"You think maybe I might have a drinking problem?" As though carried along by a force unseen, Matson's question shattered the front porch reverie. Even the cicadas seemed to cease their chirping.

Matson had been drinking daily since he was 16, in the gateway cooler at Angelo's. No DUIs, no trouble with the law. The blackout in the Cities nagged at the corner of his consciousness.

Just that one, though. No others before or since.

He was now 25. It was the first time in his life he felt compelled to gather data other than his own on this thought.

Genuinely concerned, Jim set his beer down, flicked his cigarette ash, and turned to directly face his friend.

"You don't drink to get drunk, do you?"

"'Course not." Had he not answered immediately, the silence itself would have revealed the truth.

Some fog was lifting, though he was nowhere near acknowledging it.

35.
September 16, 1981

In less than a year, the TV anchor who gathered no news moved up and out, and Matson was promoted to news director, anchor of the six and 10 p.m. news, and co-host of the noon talk show. He waited 60 days, then sat down with Bernie and pitched an idea. Lose the stand-up podium-esque news set in favor of a two-person seated set. Him and the revolving door token female. She would still do the weather; he would do sports; and they would share news anchoring duty.

It was an idea he and Jim cooked up together. Mike had the notion of two anchors splitting the duty. Jim sketched out the set design, complete with a new Channel 7 logo, and suggested Matson pitch it.

"He'll listen to you," Jim was already catching on to the centers of power and influence in the broadcasting industry. "You're talent."

Bernie loved the notion of upgrading the set, "Drag it into the 1980s." But his eyes really lit up at the thought of losing an entire full-time position. For a barber, his television production design instincts were solid, but his bottom-line budget skills were even better.

When he succeeded Cronkite as anchor of the *CBS Evening News* in March of 1981, Dan Rather signed off using "Until tomorrow." It would be a few years before Rather mustered the courage to sign off by saying, "Courage."

Matson's signoff was designed to sound purposefully

casual.

"That concludes our 7 News broadcast tonight. We'll return tomorrow—at six and 10. On behalf of (insert name of weather girl and sports guy *du jour* here), I'm Mike Matson."

At which point, he would pause, nod at the camera with self-confidence, and break into a big smile.

"Thanks for watching."

It was as though he was the 1980's equivalent of Edward R. Murrow in Hays, Kansas. Murrow broadcast from the London blitz, profoundly intoning, "This—is London."

There was no German blitz of London. Only Volga Germans, their raw hamburger, and red beer.

This—is Liebenthal.

With bright brown eyes, porcelain skin, and a dry, sardonic wit, the ingredients were there.

Sharon Kent was a child of rural western Kansas culture, and like many, matriculated as a matter of course to Fort Hays State, where she earned a pair of degrees in communications. Whether winning prize blue ribbons for showmanship with her quarter horses or performing in high school and college stage plays, Sharon's communications talent and ability was more artistic, while his was finding a solid journalistic groove.

Her father was a quiet, unpretentious farmer, her mother, a domineering personality with rigid ideas for her daughter's conduct, style, demeanor, pretty much everything.

"Sounds a lot like my old man," he told her in their courtship phase.

"My mom has some pretty lofty expectations," Sharon replied.

"I voted with my feet and then kept my distance," Matson

said, walking her through his action plan featuring Woodgate, six months before his 18th birthday.

"It worked, mostly because James E. considered it normal. 'Raise up the kids and turn 'em loose. You're on your own.'"

"My mom's the polar opposite," Sharon explained. "Raise up the kids and then try desperately to hang on to them when they eventually leave home."

Sharon still struggled with her mother's influence, which at its peak had led to a pair of hospitalizations right out of high school for "emotional exhaustion." He felt bad for her, but could not see beyond his own solution. It had worked for him, why wouldn't it work for her?

Matson may have pinpointed his old man's way of being, and Sharon had figured out her mother, but given her experience, Sharon had the definite edge in self-awareness.

He woke up drunk.

That's a first.

Sharon had a waterbed and by the time he dog-paddled his way to terra firma, she was already up and at 'em and reminded him that it was billed as a party to last the entire weekend.

"It's only 7:30 on Sunday morning," she said, emerging from the bathroom, perfectly coiffed and made up. "We're good for at least twelve more hours."

Their hosts were the parents of a colleague, who seemed perfectly at ease hanging with their daughter's friends. Daddy had bagged his limit of pheasants on opening weekend in nearby Trego County. Mom was practiced in the culinary arts as it relates to wild game prep. Pheasant in mushroom and wine sauce for dinner last night.

He abhorred mushrooms, and preferred his Riunite Lambrusco in a wine glass, thank you very much, but by dinnertime (the locals called it "suppertime") Saturday, was sufficiently past the point of inebriation to care.

The 48-hour party had discombobulated Matson's traditional hangover management. He had a whole menu of tactics that were mixed and matched to fit the circumstances. Before retiring, he would very often stick two fingers down his throat to void whatever alcohol that lingered in his stomach before it reached the bloodstream.

On the other end of the party chronology, another fav was to take a few slugs of Wesson oil before he started drinking, ostensibly slowing the rate at which the alcohol was absorbed into the system.

His tried-and-true was the four Excedrin before and after. He was purposeful in purchasing the pill bottles with traditional pop-off lids. Experience had taught him the childproof ones were often too much to manage after a night of partying.

Today, none of those tactics were deployed, and he had slept only a couple of hours. As he swam to the bathroom, he remembered: he was supposed to wake up drunk. The weekend party was engineered this way by design. Their hosts were expecting them back by 8 a.m. to kick-start the frivolity on Sunday morning.

Sharon was eager to fit in, and completely at ease in social settings. She took charge, called Jim and Tammy, who had awoken similarly on 17th Street, and told them they'd be by to pick them up in 10 minutes.

"Punch it, Matson. Some vacuum-sealed Tupperware containers of leftover pheasant are beckoning me," Jim announced as he and Tammy poured themselves into the back seat of the Corolla.

The air in the car reeked of residual partying. All four had showered, but with so much individual intake, the alcohol fumes were oozing through the pores of their skin.

36.
June 4, 1983

By the time they got married, Sharon had parlayed her television exposure into a job as exec of the Hays Arts Council. Better hours and more money. She managed an art gallery downtown, featuring the works of local artists, built relationships with deep-pocketed locals, and convinced them they were culture-minded patrons of the arts, regardless of whether they realized it.

He was thrilled. Not only did it better suit her abilities, it cleared the way for him to be the lone family big fish in a small pond.

His most vivid memory from the wedding was the preacher shutting down a photographer mid-ceremony. The bride and groom looked wide-eyed at each other and then to the preacher, silently encouraging him to let it go.

Kenny Johnston made the trip from the Cities. No Burns or Donna. No Inglewood, Jennie, or Duane the Man. No Duck. The trend lines of earlier relationships were sloping downward.

Jim and Tammy served as best man and "best woman," Matson lingo for matron of honor.

Mike and Sharon moved into a luxury four-plex with a fireplace, just northwest of the radio and TV station. He began to equate fireplaces with high-end living. The two of them dined regularly at a fancy restaurant on the top floor of a downtown bank building, where they were often recognized. Occasionally, Matson would be asked for his autograph.

Before affixing his name, he would alternate between, "Best wishes" and "Good luck."

He was in love with his wife, but down deep where it really mattered, he was more in love with the idea of being in love. Matson had begun to think of himself as a Young Upwardly Mobile Professional. He had the look, the domicile, the marriage, the cat named Thad, and the career success.

Young Upwardly Mobile implies motion and he was ready to move.

The statewide radio news network Keith Williams dreamed up in the KAKE Radio newsroom, now under the ownership of the oilfield supply boys, needed a radio news anchor/reporter. Williams had moved on, but the new management was familiar with Matson's voice and journalism from the local reports he would contribute to the network from Hays.

He left Hays with levels of skill and confidence markedly higher than when he got there. He had learned the basics of a calling so ingrained in the American culture it was protected by an amendment to the Constitution.

The glamour of local television would be traded for statewide exposure on the radio. His voice and journalism would be on the air in 60 Bumfucks.

Four years earlier, when he got to Hays, he was doing battle with the neighbors' spaghetti. When he left, he was basking in the warmth and glow of fires built in his fireplace.

Back to Wichita for a second time. The first time, he came back defeated by love, eager for the comfort of old friends and familiar places. This time he was coming back as a young married man on the move.

Confidence inexorably intertwined with ego.

The second Wichita experience was short-lived.

As broadcasters, the oil field supply boys were really good oil field suppliers. When KAKE Radio was sold and separated from KAKE-TV, only one of them got to keep the call letters, so 1240-AM became KAKZ and moved downtown. The divorce was amicable, but KAKEland was torn asunder.

Falling back on their vast reserves of experience at programming radio stations, the oil field suppliers punted KAKE Radio's successful adult contemporary format in favor of something called "The Music of Your Life," featuring big band swing music and early pop crooners.

Goodbye England Dan & John Ford Coley. Hello Benny Goodman.

On its face, the format seemed counterintuitive since their target audience was literally dying off.

The music of your death?

When a white knight in the form of a family-owned communications juggernaut out of Topeka came sniffing around the radio networks, the oil field suppliers jumped at the offer. Stauffer Communications owned the *Topeka Capital-Journal*, WIBW-TV, an FM station, and WIBW 580-AM, arguably the most important and influential radio station in Kansas.

Stauffer was a glossy, successful media company, and their purchase of the radio news, agriculture, and sports networks seemed like a natural move. Success was all but assured.

The transaction involved hardware and a pair of soft-tissued assets: the satellite system, three news-gathering consoles (which allowed recording on reel-to-reel and cassette), and some other assorted and sundry gear. To staff the radio news network, Stauffer had their eye on Matson and a colleague. He was hired as managing editor of the network, and when Stauffer picked up his moving costs from Wichita to Topeka, he knew he was upwardly mobile.

Mike and Sharon toasted their good fortune with bottles of Coors Light, and for the second time in less than a year, made plans to move.

He left Wichita with mixed emotions. It would always be home. There were far too many memories for it to be anything but. He would miss the pizza and pasta from Angelo's. Woodgate, Mr. D's, and Pogo's were already lodging themselves into his permanent consciousness. Inglewood, Duane the Man, and Duck. Life-molding relationships and experiences. Now, fond reminiscences.

Wichita was where he started drinking, and his intake had been trending up incrementally ever since. On rare occasions, Matson thought about his blackout in the Cities and that night in Hays when he screwed up the courage and asked his best friend's opinion on his drinking. Deep down, where it's uncomfortable and squirmy, he knew the truth then.

Maybe he knew Jim would defend or deflect. It's human nature.

Addicted?

Perish the thought. Jim's response that night didn't buy any peace of mind and allowed him to push the thought down deeper.

If I don't think about it, I won't have to sweat it.

That was three years ago. He sure as hell wasn't drinking any less, but the career success spoke for itself and crowded out any lingering doubts. If he was in middle management in the biggest and most successful media company in Kansas, how could he have an addiction?

The highlight of their brief time back in Wichita was the arrival of their son. Scott Michael Matson made his first appearance, happy and healthy, two weeks after his due date on an icy last day of January 1985. Sharon's OB-GYN said if they didn't induce that day, she would end up giving birth to a third grader.

When she learned she was pregnant, Sharon quit drinking and partying. He chalked this up to love and intelligence. Matson's intake never wavered. He had no fetus in the womb for alcohol to harm.

For the first time, she now had a clear-eyed view of her husband's behavior.

THE STATEHOUSE

37.
September 29, 1986

At 32 years of age, the lieutenant governor of Kansas would show the world and the voters that he was full of vim, vigor, and up to the physical, mental, and emotional rigors of being governor.

Tom Docking would barnstorm Kansas for 24 hours straight.

Four years earlier, Docking was plucked from tax attorney-obscurity in Wichita to serve as running mate to an incumbent Democrat seeking re-election and prevented by the state Constitution from seeking a third consecutive term as governor. Neither prowess in manipulating modified adjusted gross income, nor political experience, were behind the selection. He was picked for one reason only. In Kansas political circles, his last name was golden.

The son and grandson of popular Kansas governors, Docking gave off the vibe that he was running for governor not out of ambition, but obligation. By 1986, he had shucked his metal framed glasses in favor of contact lenses and crow's feet were enhanced on his campaign posters to add some seasoning.

Docking's general election opponent was Mike Hayden, the Speaker of the Kansas House. At 42, Hayden was only ten years older than Docking, and arguably, more energetic. An ambitious, outgoing Vietnam veteran nicknamed "H.V." by family and friends from his hometown of Atwood, for "High Volume," Hayden's western Kansas loud nasal twang was the stuff of legend in the Statehouse.

Hayden simply had to play "prevent defense" to win. Don't fumble. Don't give the overwhelming majority of Kansas Republicans an excuse not to vote for him. His stump speeches were stemwinders and he would often end by shouting, "Mike Hayden's the kinda guy who'll look you straight in the eye, shake your hand, and ask for your vote." Whereupon he would plunge into the crowd and do exactly that.

"Vote" came out louder and at a higher inflection than the words which preceded it, which cemented the impression of earnest hayseed, just like your neighbor.

Despite his name and heritage, Docking's personality was the polar opposite of Hayden's. Trailing in the polls, his campaign landed on a tactic aimed at illustrating their man, while a quiet, modest, green eye-shade nerd, had the stuff to be chief executive of Kansas.

Wheels up dark and early from Philip Billard airport in north Topeka, touch down in Lawrence, Kansas City, on to Pittsburg, the candidate's hometown of are-KAN-zuhz City, Wichita, Manhattan, Salina, Hays, Colby, Garden City, Dodge City, Great Bend, and 24 hours later, back to Topeka.

Six seats on the airplane. The candidate, a campaign hanger-on, and the pilot would fill three of them, leaving three seats for the media. One went to a *Wichita Eagle* reporter, one to a wire service photographer, and the final seat to an enterprising young radio news reporter representing a statewide radio news network.

Matson was eager to rip off the façade and get the scoop. He was already planning his attack.

"How does stamina make you a good governor?"

"You're 32. Doesn't pulling the occasional all-nighter

come with the territory?"

"You're a Democrat in a GOP state, behind in the polls. How is this stunt going to get you the Republican votes you will need to win this election?"

"Are you expecting a big crowd for that 4 a.m. appearance in Great Bend?"

As a journalist, the personality characteristics that he considered strengths were connected to what some would view as character deficiencies: distrust, an inclination toward confrontation, obsessiveness, and manipulation.

Unspoken tension between print and broadcast journalists would mean the *Eagle* reporter would look down his nose at him. Even as late as 1986, many old-school print reporters could not bring themselves to think of broadcasters as journalists. Too much show biz. If this guy gave him any shit, Matson was ready.

Oh yeah? At 12, I schlepped your rag door-to-door in Pleasant Valley. It sucked then, too.

You will file one story that won't be consumed until tomorrow morning, when unshaven, unkempt Wichitans in bathrobes and slippers stumble into their driveways, scratch where it itches, bend over, and fetch a bundle of newsprint.

And if it rains, it'll be soggy newsprint.

The print reporter may have had more sources and experience, but Matson had the advantage inherent in his medium—immediacy. If Docking said something newsworthy at 9:10 a.m. in Overland Park, he would have it on the air in Goodland, Ulysses, Chanute, and 57 other radio stations at 9:30 a.m. Then again at the bottom of the next hour and the next, on through to the evening.

The dirty little secret, and the campaign knew it, was the candidate did not necessarily have to meet some loosely defined newsworthiness judgment call of a 28-year-old enterprising young radio news reporter. The mere fact that Mike was given a seat on the plane meant Docking's voice would be broadcast to 60 radio stations across Kansas at the bottom of each hour, regardless of the quality or depth of the words that emanated from the candidate's lips.

In the aircraft, he was literally knee-to-knee with Docking, affording an opportunity to engage informally, feel him out, allow him to get comfortable, let down his guard. Then, and only then, would Matson whip out the cassette tape recorder and microphone to go on the record.

He would write and file reports to air during the bottom of the hour newscasts, maybe even squeeze in a couple of live reports, if the timing worked out. The plane would wait for him. Docking and his campaign saw it as free media. Matson saw it as a chance to make his bones as a political reporter.

"...here in southeast Kansas, Docking stresses his Ark City roots and finds subtle ways to remind his audience that his father and grandfather were Kansas governors, hoping that will be enough in November. With the Docking campaign on a 24-hour Kansas barnstorm, Mike Matson, Pittsburg."

"...Docking sticks to his stump speech at each stop, emphasizing his twin campaign themes of 'pride in the past, confidence in the future.' In solidly G-O-P Kansas, he'll need every Democratic vote and a significant Republican crossover, if he is to have a chance on Election Day. He's clearly banking on the family name to pull that off. With the Docking campaign on a 24-hour Kansas barnstorm, Mike Matson, Wichita."

It was all working according to plan, right up until the moment the plane encountered some turbulence high over the Flint Hills after departing Jabara Airport in Wichita, *en route* to

Manhattan. A week past the autumnal equinox, it was Indian summer in Kansas. Hot air rises.

When she saw Mike turning green, Docking's aide reached behind her seat and handed over a 30-gallon black plastic garbage bag.

"Just in case," she smiled, imagining scattershot chunks being blown throughout the cabin at 20,000 feet with her candidate in the direct line of fire barely eight hours into their 24-hour marathon.

The cookies were lost over land just west of Council Grove, and whatever psychological advantage the reporter may have had over the candidate disappeared into the bottom of the garbage bag, along with remnants of the boxed lunch stowed aboard at the downtown Kansas City airport and consumed somewhere over Greenwood County.

When the lunch was launched, the tables were turned. He now needed them more than they needed him.

Plan B. He would deplane and depart the entourage after the 4 p.m. stop in Manhattan.

He could call Sharon and ask her to come fetch him, but she was still at work and that would require daycare re-arranging, baby-driven logistics. It would be two hours before she got there, best case. He had a better idea. Dead head a rental car from the Manhattan airport, drive home and surprise her.

With the aid of being solidly on the ground, and two Pepto-Bismol tablets procured at the Manhattan Airport, his stomach settled about the time he crossed into Wabaunsee County on Interstate 70.

He had filed campaign news reports up until the network

went off the air and had plenty of supplemental material in the can to stretch through the following morning. In his mind, he'd already framed-up two additional stories with separate actualities and a wrapped package that would be network-fresh through noon the next day, at which point the shelf life for stories about Tom Docking's 24-hour Kansas barnstorm would expire.

Gastric acids subsiding, the reflection of the Kansas sunset was glaring in his eyes. Matson reached up and flipped the rearview mirror in the rented 1986 Oldsmobile Ciera to night mode and thought about the cool of the evening. Another pearl from *Ball Four*. Bouton bought into a coach's description of a pitcher's special feeling after he did really well in a ballgame. The cool of the evening. The job well done.

Four years in Bumfuck got him a seat on a candidate for governor's barnstorming plane. When the network was sold and moved from Wichita to Topeka, the new owners wanted him. A promotion, more money, more responsibility.

His reports from the barnstorm were truthful, accurate, and fair, shaded and molded by the personality characteristics that he considered strengths.

Young man on the move.

His personal life was trajectoring on a parallel plane. Sharon had parlayed her multiple degrees in communications from Fort Hays State into a professional-level analyst position with a state government utility regulating agency. They were renting a new two-bedroom townhouse on Topeka's expanding west side. All electric with a fireplace and covered parking.

Since the move to Topeka, Sharon had developed and nurtured new, friendly relationships. He was perfectly content succeeding professionally during the daytime, making a name for himself, and coming home in the cool of the evening to family domesticity.

Sharon would set up opportunities and encourage them to socialize more as a couple, with other couples. He would quote Loretta Lynn's husband, Doolittle, from *Coal Miner's Daughter*, but turn the tables on the outcome, expressing no desire to "hire one o' them thar babysitters and go honkytonkin.'"

Pogo's was ancient history. He had mastered the Hustle in the one place where mastery was demanded. He had outgrown the meat market.

"I don't have any friends here like we had in Hays, or like I had in Wichita." In his mind, his arguments were clear and clean. "It's not that I am incapable of making friends, I just don't need them. I have you and Scott."

He did not object when she started socializing without him. Great father-son bonding time, watching the ballgame, enjoying a cold one, turning the baby on to the finer points of the game, he reasoned.

Sharon's alcohol consumption would never revert to the pre-pregnancy Hays partying levels. After Scott was born, she would enjoy maybe one or two beers a week, while Matson's intake revealed a slow but steady upward creep. From this clear-minded, unimpaired view, Sharon began, slowly, to witness and interpret her husband's behavior as increasingly problematic.

To him, life was good.

Life was so good that unbeknownst to her husband, about a year after their move to Topeka, Sharon had found her own way to Al-Anon meetings, connecting with others who had loved ones in denial, and she began a careful, purposeful campaign, encouraging him to go to an A.A. meeting.

"You're joking, right?" When he saw that she was not, he

slipped deeper into denial.

There was never any physical abuse. Only emotional. The personality traits he had purposefully nurtured that paved the way for professional success, were having the opposite impact at home. He was comfortable as alpha male and had the impression she was just as comfortable as omega female.

"Why should I quit? What's the worst of our problems, that I prefer to stay home rather than go out and socialize?"

"No, I believe the worst of our problems is far worse than that." Sharon had felt the love slipping away for months. "You start drinking the moment you walk in the door and don't stop until you go to bed. Everything, and everyone else, is an afterthought."

With the aid and comfort of those who had experienced the same thing, she had begun to connect the dots between his behaviors and what she had come to believe was his addiction.

His added layer of professional success only bolstered his view. This new edge to his personality that made him a good journalist, did not change once he came home. His manner was consistent. Hers had evolved.

"I'm not an alcoholic," Mike said, beginning to wonder if maybe her mother was on to something by questioning her daughter's emotional soundness. How could she think such a thing?

"I just enjoy a few beers after work... "

Tears welled up in her eyes as she slowly turned around and wordlessly ascended the stairs.

"... like everyone!" He called after her, alone in the living room.

When it became clear the prodding and cajoling was not going to cease, he gave in and went to an A.A. meeting. Not because he thought any behaviors and attitudes needed changed. Because he wanted behaviors and attitudes to remain the same.

I went. Box checked. Why would I return? Those people were friendly enough, but it's some kind of cult for losers. I'm not a loser. I'm a young man on the move. I can quit whenever I want.

There's simply no reason to.

As he pulled the rented Ciera into the covered parking stall at the townhouse, he recognized the car parked in the street in front as belonging to one of Sharon's new friends. Andrew, a professional utility-regulating colleague.

Andrew was on the couch, suit and tie from the office, she was seated opposite him in a matching chair, but circumstances didn't matter. Matson's tone of voice and demeanor set the stage and determined the outcome.

As though scripted by an unseen screenwriter, familiar with addiction and wise to the ways of those in its grip, the three of them were just going through their assigned roles, right up until the moment Andrew got up, departed quickly through the sliding glass patio door, and scrambled over a half dividing wall in his suit and tie.

Addiction centers in the mind and Matson's was made up. If Andrew were innocent, the three of them would have had a polite conversation, he would graciously hint at his need to be going, and would leave through the front door, shaking Mike's hand while accepting vague promises to have him over for dinner one evening very soon.

The world in which Matson was living left no room for such pleasantries. It had narrowed to a worldview revolving around two points.

I am a young man on the move and succeeding professionally. By definition, I cannot have a drinking problem.

I need no one but my wife and son.

Assumptions were made and conclusions were drawn about anything that fell outside the parameters of that narrow scope.

Quickly. Impulsively.

The cool of the evening had dissipated.

38.
September 30, 1986

"It's a race to the courthouse, my friend."

The lawyer was not his friend, but he knew enough about pissed-off, impulsive young husbands to push all the right buttons.

Maybe it was the journalist in him, maybe it was the addict, but Mike's head and heart were a cloud of confusion, and he needed some hard, factual, confirmable answers. Then things would make sense. Then he could formulate a plan.

The attorney was a referral from the guy managing the campaign for the candidate in whose aircraft he had blown chunks the previous day. That morning, after writing and filing his Docking barnstorm follow-ups, Mike made a couple of calls, secured this appointment before lunch, and was gaining knowledge.

It was a typical attorney's office. The man sat in front of an ego wall, filled with framed diplomas, citations, and photos depicting his success in the practice of law.

"If you have even an inkling that she wants out, whomever files first has the upper hand in gaining custody."

It's whoever, not whomever.

Mike liked the sound of that. He was getting better at gaining the upper hand. It gave him an edge as a journalist, and he considered it a vital tool in his young-man-on-the-move kit.

Until now, the notion of divorce had never really been a serious one. He still loved Sharon, but with all her nagging and harping about his drinking, he was beginning to think maybe she wanted out.

Lately, when the thought crept into his imagination, it was surrounded by what he considered his sacrosanct responsibility as a father and the weight and depth of the potential arguments his attorney would bring to bear at the inevitable custody hearing.

"The facts are, your honor, she was at home alone with a male colleague, who ran for the patio door and scrambled over a fence in a suit and tie, rather than remain for a civilized conversation with my client. Those are not consistent with the actions of an individual with nothing to hide... "

"And, as painful and difficult as it may be to bring this up, the truth is, she has a history of emotional instability. Nothing could be more important in determining the safety and well-being of the minor child... "

Case closed.

The lawyer leaned in and recommended three actions. First, a civil lawsuit for divorce on the grounds of incompatibility. Next, a petition for custody of the minor child. Both standard operating procedure in such cases, he explained. A third filing would be an *ex parte* temporary order, which would have the practical effect of freezing two separate lives at the time it was filed. Assets, custody, attitudes, states of mind—everything—pending a hearing.

That third filing, his lawyer explained, would give Mike temporary emergency custody, with no notice given to the other parent. Legally, it would kick in the moment it was officially received by the Clerk of the Shawnee County District Court, and nothing would change until a hearing, which would likely occur within a couple of weeks.

The third order was designed for use in cases where the child was in physical danger. The lawyer did not tell him that.

Scott was in no danger. As angry and scared as he was, Mike knew Sharon was a good mother. She loved her son, and she knew her husband knew it.

Divorce and custody, sure. We'll hash it out. That third filing was pure, unadulterated spite.

Then the lawyer quit talking and stared at his would-be client. All the buttons he had pushed until now, crescendoing to the pushing of this one.

Mike looked back at the lawyer, then he looked at his hands. The right one trembled slightly, so he reached out with it and held tight to the ceramic mug of black coffee offered to him by the firm's receptionist, upon his arrival.

Pissed-off, yes. Vulnerable, no doubt. More knowledgeable about his options, certainly. The lawyer was offering one track. There was no consideration given to any others. None of it gave him peace of mind. All of the emotions started and ended with fear. He was afraid, and afraid to show his fear to anyone, including this lawyer he had just met.

If I don't do this first, she'll do it to me.

Mike had no factual basis upon which to ground that conclusion. Sharon was not aggressive, in fact, when they met, she was barely assertive. She did seem to gain confidence and footing after moving to Topeka and connecting with Al-Anon, even though he believed her underlying premise and assertions were entirely off base. He had no doubt being blindsided like this would provoke anger.

Especially when she got popped with that *ex parte* action. Anger would seem a reasonable reaction.

The lawyer's eyes continued to drill holes in him. His silence, purposeful.

If it were all innocent, Andrew would not have scrambled out and over the patio fence.

"Let's do it."

"I'll file them this afternoon, right before the clerk's office closes," the lawyer said. "Make damn sure you have physical custody of your son by 4:30 p.m."

The Corolla clock read 12:05 as he left the lawyer's office. Just shy of four-and-a-half hours before he would pick up Scott from daycare. Four and a half hours before his *ex parte*-life would kick in. He drove home, packed a suitcase with a few days' worth of his and Scott's clothes, grabbed a sleeping bag and pillow, filled the diaper bag, and folded the playpen.

Across the street from their townhouse, a new apartment complex was nearing completion. He signed a six-month lease effective October 1. Even though that was a couple of days away, because he asked, because he was on the radio and a young man on the move, the apartment complex manager gave him the keys and said it was okay to start moving in some of his stuff right away.

"Possession is nine-tenths of the law," his attorney would have said.

The Crown Colony complex was so new, the apartment buildings on the north end, which butted up against I-70, were in the finishing stages of construction. His was on the opposite end, away from the Interstate, a one-bedroom with a walk-in closet, which he would convert to a bedroom for Scott.

He would measure the space and suit up James E. to whip up a 14-month-old kid-sized bed frame that would fit in the closet and still give his son room to maneuver. He would find a mattress outfit and have one custom made to fit the frame.

When he picked up Scott at 4:30 p.m., a full hour early, he maneuvered the daycare provider into a corner and gave her his pitch, honed on the way over.

"Really sorry to put you in a tough spot, but Sharon and I are splitsville. It may get tense, we both love Scott and want this to be the least disruptive on him as possible. She may call you later, maybe in a panic."

The daycare provider's eyes widened, rapidly determining she had no options, even if she wanted to intervene. Mike is Scott's father. He picked up the kid like he does every evening.

"Tell her the truth. I picked up Scott and he is safe. I intend to call Sharon this evening. Please feel free to tell her that."

Most days, after anchoring the 4:30 p.m. radio network newscast, Mike's day was done, and he would fetch the baby from daycare and nearly always beat her home. This day, upon entering an empty townhouse, she would assume her husband and son were running a bit late. Her first call would be to the daycare provider. She might call the radio station and learn that her husband had taken the day off after writing his Docking follow-ups.

His intent was to get to her before she made either of those calls.

From a pay phone in the clubhouse of the new complex, he had one message for her. Scott is with me, and he is safe. He thought she would assume he was still pissed off about Andrew, that he would cool down and return home soon.

Only when hit with the three legal actions the next day would the real emotional shitstorm rain down and what little goodwill remained between them would dissipate. He said nothing about them.

Of course, she would be angry, but she would also feel scared, and when the enormity of the court filings hit her— that the law now stipulated her to stay away from her baby until a court hearing that had yet to be scheduled—she would feel helpless, even powerless.

"Be pissed, but don't be scared," he was resolute in his manipulation. "You know me. I'm a great father. I can't trust you, but you can trust me."

Scott was excited about the new place and didn't seem to notice his mother was not there. As if to prove to himself and this child's mother he was a man of his word, Matson fed the boy dinner, took him on a walking tour of their new home complex, and played with him until bath and bedtime.

Outfitted in a blue flannel sleeper onesie, the boy was happy and content in the playpen. Especially when he lifted up a blanket and found Myra, his stuffed plush bunny. Short for "my rabbit," named in an earlier, happier time.

"My-wuh," he lit up as he pulled her close and tried to fight back sleep.

"Wuv you, Daddy."

"I love you too, son."

He made sure the boy was asleep before leaving his side. He and Sharon often talked about their good fortune that the kid was a good sleeper. Scott had been sleeping through the night since he was two weeks old.

Tiptoeing into the kitchen, he quietly moved their dinner dishes into the dishwasher. Didn't think to grab any Cascade during his townhouse grab-and-go, but he did bring the essentials. Snagging a pair of twin silver bullets, he pulled his only stick of furniture—a lawn chair, a wedding gift from Jim and Tammy, now that he thought of it—onto his new apartment patio.

The sun had gone down an hour earlier. He thought about

the day's actions, formulating a narrative for public consumption. Before he met Sharon and they had a baby, his mother had described him as a family man without a family. He'd have to find a way to clue her in.

Simple, Mom, she was screwing around on me. She left me no choice.

Probably because he felt he had to, the lawyer, now his lawyer, barely mentioned the possibility of a settlement. His lawyer was not in the marriage reconciliation business.

Scott would grow up the child of a broken home. Nothing could be done to change that now. He had unilaterally torn it asunder. In the all-important race to the courthouse, he was victorious.

Young man on the move.

The darkness was interrupted by lamps positioned near where the apartment complex sidewalks intersected. He leaned out over his patio enclosure, looked north and saw three of them, the furthest two, lower and dimmer, forming a sort of telescoping artist's perspective. He hadn't noticed them in the daylight when he took Scott around.

Back in an apartment complex. Woodgate. Indian Hills. Amidon Place.

This place puts all those to shame. Top of the line. I have my own washer-dryer unit, right in my apartment. Crown Goddamn Colony.

He drained the first bullet and launched seamlessly into the second. He would need to down the whole twelver to catch a buzz, but not tonight. Two full days of mental and emotional stress hit hard as he glanced at his watch. 9:15 p.m. The day/date read "TUE 30."

It had been 27 hours since he felt the cool of the evening.

He took a long, deep pull from his second bullet and counted backward on the calendar.

His marriage lasted three years, three months, three weeks,

and three days.

She wanted me to quit drinking. She's delusional.
Leave me alone.
She wouldn't, so I took some action.
I don't have a problem.

39.
October 16, 1986

Whatever momentum and advantage he may have had with the ambush faded by the time the court hearing rolled around and he got in front of a judge. Divorce? Work out the specifics and report back to me. Custody? That'll take a while, let's feed it into the system. *Ex parte* temporary emergency custody?

"This motion is dismissed." The judge was emphatic.

Mike glanced at Sharon's lawyer, who was smiling, waiting for the judge to say, "with prejudice."

"We'll do joint custody, pending a formal hearing to determine permanent custody of the minor child."

The judge appeared ready to shuffle Matson v. Matson to the pending stack and move to the next case. Instead, he paused, then looked directly at Mike's lawyer, frowning.

"You know better, counselor."

The next six months were a blur of lawyers, judges, social workers, and mediators. As he gained new knowledge and experience in maneuvering the domestic juris prudence system, Mike sensed he was losing the upper hand, bounced his divorce attorney and hired a new one, this one female. She was a pro, less of a shark than the first guy, and he liked the optics.

"Municipal code" and "egress in the event of a fire" are what stuck with him after the court-ordered domestic inspections. Some planned, some purposefully spontaneous.

The social workers were practiced in showing no emotion, but Mike got the impression they had seen more than their share of shitty fathers, and he was being judged and lumped in with the alcoholics, addicts, and guys who thought only of themselves.

Sharon's arguments were legit, he did drink too much, but he had no idea if the social workers had access to her pleadings and hence, no way to know if they came armed with preconceived notions. He was cognizant enough to realize his "perhaps you've heard me on the radio" schtick would be counterproductive but felt uncomfortable and squirmy with putting forth his version of the truth.

I love my son, I am a productive member of society, performing Constitutional commitments.

The social workers seemed unmoved by his arguments, that the first-floor bedroom window was mere steps away. That he stored nothing in Scott's "bedroom," instead shoving his hang-up clothes and shoes in the hall closet near the front door. Nothing was stored on the upper wire shelf rack that could potentially fall off and bonk the kid on the coconut. Matson had even removed the closet door and stowed it in the small, enclosed storage space outside, off the patio.

He showed off James E.'s kid-sized bed frame and accompanying custom-made mattress, seeking to give the impression it was a small, workable bedroom, just right for a two-year-old. He wanted to say, "Surely you've seen worse, from fathers who lack the imagination and innovation to engineer these sorts of temporary workarounds. Surely this proves I am fit for full-time custody... "

He wanted a little credit for his common sense and creativity to be included in the box they were checking for the judge. If the social workers were aware of the case Sharon was making, he wanted to hide that truth and cast their attention elsewhere, to color the conclusions they would draw.

Manipulations and window dressing aside, the hard truth was unavoidable.

The boy slept in a closet.

In anticipation of, "He puts the kid in a closet, Your Honor," by the time of the permanent custody hearing, Matson moved to a two-bedroom townhouse on Topeka's west side, bounded on either side by single mother neighbors.

I guess these are now my people. I guess this is my 'community.'

He traded the Corolla for a 1989 fire engine red Camaro Rally Sport. No subtlety. The single mothers may as well see him coming. Finally, the muscle car he had dreamed of since drivers ed with Inglewood. Scott loved it as much as he did.

"Go fast, Daddy."

"Strap in, son."

As the drama subsided, the momentum shifted to Sharon. After getting her head and heart around the case—and her client—his new lawyer began to manage Mike's expectations.

"There is virtually no chance you will be granted full custodial custody," she warned. "Right or wrong, the courts nearly always default to the mother. Swing by Blockbuster and rent *Kramer vs. Kramer*. It's instructive."

Mike tried to suggest a "This is the 1980s, time for a thoroughly-modern-father's-rights" approach. As a man with enhanced community stature and access to the media, he could bring some disinfecting sunshine to antiquated gender roles and musty inherent system inequalities.

"That would require you to talk out loud about what got you here," she cautioned. "Are you ready to answer questions about your drinking on the radio, TV, and in the papers?"

They both knew it was the kind of question that did not require a verbal response.

The ruling was joint custody. Literally half of Scott's time would be spent with his mother, the other half with his father. His lawyer was thrilled and counseled him that it was a huge victory, the absolute best that could be hoped for, given the circumstances.

Their main ammunition against each other—she used to be bananas, he's a raging alcoholic—cancelled each other out and the system was left with the facts. Both parents loved their son. Both had steady, professional jobs. As custody cases go, the system considered this one was easy and painless.

His life became a dichotomy.

Without Scott, he led with the Camaro.

Larkin and Tammy had gone their separate ways for reasons that were not entirely clear. Tammy returned to Longmont, Jim landed a job in southern California, and Mike flew to the West Coast a few times. Enough that he learned the Burbank airport was less of a hassle than LAX. Jim lived in Arcadia, at the base of the San Gabriel mountains.

Jim and Tammy had split up. Mark and Jennie had split up. He and Sharon had split up. Duane the Man remained blissfully unmarried. Maybe he was on to something.

Some trips west, he and Jim would connect and the two of them would exchange laundered versions of their matrimonial dissolution at sporting events. Santa Anita racetrack, Dodger Stadium, Anaheim Stadium, and Memorial Coliseum to watch Mike's favorite quarterback, Dan Marino, outduel Howie Long and the L.A. Raiders.

Mike had connected with the Miami Dolphins as a kid in 1970, when Don Shula led the aqua and orange to their first-ever playoff berth. In 1984, the season of Sharon's pregnancy, the Fish went 14 and 2 and made it to Marino's only Super Bowl, losing to Joe Montana and the 49ers. Mike had come within a dorsal fin of talking Sharon into naming their son Dan Marino Matson.

Other times, he would sit alone on the beach, drink beer and fantasize. He started in Santa Monica and worked his way south through the beaches of Venice, Manhattan, Redondo, Huntington. He had no idea what he was looking for, but he felt something resembling peace of mind at Laguna Beach in Orange County.

He would rent convertibles, put the top down, and listen to KNX 1070-AM, L.A.'s all news, all talk station, with live traffic reports from helicopters, live reports from the scenes of spot news, cop shops, and city halls throughout the Southland, and exclusive enterprise broadcast journalism not found in the *Los Angeles Times.*

Smooth, seamless transitions. Quarter hour maintenance. Hot track the quarter hour with traffic and weather. Traffic would vary but the forecast would be consistent. Sunny and warm. Major market radio. Hollywood. The pinnacle.

I could do that.

If L.A. was pollution and grunge, Orange County was shiny and clean. Most days, he couldn't even see the San Gabriels because of the smog. At Laguna Beach, when he would flip over on his stomach to ensure an even tan, Mike would gaze over the top of his Ray-Ban Wayfarers at the Santa Ana mountains, looming bright and clear.

He knew he was in the right place when a stunning blonde walked by, clad in a fluorescent lime green bikini with matching fluorescent lime green sunglasses frames, sucking on a fluorescent lime green popsicle.

Hi there. If you've ever traveled through Kansas, perhaps you've heard me on the radio. I'm on the air at the bottom of the hour in 60 Bumfucks.

With Scott, he was the loving, attentive father. Determined to ensure his son grew up as normal as could be expected coming from a broken family.

No doubt, because of the divorce and the guilt, his relationship with his son transitioned into one of buddies. Scott got everything he wanted. Matson didn't have the heart to say "no" very often and when he did, it often morphed seamlessly into "maybe," then "we'll see," which as a practical matter, became "yes."

Nothing was lost in translation.

The boy wanted new toys, but every-other-weekend visits to Toys R Us and Hypermart could be expensive, so they struck on the notion of garage sales. They would cruise Topeka garage sales in the Camaro with rules laid down beforehand.

"You can get three toys, total. We'll go to as many as six garage sales." The idea was to teach some arithmetic and spend no more than 4 or 5 bucks on three new-to-him toys every time he'd visit the old man.

"If I don't find three that I like anywhere, then can we go to Toys R Us or Hypermart?"

"We'll see."

The kid had his old man wrapped around his three-year-old fingers.

At home in the townhouse, Mike would not start drinking until he put the kid to bed, then he had some catching up to do. By then, his body had become increasingly tolerant, and it took more and more beer to achieve the desired objective. "Mass quantities," the Coneheads said.

One night after putting Scott to bed, he polished off the four remaining cans of a Coors Light twelve and found himself frustratingly sober and out of beer.

The clock on the stove read 9:44 as he opened the cupboard door beneath the sink to toss his last remaining empty.

He eased up the stairs and stood in his son's bedroom doorway for a full two minutes. A real bedroom, with a twin bed, furniture, a toybox, poster of Dan Marino on the wall, windows, curtains, and a closet. The works. Blissfully sound asleep on his back. Slow and shallow breathing. Myra, who went with Scott wherever he was sleeping, was perched upright near the boy's head, one ear flopped, the other upright, as though on silent vigil.

What if he wakes up, calls out, and I'm not there? Poor kid'll be scared to death.

He'll tell his mother. What's the legal definition of child abandonment? Neglect? Endangerment? Joint custody could be reduced. Maybe to nothing.

I'll only be gone 15 minutes. I can't go to jail for being gone 15 minutes.

He could ask one of the single mother neighbors to pop over for a 15-minute babysitting gig. But that would mean she'd have to leave *her* kid alone. And he'd have to explain why he was asking this favor.

Well, I'm frustratingly sober and out of beer.

From the front window, he looked northeast and saw the

lights of Fairlawn Plaza. It would not be busy this time of night. He could get in and out quickly. He went back to the kitchen and peered out the window at his Camaro in the carport, as though the car defined him and could provide answers.

When he got back, he raced up the stairs. Still sleeping peacefully, though his son had rolled over.

Thank God.

Myra was now next to him, on her side, both ears flopped down.

There's always a choice, Myra.

40.

December 14, 1988

It had been two months since he had checked himself into rehab. Thirty days since completion. Sixty days since his last drink. He remembered it vividly, hoisting a can in silent celebration as Kirk Gibson hobbled around the bases after a game-winning blast off Dennis Eckersley. Two outs, bottom of the ninth. It was a once a generation World Series moment. A fitting sendoff.

What better way to enjoy the last beer that I will ever drink?

He had always rooted for the Dodgers in their World Series clashes with the Yankees and visiting Dodger Stadium had given it legitimacy. He didn't love them like the Royals, but he didn't need to. All he needed was a rooting interest. A team to drink to.

Mike struggled mightily with the concept of living the rest of his life without ever taking another drink, but the dichotomous life had to end.

With Scott, a loving, attentive father counting the hours until his son went to bed so he could drink. Without Scott, his world had become like it was at Amidon Square. Back then, his outlying working hours kept him isolated. But he was working days now, surrounded by people.

No friends of the Inglewood, Duck, Duane the Man, or Jim Larkin depth. No casual friendships, either. Not because he didn't have the skills to build relationships, because his priorities had narrowed to himself. On occasion, he would drunk dial old girlfriends. To rekindle old flames. To hear a voice.

Friendships imply mutual trust. These days, on the rare occasions when he was around people socially, he'd get frustrated because everyone else drank too slowly and he would find ways to extricate himself so he could go home and drink at his speed.

The dichotomy only seemed to be getting worse. Successful professionally, failing at home, where it's supposed to count.

His pattern had become consistent. Home after work and drink until he passed out. He would generally make it through Carson and tended to pass out during Letterman. At some point in the night, he would wake up and trudge the stairs to his bedroom. He slept in sweatpants and a long-sleeved T-shirt and would change into them after arriving home. No one was coming over, he wasn't going anywhere, and the path from passed out on the couch to passed out in bed was one of least resistance.

He knew his own tendencies.

His expectations of rehab were that he would enter this system and emerge on the other end cured. It was outpatient, 6 p.m. to 11 p.m., Monday through Friday for four weeks, allowing him to continue to succeed professionally in the daytime without anyone knowing about how he was trying to address his domestic failures.

If he were to tell his employer, it would expose weaknesses and ruin his carefully constructed, upwardly mobile façade. Someone at Stauffer would find out, though. The company's group health insurance was recently expanded to cover "mental health and behavioral issues." Maybe a bookkeeper in HR who would process the claim? He would just have to take his chances.

He would be cured in suites of a medical arts office building on the south bank of Shunganunga Creek near 29th and Fairlawn in Topeka. He had found it in the Yellow Pages, under "addiction treatment," between "actuarial consultant" and "advertising/direct mail."

The cure was designed around the 12 Steps, which premised a spiritual component. Patients were encouraged to find a "higher power." He soon caught on it was a nomenclature sleight of hand traced directly to the founders of A.A., who a half century earlier, had encountered hardcore non-believers who wanted to get sober and needed some window dressing.

Mike had no trouble admitting his belief in God, but that's all it was, one-layer-deep belief based on front of the room knowledge passed on solely through a Christianity template, the blanks of which were never really filled in.

For the first time in his life, however, Matson began purposeful conversations with God.

"God, please help me make it through this day without taking a drink," followed immediately with, "please help me to understand your will in my life."

For the first time, rehab forced him to dig a layer deeper— forced him to have the next thought.

All he had to do was open his eyes to get a clear picture that his will, his plan, was not working. His will got him to chemical dependency rehabilitation on the banks of Shunganunga Creek in Topeka, Kansas, in the middle of the 1988 World Series.

Each evening was kicked off with all the patients gathered in a circle in group therapy.

"My name's Sam and I'm an addict."

There was a distinction, apparently, between the

chemicals to which they had succumbed. "Addict" was reserved for those who abused drugs, generally pot, cocaine (crack and powder), meth, or heroin. "Alcoholic" was set aside for those who drank too much.

Matson's addiction was limited to alcohol. Smoking pot gave him a headache. Back in the Mr. D's/Pogo's era, he had been known to pop Dexedrine when pulling all-nighters. They called it speed, an amphetamine that bounced him off the walls. He had tooted a few times, but fear and the price tag put the kibosh on whatever long-term cocaine aspirations he may have harbored.

The treatment did little to knock down what was then an enormous psychological chasm between those addicted to illegal substances and those hooked on a legal chemical. Though Matson was physically, emotionally, and clinically addicted to alcohol, under these rules, he was not an addict, just an alcoholic.

"My name's Sue and I'm an alcoholic codependent... "

"My name's Pedro and I'm an addict/alcoholic... "

Around the circle they went. The woman sitting next to him, ten years older, hoop pearl earrings with a black Lucite Coco Chanel logo, blonde 'do like Marie Fredriksson of Roxette.

"My name's Sandy and I'm a codependent addict/alcoholic... "

Wow. The trifecta.

"My name's Mike, and I'm an alcoholic... "

It was not that hard to say out loud. These people didn't know him, and they were all there for the same reason. And it had the added benefit of being true.

He had no clue what "codependent" meant, but the journalist in him needed to know. He picked up a pamphlet titled, "What is Codependency?" on the way out one evening and read it at home.

They musta stayed up all night thinking up that pamphlet title.

"An excessive emotional or psychological reliance on a partner, typically one who requires support on account of an illness or addiction."

Can you be codependent without a partner? He was a wreck when Malea dumped him. But he took action. Quizzed out of the last quarter at Brown and got a foot-in-the-door job. He was in a bad place when he was convinced Sharon would dump him, but he took some action. Ambushed her with divorce, custody, and an *ex parte* order that kept her away from her child.

On the other hand, he didn't necessarily relish the thought of being considered just your run-of-the mill, dime-a-dozen lush.

How could he have "an excessive emotional or psychological reliance on a partner" if he lived alone? He hung his hat on that technicality and presented himself as strictly an alcoholic.

In addition to all this mental, emotional, and spiritual healing, there was a separate, practical concern that explained the lingo. If the patient suffered from a second malady, in addition to addiction, insurance companies tended to pony up more.

When it came to getting cured, there was a lot to think about.

A couple of other tidbits stuck with him. "Quit drinking and/or using" was a broken record among the counselors.

Duh. OK. Simple as that. If I could do that on my own, I wouldn't be here.

"Stay away from your old crowd."

No problem. I live and drink alone.

He also worried a lot about the biology he learned about addiction. The brain's chemical structure is impacted by chemical abuse and the changes stay with you long after the intake has stopped. This change in brain structure increases the risk of relapse.

In other words, getting cured was not going to be as simple as he thought, at least structurally. When he was sick, he'd go to the doctor. If his car needed a new U-joint, he'd call his best friend. If he was nearsighted, he'd get new glasses. There was always someone smarter, some subject matter expert, some system designed to solve his problems.

Cure me, goddammit.

Rehab reintroduced him to A.A. and moved him off his previous "loser cult" conclusion, drawn after attending one meeting, solely to get his wife off his back. In hindsight, he wondered if maybe that was an impulsive decision, especially since that wife was no longer around.

As a group, the rehab crowd took field trips to A.A. meetings, in two separate venues.

The first was an A.A. meeting house, filled with smoke, grizzled old-timers, folding metal chairs, and bad coffee. The second was a sleek, ultramodern building on the Menninger Clinic campus, tucked into rolling hills north of Interstate 70 that spilled into the Kansas River. He connected with the ambience. No smoke, dim lighting, comfortable furniture, and high-end clientele from all over the world.

If indeed he had a screw loose, he liked the thought that it could get tightened at a world-renowned head shrinking shop, rubbing shoulders with movie stars and NFL quarterbacks.

Sixty days in, the only things that had really changed were the rote prayers and his alcohol intake. From a twelver a night to nothing. He was still isolating. He did go to the Menninger meeting, but only once a week.

Reaching for the remote, he punched up KSNT, Channel 27, the Topeka NBC affiliate. He had what he considered a personal connection with two of Johnny Carson's guests this night.

Everyone from the old crowd bonded with Steve Martin's anti-comedy, conceptual humor, his secret sense of superiority. Michael J. and Duane the Man were among the thousands who jammed Kansas Coliseum in Wichita when he came for a concert during Martin's "white suit/arrow through the head" years.

Actress Helen Shaver had starred as *Jessica Novak*, a short-lived 1981 series on CBS about a token female reporter at a Los Angeles TV station who longed to report the big stories. *Jessica* survived long enough for Shaver to record a personalized promo that aired throughout the High Plains during his big fish, small pond era.

"... I only wish I had a News Director like Mike Matson. He's so adorable... and such a good journalist. See what I mean every weeknight at six and 10 on KAYS, TV-7."

If I am going to live my life vicariously through Hollywood stars and big-league ballplayers, it would go down better with a buzz.

On the way back from the liquor store, ice cold Coors Light twelver resting comfortably in the passenger seat, Mike was not sad or disappointed in himself. Nor was he happy or excited. If forced to pinpoint his feelings, he probably would have said relieved.

I no longer have to worry about how I will live the rest of my life without ever taking another drink.

41.
August 16, 1989

"Mr. Matson, I pulled you over because I observed you weaving outside the confines of your lane. Have you been drinking?"

Yeah, but I'm not drunk. You shoulda seen this guy I was with. Slurring his words, damn near fell down trying to get into his car.

"Yes, I was at the bar with a friend."

The guy he was with was not a friend, he was actually a journalistic source, who worked in a key state government agency and had pointed Matson in the right direction on a couple of news stories. The source had asked if he wanted to hit a couple of bars and Matson agreed. Not because he liked going out; he didn't anymore. He did like nurturing relationships with confidential news sources.

"Step out of the vehicle, please." The cop pronounced it VEE-hickle.

It's VEE-uh-cull.

Matson was convinced that he maneuvered the "nine steps, heel-to-toe, turn on one foot and come back the same way" test with skill and grace. The cop wasn't giving away anything.

"Blow into this," handing him a gizmo with a tube sticking out if it. Mike knew he had the right to remain silent but was unsure how that applied to respiration. He did want to convey cooperation, so he blew.

The cop went back to his cruiser and radioed in to ensure this guy was not a fugitive on the lam from justice, wanted for all sorts of heinous crimes in multiple jurisdictions. Matson remained, leaning against his Camaro. He considered climbing back in to wait but worried the cop might think he was impatient and uncooperative, so he just stood there, hands in pockets.

I'm not drunk. I know my metabolism.

Mike was lost in the reverie of picking up a twelver, going home, and getting drunk. As the cop made his way back to him, he wondered if an apology would ensue.

"Turn around. Place your hands behind your back."

It didn't really register until he heard the second handcuff ratchet into place.

"Mr. Matson, I am placing you under arrest for driving under the influence," Not his first rodeo. All business. "Your breathalyzer test registers over the legal limit."

The cop led him to the back door of the cruiser, Mirandizing *en route*, blue and red bright flashing lights getting brighter with each step.

"Watch your head." Be nice to the first-time offending middle management white guys driving fire engine red Camaros.

"Any questions?"

"What'll happen now?" Mike liked to be in control. Any scrap of information would help him get back there and ward off panic.

"I'm gonna take you downtown, where you'll be booked and processed."

The fear was hitting hard, just like graduation night at Levitt Arena. That fear was grounded in saving face. This one traced upstream to saving his freedom. Getting arrested for drunk driving is a bit more serious than finding a girl to walk with to the strains of "Pomp and Circumstance."

"Then what?"

Anything less severe than, "Overnight in jail, ya criminal," would make him feel a little better.

"Hard to say." The cop was practiced in not communicating anything that could be construed as promises that could not be kept.

"Booked and processed" involved mug shots, fingerprinting, and a lot of sitting in a holding area. It was August. He was wearing khakis, penny loafers, no socks, and a long-sleeved pink chambray shirt with the sleeves rolled up, purchased earlier that summer in Laguna Beach.

He joined three others in the holding area, each at varying points along the chronological spectrum of being booked and processed. Mike sized up his fellow alleged criminals and very quickly determined he was the only courtesy boy clad in togs from Southern California.

Nearly three hours later, he was released on his own recognizance after signing a written promise to appear in court as required. The cops asked if there was someone he could call to pick him up.

Who would he call at two in the morning? Sharon had moved to nearby Lawrence. With their son. The single mothers were sound asleep. Last time he checked, Inglewood was in Colorado Springs. Duane the Man and Duck were in Wichita, Jim Larkin was just down the road from the Santa Anita racetrack.

"No, I'll call a cab."

He remembered someone at the police station telling him not to drive again that night. If he got pulled over again, it was the slammer for sure. Easy for them to say. As a practical matter, how was he supposed to get where he needed to go?

Fearing the cabbie might be a stoolie, he gave instructions to be dropped off a couple of blocks from where he was arrested. As he walked back to his car, he wondered if he would have been pulled over driving an '81 Corolla or '73 LeMans. A fire engine red Camaro is hard to miss when it's not weaving in and out of the confines of his lane. That's sorta the point.

He climbed in, fired it up, cranked the air conditioning wide open, and just sat there for a couple of minutes. The radio was tuned to 580 WIBW, right where he'd left it, listening to the Royals before meeting his source at the bar. Bret Saberhagen went seven strong and Jeff Montgomery shut down the White Sox for a two-inning save.

The top of the hour CBS Radio Network news featured a report from Graceland, on this 12th anniversary of Elvis' death.

That night, he had to know why Laura Wilson was doing him wrong. He had to know so badly that he drove to her house and stalked her until she came home.

Twelve years, three cars, one blackout, a launched career, a failed marriage, a four-year-old son, an unsuccessful rehab, and one arrest later, he sat in his "look at me" car, cold air blowing over him, and obsessed anew.

What if someone finds out? What if I'm convicted?

He creeped home on side streets, avoiding the main arteries.

Don't look at me.

Clearly, he would need a new lawyer. No way could he ask his divorce attorney. Can't have the woman who stood up in court and argued he didn't have a drinking problem defending him on a DUI.

His new lawyer was the boyfriend of a girl with whom he rehabbed at Shunga. About his age, fluent on how the Shawnee County criminal justice system would react to first-time offending middle-management white guys who report the news on the most important radio station in Kansas and 59 others across the state.

"If you admit guilt and make it twelve months with no additional DUIs, it'll be as though it never happened."

By entering into a diversion, adjudicating Matson's DUI would be perfunctory.

"How would you feel about voluntarily going back to rehab? It'll sweeten the pot."

Mike could have kissed him. Diverting the entire prosecution of the case. It was all buttoned down and self-contained. Sharon didn't need to know about it. Stauffer didn't need to know about it. It's almost as if it didn't happen.

Like the blackout in the Cities, the handcuffs, mugshots, and fingerprints in Topeka would be just another skeleton in his closet. No one would know. Plus, now that he'd been through it once, he knew what to say in rehab.

"Hi! My name's Mike, and I'm a pink chambray shirt-wearing, middle-management codependent addict/alcoholic!"

The diversion scared him even more into staying home. He replayed the night of his arrest over and over, second-guessing his decision to go barhopping with his source.

How many times had he driven drunk? How many times had he made it where he was going without incident? It was the same answer to both questions.

Countless.

Mike made it 70 days after completion of his second rehab before relapsing.

He couldn't pinpoint why. Boredom, restlessness, ease, and comfort, maybe. He did know he was an alcoholic and would often stop there, when trying to self-analyze his motivation. He did begin to wonder if maybe he was "constitutionally incapable of being honest with himself," part of the 12-step mantra.

"There are such unfortunates," the mantra cautioned, "they are not at fault. They seem to have been born that way."

If he was truly incapable of self-honesty, what does the rest of his life look like? He genuinely wanted to quit and was still reciting the rote prayers.

There's one surefire way not to get DUIs. Stay home and drink. Can't get arrested for Staying Home Under the Influence.

He was doing Topeka a favor.

42.
November 6, 1990

"It is seven-fifty-one, you're listening to election coverage on 5-80 Radio W-I-B-W. C-B-S News, C-N-N and other networks are predicting Joan Finney as the winner in the race for Kansas Governor. Let's go live to the Kansas Expocentre, where Governor-elect Finney's making her way to the microphones amid a sea of supporters and well-wishers... "

He designed an elaborate, precisely-timed programming clock to allow the 60 Bumfuck radio stations to air their top of the hour national news, fill in with local coverage, then join the statewide network to hear the dulcet tones of Mike Matson anchoring live radio coverage from the studio of the network flagship station, WIBW 580-AM.

"Double-you-eye-bee-double-you." The pronunciation lessons at Brown had stuck.

Matson was jockeying one correspondent at the Republican watch party, another with the Democrats and a pair of inhouse pundits, a professional political operative from each party, steeped in the trends, familiar with the candidates.

A year after buying the network and purposely keeping the journalism and the personnel who produced and reported it separate from the big radio station, the General Manager of WIBW-AM had a Bernie Brown moment. Since the big radio station and the network were producing the same product—radio news—let's merge the newsrooms and bask in the glow of all the efficiencies that will naturally ensue.

Matson was promoted to News Director of the combined

operation, which meant he split his time between the network newsroom on one level of the building and the shared WIBW-TV/Radio newsroom on the lower level.

After five years in radio news for Stauffer's network and flagship station, the election night coverage was to be his radio swan song. In the one part of his life that was working, Mike had decided to double down. He was focused on a career move into politics, not as an office holder, but as a spin doctor. He wanted one job: to be press secretary for the governor of Kansas.

He had seen enough of the way elected officials and their staffs worked to feel confident in his ability to do that job and had concluded that being on TV every night was the path to opening that door. He reversed Donna's late-night advice when he was a KAKE-TV tech pining for radio and she was toiling at the point of entry for the Earth's enema.

There's a television station, right fucking there.

Mike maneuvered his way into the WIBW-TV Statehouse reporting gig. It was a three-way negotiation, with the general managers of the TV station and the radio properties. For the first time ever, his parallel lives met. Matson tried a novel approach. He told the truth. He suffered from a chemical dependency problem and needed 30 days to lick it.

His last day on the radio would be the Tuesday before Thanksgiving. He would start on TV after New Year's Day, 1991.

That night, four-term Democratic Kansas State Treasurer Joan Finney was elected governor of Kansas, ousting Mike Hayden, who apparently did not shake enough hands, look enough people directly in the eye, and ask for their votes.

Finney had come of age as a staff hanger-on to longtime Kansas GOP stalwart Frank Carlson, during a time when the expectations of women in those roles didn't get much beyond running the mimeograph machine or fetching coffee. She ran for the U.S. House in 1972 as a Republican and lost. When the men she thought of as her GOP mentors tried to block her from running again, she switched parties, carried a chip on her shoulder, and never looked back.

Quirky, marching to her own drummer, Finney did not fit the traditional politician mold. On the campaign trail in '90, she said out loud that she believed fervently it was her destiny to become governor of Kansas. Joan Finney would take office in January the same time Matson took over as WIBW-TV Statehouse reporter.

A journalistic gold mine.

But first, another crack at getting cured.

"In addition to the addiction, do you find yourself feeling depressed?" The admissions counselor had the tone of voice and body language that often led to the answers she wanted to hear.

He didn't really, at least not in the clinical sense, but he remembered the dual diagnosis from Shunga Creek, and manipulation had become a default knee-jerk reaction.

"Yes, I'm afraid I do," doing his best to look sad.

Mike would spend Thanksgiving and Christmas in rehab. He was fine with it. Had he been with family, he'd have just been fidgeting to leave early, anyway.

The Cedar Ridge Drug and Alcohol Rehabilitation Center was perched atop a hill overlooking Interstate 435, which served as sort of a beltway ringing the greater Kansas City metropolitan area. The street address was Shawnee, but since the suburbs on the Kansas side all ran together, many people thought it was actually in Lenexa.

Cedar Ridge was situated just across the freeway from the Tomahawk Hills Golf Club, the oldest golf course in Kansas City, carved through the woods and streams into Johnson County hillsides in 1910. The Johnson County suburbs had grown up around the golf course and now it dovetailed perfectly with the image Johnson Countians like to portray.

Mike had called the lead counselor at Shunga Creek seeking advice on inpatient rehab, rationalizing that two outpatient stints didn't take, but surely an intensive four-week cloister would do the trick. The Shunga Creek counselor recommended Cedar Ridge.

When Mike learned it was in Johnson County, he was all in. Close enough to Topeka to be convenient, but far enough away to be considered a specialty.

The admissions counselor asked to see his shoes. He dug a pair of Cordovan penny loafers out of his bag for inspection and lifted up one foot, proudly displaying L.A. Gear high tops with Velcro.

Only later did it dawn on him why they were confiscating shoelaces. He caught on after the cafeteria attendant refused his request for a paring knife to slice a banana to top off his Honey Bunches of Oats.

You'd have to work pretty hard to slit your wrists with a table knife, but they do the job on bananas.

In a rare second thought, he wondered if these preventive measures stemmed from actual experience. Just because he was faking depression didn't mean all his fellow inpatients were.

When he called Sharon to say he'd be out of pocket for 30 days, she negotiated a hard bargain. Clearly happy to take Scott, now just a couple of months shy of his sixth birthday, during Matson's allotted joint custody time. She would even bring him over to Johnson County during visiting hours, but don't expect her to come for family day.

"I can't argue with that," he said, genuinely appreciative of her civility. "We're not really much of a family anymore, anyway."

As more time passed since his *ex parte* ambush, their interaction had improved. When she came to him the summer before Scott started kindergarten with a new time share proposal, she expected another bruising knockdown-dragout, but he didn't put up a fight. Her argument—that the boy needed to be anchored in one home as he starts school—was true. Mike's time with his son decreased from literally half the time to every Tuesday evening and every other weekend.

Their Tuesday evenings in Lawrence were spent at Furr's cafeteria, where the kid could pick and choose his own dinner, and at a video arcade, plugging quarters into *NBA Jam*. Scott would suit up Dan Majerle and Dennis Rodman ("He's on fire!") who would rain three's and bury the random second stringers Matson purposefully selected. ("Can't buy a bucket!")

Mike and Sharon agreed to the change without mediation, and her lawyer had the order worked up as an addendum to their custody case. The thought that it actually freed up more time to do more drinking was always close to the surface. An implied given. He didn't even bother trying to justify it.

The Cedar Ridge dining room faced south and west and offered a panoramic view of the freeway. Breakfast was at six a.m., still dark. Headlights heading north, taillights heading south. At lunch and dinner, if you really looked, you could make out portions of the golf course across the Interstate.

Sunday afternoons were spent gathered around the TV watching Steve DeBerg, Barry Word, Derrick Thomas, and the Kansas City Chiefs. During a beer commercial, Mike felt compelled to point out to his fellow rehabbers that he'd seen DeBerg in action in person, quarterbacking the Broncos that Sunday afternoon eight years ago when his good friend Jim Larkin took him to his first NFL game in Denver.

There was a community phone, but only collect calls were allowed. That's okay, there's really no one to call. All the close friendships had disappeared. He was too proud and embarrassed to call any of them, anyway. Inglewood, Duane the Man, Duck, Larkin. What would he say?

"Well, I'm in rehab again."

"Whaddayamean, again?" No one knew anything about the first two.

They'd sympathize, feel bad or sorry for him. Tell him to hang in there. Then what?

Like Shunga Creek, the Cedar Ridge curriculum was grounded in the 12 Steps. No field trips to A.A. meetings, though. The patients were sequestered and not leaving, so A.A. meetings came to them. As many as a half-dozen people in recovery would take turns leading an in-house meeting every evening after dinner.

Mike knew the lingo, knew what to say, but unlike outpatient, these counselors saw him 24-7, called him on his bullshit, and encouraged him to dig deep.

During a two-on-one therapy session, when Mike sought to arrange the three chairs, the counselor saw a teachable moment.

"Do you see how manipulative you are?" pointing at the three chairs. "You're trying to arrange these chairs to suit your needs, to give you comfort, so that you have some sort of perceived advantage."

Two weeks in, Sharon kept her promise and brought their son over for a Saturday afternoon visit. It was not inconvenient for her. Cedar Ridge was only a half-hour from Lawrence.

Scott rushed to his arms and lit up. "Are you feeling better, Daddy?"

They'd both told him he was sick and needed to spend this time in a hospital to get better.

"I am, son."

The three of them sat at a picnic table in the courtyard. Once Scott saw that his father looked good, was not in a hospital bed, on crutches or covered in bloody bandages, he relaxed. He sensed something was wrong with his father, but it was unseen, invisible.

Their son had brought along some toys, including an eight-inch King Kong Bundy, professional wrestler action figure.

"'Member when we got this guy?" Scott walked mini-Bundy across the picnic table and punched the figure's three-inch arm toward his father. "At one o' those garage sales?"

"I do, son."

He didn't bother trying to stop the tears. The sadness hit him like a wave at Laguna Beach, washing over him, but not dissipating.

"It's okay, Daddy." Genuinely concerned, Scott dropped King Kong Bundy, came around the table, and hugged his father.

"You'll feel better soon."

"I already do, buddy." He looked across the table at his

ex-wife, who was also misty.

Despite all our strife and confrontation, how did we get so fortunate to have a kid this empathetic at such a young age?

As a parent, Mike was determined to be the anti-James E. Was that just going to be lip service? How, exactly, would that work if he could not stop drinking? He could not hide it forever. Sooner or later, the kid would catch on. Maybe he already has.

He imagined the two of them driving back to Lawrence, his son questioning his mother about his father's well-being. He knew Sharon would do and say all the right things and then the sadness submerged him a couple of fathoms deeper. It struck him that when she got pregnant a half-dozen years earlier, she had always tried to make the best of their circumstances and never bad-mouthed Mike around their son.

She knew he had an addiction problem long before he did. Sharon also knew there was absolutely nothing she could do to change her husband's behavior, before, during, or after the dissolution of their marriage. Al-Anon had taught her these things. When he analyzed his role, he had begun to see—for the first time in his life—that every thought, every scheme and plan, every subsequent action was grounded in self.

His will.

God, help me to recognize your will in my life.

When he went to bed that night, he added another prayer to the inventory of rote recitations.

God, please give me the willingness to be willing.

When he shared these feelings with his counselor, expecting absolution, or for her to say something to cheer him up, all she said was, "Those feelings seem legitimate and genuine."

43.
January 8, 1991

The staircase steps were small and closely spaced on purpose, designed for children. Taking them one at time felt like a lot of work without much visible progress. Two or more at a time was just as uncomfortable.

The comfortable balance was never found.

Stauffer's broadcast operations (one TV station, two radio stations, and the three radio networks) were housed in a building that started life as a schoolhouse for orphans on the Menninger Clinic campus, high atop those hills that sloped down to the Kaw. The actual original orphanage was a building right across the parking lot, now used as the Menninger outpatient unit.

The back door to the broadcast building opened to the north, affording a view of Menninger's historic clock tower. Many of the sleek new campus structures could be seen from the TV newsroom's east-facing windows and it was not uncommon for the broadcast journalism professionals to gaze out on individual or pairs of Menninger patients, strolling the grounds.

"Nut—or not?" was a favorite newsroom game. Mike joined in, careful to hide from his colleagues the tidbit that a year and a half ago, at least one night a week during the A.A. meeting at Menninger, according to their definition, one among their brethren was a nut.

Back in Topeka and back on TV for the first time in a half-dozen years, Mike hit the ground running. As Statehouse reporter for WIBW-TV, he had a hole to fill every night. He was the only reporter in the newsroom with a very specific beat, the cottage industry in a state capital—government and politics.

Filling the hole meant enterprising a news story. Every day. These stories would make the air and be consumed by television viewers in one of a host of ways.

A pre-recorded "package," complete with a recorded "standup," featuring Matson on camera spouting part of the narrative script on camera, often used as a bridge between competing arguments; a "live shot" from the Statehouse, ad-libbing in and out of a pre-recorded package, both of which involved writing a script; selecting "sound," which generally involved at least two comments from people he had interviewed, and whatever "natsound" from the b-roll footage was applicable.

Next was "voicing" the script and editing the package, which required two connected behemoth ¾-inch videocassette recorders, one to play, one to record. This work was done in one of two places: in an edit bay at the TV station, or in his statehouse office.

A half-dozen standalone offices on the first floor of the Kansas State Capitol were reserved for the news media. WIBW shared theirs with two other Topeka TV stations and a handful of radio stations, but since WIBW was the only station in the market with the ratings, influence, and resources for a full-time political reporter, most of the time Mike and his videographer had the space to themselves.

If Mike's story did not warrant a 90-second package, he would work up a 45-second "SOT," writing a script the anchorperson would read, leading into "Sound on Tape," known to the masses as a "sound bite." Sometimes trailing with more video, sometimes directly back to the anchor for the next story.

If his story fell even lower in the daily news prioritization, he would write a "VO," a 30-second script for the news anchor to voice over corresponding video. "Wallpaper," in newsroom parlance. At the bottom of the television news food chain was a "reader," two or three sentences, with no video, read by the anchor staring intently into the camera, often accompanied by an electronically generated graphic still image depicting the subject matter.

All these vehicle delivery judgment calls were made by the producer.

In his live shots from the Capitol rotunda, he would tell it like it is. Governor Finney cornered him once on her way out of the office, stood off to the side out of the shot, and listened, as he reported on the challenges the Democratic governor was having working with the Democratic majority in the Kansas House.

"Mike, why do you have to be so mean?"

Live shot over, he tried to engage her.

"Governor, it's not personal. It's journalism."

They were both a little bit right and a little bit wrong.

Some reporters pushed for live shots just to get their mugs on TV. Matson didn't object to live shots, he was good at them, but if the whole idea was to impart information, to scrub the unwashed masses clean with the straight skinny, a pre-recorded package was the way to go.

In radio news, he was "writing for the ear." In TV, the story could be more effectively communicated with compelling visuals and natural sound. He tried to reserve his live shots for stories when he was short on compelling visuals.

Since the market was bigger than Hays, WIBW-TV had

significantly more locally-produced programming, and as a result, more warm bodies in the newsroom. *Live at Five*, which checked the feature/community service box, joined the farm news-oriented noon show, and the traditional news-weather-sports six p.m. and 10 p.m. broadcasts.

Mike's TV news stories had a roughly 15-hour shelf life. They "debuted" at six p.m. and versions of them aired at 10 p.m. and in the following morning's twice-an-hour, four-minute local cut-ins during the *CBS Morning News*.

Now, he was really in what Roxanne had described as the "look at me" business and that briefly worried him when he relapsed again after 90 days. But he reverted quickly to familiar, comfortable thinking.

I can separate these two lives.

A couple of weeks into third relapse, as he picked up his mail, Mike noticed a letter addressed to him in his own handwriting. He momentarily scratched his head, then it hit him. An exercise at Cedar Ridge; his primary counselor had him write to himself, describing how he would feel if he relapsed.

He tore it up and tossed it without opening it. He knew what it said. Shit he didn't want to read.

He obsessed over how she found out. Double agents at the liquor store? Hidden camera out by the pool? Or did she just size him up after being around him 24-7 and know it was a certainty?

44.

August 3, 1991

The top button of his 100 percent cotton, button-down white Oxford (light starch applied at Scotch Dry Cleaners, $1.10, not 110¢, per shirt) was undone. The half-Windsor knot of his maroon and grey paisley necktie hung about an inch below where it started the day.

Elastic maroon braces, trimmed in navy, buttoned inside the waistband of his pants, stretched with him as he climbed out.

The top-to-bottom pleat in his cuffed grey dress slacks remained crisp. The argyle socks, colors matching the necktie, were pulled up immediately after he shut off the ignition.

Before he climbed out of the Camaro, he glanced in the rearview and ran a hand through his hair. After exiting the car and before emerging from beneath the carport, where all his neighbors would see, he had wiped the toe of each shoe on the back of the opposite knee to ensure a quick shine.

If his hands weren't full, Matson would have hooked a finger on the collar of his brass-buttoned double-breasted navy blazer and toted it over his left shoulder.

Young man on the move.

Black leather briefcase slung over his right shoulder, nightly Coors Light twelver in his left hand, keys in his right. Despite August in Kansas, he kept the blazer on. There was nothing of significance in the briefcase, and he sure as hell didn't plan on doing any work at home, but it matched his shoes, the leather strips that connected his suspenders with his pants, and the image he sought to convey.

Just in case someone from the building was looking at him.

Two keys for two doors. An outer plate glass, separating the important people who live there from the riffraff who might otherwise seek to enter.

One building, two separate street addresses. Individual storage spaces in the basement, a shared coin-operated laundry in the basement, and a swimming pool. The buildings were a stone's throw from the south branch of Shunganunga Creek, nestled in a low draw that long before pioneer settlement was a brook that fed into the Shunganunga. The area was still populated by a thick grove of cottonwoods, maples, and elms, a purposeful development feature around which the buildings were designed and built.

The result was a swimming pool like an oasis with a natural shady canopy. If one sought to lay by the pool and get a suntan, one had to be really purposeful about chasing the sun, there was so much tree shade. Mike took it upon himself to skim the leaves from the pool with a net on a long pole. Since he was such a good neighbor, every single leaf needed to be fished out.

Every leaf. Every time.

Each unit had a balcony and a fireplace. His balcony featured two flowerpots containing marigolds. He knew nothing about planting and growing flowers except that he liked the color of marigolds.

His neighbors managed their fireplace ambience one blaze at a time, making do with little bundles of firewood purchased from Dillon's supermarket in the nearby Brookwood Shopping Center. Now a fireplace aficionado, Matson had procured an entire cord and arranged with the landlord to have the logs stacked neatly between a pair of trees down in the draw.

When they saw him traipsing to and from the draw bearing said logs, a couple of neighbors had the temerity to inquire whether this was, in fact, a community cord.

"No, indeed," came the emphatic response.

He shared his wood with only certain of his neighbors.

From the time it opened around Memorial Day until it was buttoned down for the season after Labor Day, he became a regular at the pool with a book, newspaper or magazine, and the requisite cheap Styrofoam cooler.

On his single-dad-weekends, they'd see him in the pool playing keep away or water football. They would see him bonding with his son, letting him win. Being a buddy.

The rest of the time, sixteen years later, it was Woodgate redux. At least he thought it could be.

Hi there. Perhaps you've seen me on TV?

Maybe they know I'm an every-other-weekend Dad and want nothing to do with me.

Maybe they see how much I drink.

Some of the units were privately owned condominiums. Others, like his, were rented apartments. Still, when he referred to the place he lived, he called it his "condo."

The door to his "condo" had two locks. One in the doorknob and a separate deadbolt, same key for both. He always ignored the doorknob lock, and after the deadbolt moved smartly to its unlocked position, he leaned into the door with his right shoulder, reaching across with his right hand to flip a switch on the wall to illuminate a floor lamp across the front room.

Nothing.

"Chrissakes... "

The irritability he inherited from James E. seemed more

pronounced lately.

The blinds and accompanying drapes were pulled on the sliding glass balcony door, so he felt his way across the room to the dining room, where he deposited his keys, brew, and briefcase. Now empty-handed, he reached over and punched the dimmer switch on the wall, controlling the hanging faux chandelier that on any other day, lit up the dining room. Its rectangular mirrored panels would cast little glimmering patches on the dining room ceiling and walls.

Pogo's. A goddamn subculture.

Nothing. Just darkness. It began to sink in as he reached around and tried the kitchen lights.

Oh for three.

There was only one course of action. Feeling his way back to the front door, he slid over to Dillon's and bought a bag of ice. Six cans in each sink, surrounded by equal amounts of ice.

He set a flashlight on the dining room table, pointed toward the ceiling, casting enough of a circle of light to allow sink access.

In the semi-darkness, with each vanquished solider, another deeper thought. He had long since passed the point where he could excuse the addiction. Awareness is a bitch. Knowledge is a pain in the ass. Awareness and knowledge were not enough. Nothing was working.

We admitted we were powerless over alcohol—that our lives had become unmanageable.

The first of the 12 Steps finally began to hit home. As he sat in the dark, not really enjoying the beer, he engaged in some of the self-introspection that started at Cedar Ridge.

My first thought was not, 'How has my life become so unmanageable that my electricity was shut off?' My first thought was, 'How'm I gonna keep this beer cold?'

That problem had been solved and he grasped at that accomplishment.

That's a victory?

Nothing is more demoralizing to the addict than the intertwined, rock bottom realizations that you are truly, madly, deeply addicted and the unfathomable desperation of being unable to stop.

He was 33 years old. He had been drinking every day since he was 16 years old. More than half of his entire life. He had been trying to stop for three years. Three rehabs in three years. Divorced, DUI.

He had quit paying his bills and had maxed out a pair of credit cards. The bills just piled up in a wooden bowl on the dining room table. Even in the dim illumination from the flashlight, the bold red letters screamed off the Kansas Power & Light envelope atop the stack: FINAL NOTICE.

The property taxes on the Camaro were a year overdue. The little decal in the upper right-hand corner of his license plate was the wrong color. He could get pulled over. His workaround was to Scotch tape a maple leaf over the expired decal. He positioned it so it would look like it been blown by the south Kansas wind and just happened to lodge itself there.

Surely the cops won't see it.

Gosh, officer, thanks for the reminder. I've been intending to get that taken care of. Perhaps you've seen me on TV?

If you ignore it long enough, maybe it will go away.

Or maybe it won't.

The dichotomy.

On TV every night. Award-winning broadcast journalist with a scoop a week. Sometimes two. Imparting knowledge, serving the community. Filling the hole. Glib, erudite, functioning optimally. A courtesy boy, come full circle.

At home, alone, spiraling down.

How can these two lives co-exist?

It was not the first time he had considered it that way.

He opened the glass door to the stereo components and punched the power button on the tuner. Muscle memory. Music as distraction.

Silence.

Oh yeah, idiot. No juice.

This will be my last twelver. He had said that so many times before, he knew it could not be true.

Three years earlier, when he checked himself into rehab for the first time, he could not imagine living the rest of his life without drinking. He could grasp concepts, he could get from point A to point B, but this one was beyond him. He understood the structure—denial, awareness, and action.

He understood that his actions—three rehabs—did not work. The panic seized him as he sat alone in the dark.

Thank God Scott was not with him. He'd have to find a way to get the electricity turned back on before he came over next weekend. Or find an excuse and ask Sharon to keep him.

God. Why was he thanking Him?

Help me make it through this day without taking a drink.

Give me the strength to recognize your will in my life. My will is not working.

Give me the willingness to be willing.

He passed out on the couch during the time Letterman would have been on, had there been electricity. Awakening a couple of hours later, he shuffled to the bathroom in the dark and shook our four Excedrin. Changing into his sweatpants and T-shirt, he hung his gray dress pants on the corner of the bedroom door, crawled into bed, and passed out again.

EPILOGUE

The next morning, I got up and went about my business. Figured out a way to get the electricity turned back on. I didn't feel any different, I just didn't drink.

By itself, that wasn't a new phenomenon. I had stopped drinking hundreds of times. Stopping wasn't the issue. Staying stopped was the logistical or management nut that could not be cracked. After the first rehab, I made it 60 days before relapsing; 70 days after the second; and 90 days after Cedar Ridge.

This time around, the 91st day was on Halloween. Scott dressed up as Batman, and he had already trick-or-treated in Lawrence, but I brought him to Topeka for a two-fer. I wasn't going to 12 Step meetings or hanging out with people in recovery. My only proactive measure was reciting the rote prayers. I went to work, filled the news hole, came home, and didn't drink.

Eventually, I solved my financial mess and started paying the bills. The scotch-taped leaf came off the Camaro's license plate.

Ninety days became 120 days, six months, a year. Two years. The addiction appeared to be gone and I felt "cured." Finally.

By 1994, Joan Finney's idiosyncrasies could no longer be glossed over. Her internal polling reflected that Kansas voters were done with her, so she wisely chose not to seek re-election. Now three years sober, I found a candidate for governor with whom I was simpatico, personally and politically, and did what

I do best.

Manipulated to get what I wanted.

Bill Graves admired my ability to communicate, the nightly exposure I had on TV, and the fact that I was respected by the Statehouse media corps, broadcast and print. Reporter and candidate danced around each other for months, while I worked a friend in Graves' inner circle. Graves was the kind of manager who would offer the job, only when it was certain the answer would be yes.

Overnight, I switched sides of the camera and went from being the one asking the penetrating questions to the one answering them.

At about the same time, I met a person who saw through the bullshit façade and called me on it—the first to actually do that out loud. Jackie McClaskey took one look at the Camaro, dubbed it the "penis-mobile," and within six months, I was driving a monogamous relationship-friendly 1995 Ford Thunderbird.

A dozen years into our marriage, my self-driven nature and manipulative ways resulted in a husband-wife dialogue that ended with, "You're such an asshole."

But I knew how to fix that: go see a head shrinker, manipulate an outcome of American Psychological Association-sanctioned absolution, and revert to the status quo. Five minutes into my soliloquy, the psychologist thrust his arm toward me, palm first.

"Enough," he said. "You're an addict. Get back to the 12 Steps."

Whaddayamean? I'm already cured.

This time around, I took comfort in the process and structure and came to fully, deeply understand that addiction centers in the mind. There are upstream mitigating factors and, while abstaining isn't the cure, it is the key to clearing the psyche and soul to allow for the vital introspection.

The traditional 12 Step model is to surround yourself with fellow addicts, form bonds, and build confidence in the group setting, all the while inching toward spiritual awareness and action. The template calls for surrender, throwing in the white towel. Take it, God. I can't handle it anymore.

Mine didn't work that way.

On August 3, 1991, I polished off a 12-pack of Coors Light in the dark and have not had a drink since.

Why?

There's only one explanation: The obsession that fed the compulsion was removed.

It may come across like revival tent laying on of hands-speaking in tongues-miracle-ish stuff. But I have since learned my experience isn't unique. Many in recovery share similar stories and experiences, yet it's hard to describe what it's like.

Seventeen years of drinking every day and a life that is built around one thing. Then, one day you wake up, and that feeling is gone. Vanished. It's just not there. I didn't realize it at the time because of my previous pattern of abstinence and relapse in the three years of trying to stop.

My interpretation is there are three components to my recovery: awareness, obsession removal, and what I do with it. God did the middle task. The rest is on me.

That train of thought led to a backward inventory of traits and behaviors, deeper thinking, and the inevitable journalistic-driven questioning of God's motivation. Let's get an interview, a live shot from heaven. At the very least, a pithy SOT for the 10-strip.

Maybe God does answer rote prayers. The 12 Steps posit that "no human power" can relieve addiction. I'd just lived through three years of trying, three years of my will. Maybe I was spared for a reason. Maybe it was to get smarter about addiction, repair the relationship with my old man and write a couple of books about it. Or maybe that's just my all-powerful ego.

The Methodist belief in prevenient grace, a divine love that surrounds all humanity and precedes human decision, began to hit home. The grace prompts our first glimmer of understanding God's will. It also awakens what John Wesley described as "an earnest longing for deliverance from sin and death and moves us toward repentance and faith."

The traits and behaviors, developed during and since childhood, led me down a path that ended in addiction. I suffered financial and legal trouble, held loved ones at arm's length, and wrecked a perfectly good marriage.

My fault. My fault. My most grievous fault, as the Catholics say.

But my first glimmer of understanding about God's will did not come until after I realized that mine wasn't working. Finally, points B through Y. Maybe Thoreau was on to something. At the depth of my addiction, I couldn't see the bullshit rationalization in the dichotomy of career success and quiet, isolated desperation.

Gratitude is a behavior that has surfaced in recovery. Despite the loss and the heartbreak, I am thankful for all the experiences chronicled in this book. If I could go back, I wouldn't change a thing. For two reasons: First, I can't. But more importantly, the life I have led has put me in a position to do my part to knock down the stigma that still exists surrounding addiction.

One of the hazards of creative non-fiction is the non-fiction. This is two books in a row in which I have had to dredge up some previous unpleasantness. When you are in the throes of reliving unpleasantness, the effects linger when you emerge from the writing and try to merge seamlessly into real life. A friend in whom I confided during the writing of this book likened it to conducting a self-appendectomy without the benefit of anesthesia.

Addiction centers in the mind. Things are happening that you don't even know are happening. So, even though I have identified and named the traits and behaviors, and even though I recognize them, it doesn't mean I have lost them. I was born with them and will die with them.

When I reflect on the societal norms and expectations of the '70s and '80s, it dawns on me how much the world has changed, and how I have changed with it.

When I finally came to grips with my addiction, I could not imagine living the rest of my life without ever taking another drink. A dozen years ago, I could not imagine ever publicly sharing the truth about my motivations and actions while deep in addiction's clutches. So strong was the power and sway of societal stigma.

I am not cured. I am in recovery from an addiction that brought me to my knees. What I do with that gift is entirely an act of my will and an evolution of my soul.

Now, about that Oscar nomination…

AUTHOR'S NOTE

It would be years before I learned what I experienced that September 1978 night in the Cities has a name: blackout. Turned out, the Olde English 800 was not beer but malt liquor with an 8 percent alcohol content, compared to roughly half that in Old Style beer. It looked and tasted like Old Style, but its kick was twice as potent.

Memories are formed by receptors in the brain. I drank so much alcohol, so fast, that it caused a disruption in the link between short-term and long-term memory. Too much alcohol, too fast, basically fries the short-term, so the memories cannot form. It overloads the brain. Blackout is the result. It's a form of amnesia and the memory loss is permanent.

I never shared my blackout with anyone until years later, in recovery. Then I learned that blackouts are a red flag warning sign of addiction and that they often come after years of abuse. Mine happened at age 20. I had only been drinking for four years, but I had been drinking every day for four years.

The blackout, the DUI. The obsession that morphs into stalking. The impulsiveness that led to a legal ambush of the mother of our child. These were highly visible, early symptoms of addiction.

The personality characteristics that I considered strengths were connected to what many would view as character deficiencies: distrust, an inclination toward confrontation, obsessiveness, and a level of manipulativeness. These too were symptoms, but more insidious, hidden behind descriptors without stigma that led to professional success—assertive, leader of people.

The immediacy of broadcast journalism didn't help. Get the story on the air. Now. By definition, that work was an impulsive action.

To write this book, I traveled back in time, immersed myself in the music, watched the movies and TV shows, and grew my hair long. Most importantly, I reconnected with people I loved, lost, or let go.

Kenny Johnston finished the 12-month term at Brown and followed me to KAKE-TV where, like many of us, he worshipped *Kaleidoscope* cohost Mogie Langston from afar. It would have never worked. She was talent, he was tech. Kenny eventually landed a job at KSTP-TV and returned home to the Cities.

Mitch Burns bounced up and down the radio dial for a few years, then found a career in the Army. Mitch ended up in his home state, in the Madison suburbs.

Donna Hansen, *aka* Donna Kasey, took her own advice, did the requisite six months at the point of entry in Oelwein, then moved on to WNFL in Green Bay, springboarding her to the big leagues in Detroit and Washington, D.C. *En route*, she sang for a blues-rock band and became the voice for the Piggly Wiggly supermarket chain.

The four of us reconnected in Donna's hometown of Arlington, South Dakota in the spring of '82, when she married an up-and-coming sportscaster she'd met along the way. That marriage didn't take, either.

Inglewood and I reeled in the years over spaghetti and meatballs at Angelo's and I took his temperature on me writing a creative non-fiction book about his father's disappearance. He was warm to the idea, but his mother was not. Too bad. Coulda been a helluva book.

Duck and I reconnected at Olive Garden in Derby, a Wichita suburb. (I detect an Italian cuisine trend.) We reminisced about having each other's backs and reflected on those years not so much as drama, but as life experience. Every party, every youthful indiscretion, every circumstance adding up to understanding, wisdom even.

The Garvey'd priceless stamp of legitimacy.

In one of those strange "small world" twists of fate, Duck met, fell in love, and married a kid from the Heights class of 1975 who suffered from a neurological condition that caused his hands to shake. So, of course, at Heights, he was nicknamed, "Steady." He was killed in a car accident not long after they were married.

I felt pretty shitty, twice.

When Duane the Man and I found each other again, the decades since we personified the goddamn subculture just sort of fell away, and we picked up right where we left off. Crashing through a downtown Wichita storefront on New Year's Eve. My God, that's a story for the ages that deserves to be immortalized.

Jim Larkin returned to Colorado. We met up at a Rockies game in Denver and these days stay connected via text, especially during the World Series.

Malea (Sisk) Hayhurst helped me color around the edges and fill in some blank spaces. There's something nostalgically poignant about reconnecting with a true love, decades later. The feelings are long gone, but the familiarity remains.

Then, there are the places.

KAKE-TV still stands in the building on West Street in Wichita where I got my foot in the door. KAKZ Radio née KAKE is long gone. KAYS-TV was sold and changed its call letters, KAYS Radio is still going strong in Hays and is a gem in the Eagle Communications family.

In Topeka, Stauffer split up WIBW-TV, the radio stations and the networks, and sold them for parts. For the better part of a dozen years, the building that started life as a school for orphans sat vacant on the Menninger campus, visited only by vandals and ghosts of broadcasts past. The old school went up in flames a few years back. Even though I had long since left the business, I couldn't help feeling a little orphaned myself.

Only by looking backward does one capture a sense of "you don't know what you've got 'til it's gone." I feel fortunate to have worked for three of the premier locally-owned broadcasters in Kansas. Martin Umansky at KAKE, Bob Schmidt and Ross Beach at KAYS, and the Stauffers at WIBW. Much has been lost in the evolution of terrestrial broadcasting, not the least of which is the depth and quality of the journalism, but that's a whole 'nother book.

Brown Institute moved to the first ring of St. Paul suburbs and became Brown College. The doors were closed forever in 2016, but her alums are scattered across the globe and, of course, there's a Facebook group.

In Johnson County, Cedar Ridge became KU MedWest, a comprehensive medical care center, part of the larger University of Kansas Health System, where my son, Scott, now works as a pulmonary research physician.

In Wichita, Joe Vosburgh Wallpaper is long gone. There's a bridal shop there now and I notice there are some ginormous planters out front, ostensibly protecting the storefront from the odd, errant New Year's Eve 240Z.

The Wichita Club has faded into a bygone cultural era.

Woodgate is still around. Now almost a half-century old.

The Twin Lakes Shopping Center is a shadow of its former high-end self. The theatres, the private dinner club, and

Safeway, all gone.

Kings-X was razed to make way for a CVS Pharmacy.

Mr. D's is now a truncated ALDI discount supermarket. I popped in a couple of times while writing this book to feel the vibe. The east-facing limestone edifice still stands, but everything else has been refurbished and retrofitted.

As I wandered the aisles, I wanted to buttonhole the ALDI's workers, ask if they shared a camaraderie, inquire about their *esprit de corps,* make certain the price on the milk gallons was properly configured. I wondered if they had nicknames.

"If it's there, don't lose it," I would counsel. "Be purposeful about hanging on to it—and each other."

Pogo's has been chopped up into various retail spaces, including an outfit that takes digital inkless fingerprints. I was there a few years back to get squared away for TSA pre-check. I felt compelled to mention to the Gen Z fingerprinter she was working in hallowed space that once held deep meaning to the Wichita high school classes of the late '70s. She was polite, but I'm not sure she got it.

When I walked out, I lingered for a while on the sidewalk and reminisced. It was a gorgeous day in the city where I came of age, my hometown. My imagination transported me back in time and I could smell the Love's Baby Soft, see the strobes, taste the beer, feel the four-on-the-floor beat.

Then I climbed into my 2012 Ford Escape, punched up satellite radio '70s on 7, and drove home, awash with gratitude.

Mike Matson
Manhattan, Kansas
Autumn 2021

ACKNOWLEDGEMENTS

I am blessed with a good memory, almost granular for certain events and circumstances, which comes in really handy when you're writing a book about your own life. The journalist in me likes the notion of confirming the facts and Kari Schmidt, Brenda Paske, Teri Roberts, and Becky Kiser helped me do just that.

Rick and Denise Musser double-checked my memory on logistics in the Cities and all of their rings of suburbs. George Benton offered vital Pogo's data.

Kathy Sifrit was invaluable in offering first blush reactions.

Christie Appelhanz, Dea Mandery, Valerie Parkinson Rupp, Scott Richardson, Brandi Buzzard, Jake Huyett, Juliana Proffitt McCully, and Heather Lansdowne lent their talent, advice, and direction-pointing.

My gratitude to Sheryl Krusemark, Duane Smith, Malea Hayhurst, and Jim Larkin for coming out to play.

Gene Rump, Bob Davis, Jack Oliver, and Mogie Langston—the stars—trusted me enough to allow use of their real names. Ditto Bruce Browning.

John Schlageck and Harry Watts provided exactly the right amount of rah-rah at exactly the right times.

I was three years sober when I met Jackie McClaskey. My disco is her big hair, head-banging music. This book would not have happened absent her gifts of time, grace, and forbearance.

Scott Matson, whose innate empathy led to a career in medicine. At 13, I asked Scott to stand up for me when Jackie and I were married. In toasting the bride and groom, he hoisted his sparkling water, said, "Unaccustomed as I am to public speaking... " and proceeded to ad lib with heartfelt eloquence. In every sense of the word, my son is the best man.

My sister, Viki Matson, the only other person on the planet to carry the weight and depth of the James E. vestiges.

The author's columns, along with photos and music playlists that synch with the *Courtesy Boy* chronology, can be found at:

www.mikematson.com

Made in the USA
Monee, IL
17 November 2021